D1730399

MOVING SCENES

THE AESTHETICS OF GERMAN TRAVEL WRITING ON ENGLAND 1783–1830

LEGENDA

LEGENDA, founded in 1995 by the European Humanities Research Centre of the University of Oxford, is now a joint imprint of the Modern Humanities Research Association and Maney Publishing. Titles range from medieval texts to contemporary cinema and form a widely comparative view of the modern humanities, including works on Arabic, Catalan, English, French, German, Greek, Italian, Portuguese, Russian, Spanish, and Yiddish literature. An Editorial Board of distinguished academic specialists works in collaboration with leading scholarly bodies such as the Society for French Studies and the British Comparative Literature Association.

MHRA

The Modern Humanities Research Association (MHRA) encourages and promotes advanced study and research in the field of the modern humanities, especially modern European languages and literature, including English, and also cinema. It also aims to break down the barriers between scholars working in different disciplines and to maintain the unity of humanistic scholarship in the face of increasing specialization. The Association fulfils this purpose primarily through the publication of journals, bibliographies, monographs and other aids to research.

Maney Publishing is one of the few remaining independent British academic publishers. Founded in 1900 the company has offices both in the UK, in Leeds and London, and in North America, in Boston. Since 1945 Maney Publishing has worked closely with learned societies, their editors, authors, and members, in publishing academic books and journals to the highest traditional standards of materials and production.

STUDIES IN COMPARATIVE LITERATURE

Studies in Comparative Literature are produced in close collaboration with the British Comparative Literature Association, and range widely across comparative and theoretical topics in literary and translation studies, accommodating research at the interface between different artistic media and between the humanities and the sciences.

Moving Scenes

The Aesthetics of German Travel Writing
on England 1783–1830

ALISON E. MARTIN

LEGENDA

Studies in Comparative Literature 13
Modern Humanities Research Association and Maney Publishing
2008

Published by the
Modern Humanities Research Association and Maney Publishing
1 Carlton House Terrace
London SW1Y 5AF
United Kingdom

LEGENDA is an imprint of the
Modern Humanities Research Association and Maney Publishing

Maney Publishing is the trading name of W. S. Maney & Son Ltd,
whose registered office is at Suite 1C, Joseph's Well, Hanover Walk, Leeds LS3 1AB

ISBN 9-781-906540-08-1

First published 2008

Printed in Great Britain

Cover: 875 Design

Copy-Editor: Nigel Hope

CONTENTS

ACKNOWLEDGEMENTS

This project could not have been undertaken without a postgraduate studentship from the Arts and Humanities Research Board. The trustees of the Tiarks German Scholarship Fund of the Department of German, University of Cambridge funded foreign travel for conferences and archive research throughout my three years of study. A substantial grant from the Conference of University Teachers of German enabled me to present a paper at a conference in Boston, USA, in March 2003. On numerous occasions, Christ's College, Cambridge funded attendance at conferences and seminars in the UK and abroad. The Sir John Plumb Charitable Trust and the British Comparative Literature Association made generous contributions towards the costs of publishing this manuscript and I am most grateful to them, as also to Professor David Wells and the Modern Humanities Research Association.

My thanks go first and foremost to Joachim Whaley for agreeing to supervise this project in the first place and for guiding it, with characteristic humour and enthusiasm, to its conclusion. His help and support in its pre-publication phase were invaluable. The following have also read sections and chapters of this work at various stages, giving highly detailed, constructive criticism: Jeremy Adler, Nicholas Boyle, Hilary Brown, Jonathan Conlin, Rüdiger Görner, Barry Nisbet, Susan Pickford, Ritchie Robertson, Margaret Rose, Elinor Shaffer, Martin Swales, Godela Weiss-Sussex, and Wim Weymans. Thanks go to Graham Nelson and Nigel Hope at Legenda for their useful queries, patience and valuable advice.

Exemplary assistance has been provided by the staff of the Rare Books Room at Cambridge University Library, Ann Toseland (Microfilm), David Lowe, and Christian Staufenbiel (Accessions); the British Library; the Stadtbibliothek Hannover; the Rare Books rooms at Münster University Library, the Thüringische Landes- und Universitätsbibliothek, Jena, the Universitätsbibliothek Leipzig, and the Universität- und Landesbibliothek Martin-Luther-Universität, Halle-Wittenberg. Horst-Eberhard von Horstig kindly granted me access to some of the unpublished material pertaining to his great-great-grandfather, Carl Gottlieb Horstig. Brigitte Klosterberg of the Franckesche Stiftungen at Halle facilitated access to material on August Hermann Niemeyer, while Andreas Grape provided me with copies of Niemeyer's 1819 correspondence from England.

I owe a great debt of thanks to Pat and Ian Martin, and friends in England, Belgium, and Germany, who remained a constant source of good spirits and encouragement throughout the writing of this book. Ursula Mack energetically hunted down secondary literature in German which was inaccessible from England. Björn Zehner, above and beyond his stalwart support of the project as a whole, was of inestimable help with all matters technical. He has also continued to remind me of the world beyond the bounds of eighteenth- and nineteenth-century travel writing.

Part of Chapter 1 appeared in a much shortened form in 'German Travel Writing and the Rhetoric of Sensibility: Karl Philipp Moritz's *Reisen eines Deutschen in England im Jahr 1782*', in *Cross-cultural Travel. Papers from the Royal Irish Academy International Symposium on Literature and Travel, National University of Ireland, Galway, November 2002*, ed. by Jane Conroy (Berlin: Lang, 2003), pp. 81–88. Part of Chapter 2 appeared in 'Travel, Sensibility and Gender: The Rhetoric of Female Travel Writing in Sophie von La Roche's *Tagebuch einer Reise durch Holland und England*', *German Life and Letters*, 57 (2004), 127–42. Parts of Chapter 5 appeared in 'The Traveller as *Landschaftsmaler*: Industrial Labour and Landscape Aesthetics in Johanna Schopenhauer's *Reise durch England und Schottland*', *Modern Language Review*, 99 (2004), 991–1005 and 'Sympathy and Spectacle: *lebende Bilder, Attitüden* and Visual Representation in Johanna Schopenhauer's Travel Writing', *Publications of the English Goethe Society*, 73 (2004), 19–38. I thank Jane Conroy and the editors of *GLL, MLR*, and *PEGS* for their advice in the writing of these papers.

A. E. M.
June 2008

LIST OF ABBREVIATIONS

ADB	*Allgemeine Deutsche Bibliothek* [*General German Library*]
ALZ	*Allgemeine Literatur-Zeitung* [*General Literary Newspaper*]
AR	*Analytical Review*
BM	*Berlinische Monatsschrift* [*Berlin Monthly Journal*]
CR	*Critical Review*
DK	*Der Kosmopolit* [*The Cosmopolitan*]
DM	*Deutsches Museum* [*German Museum*]
DKV	Johann Wolfgang von Goethe, *Sämtliche Werke*, 40 vols, ed. by Dieter Borchmeyer et al. (Frankfurt a.M.: Deutscher Klassiker Verlag, 1985–)
FGA	*Frankfurter Gelehrte Anzeigen* [*Frankfurt Learned Advertiser*]
GAgS	*Göttingische Anzeigen von gelehrten Sachen* [*Göttingen Advertiser of Learned Affairs*]
GLL	*German Life and Letters*
MgS	*Morgenblatt für gebildete Stände* [*Morning Paper for the Educated Classes*]
MLR	*Modern Language Review*
NA	Schiller, Friedrich, *Werke. Nationalausgabe*, 43 vols, ed. by Julius Petersen et al. (Weimar: Hermann Böhlaus Nachfolger, 1943–)
NADB	*Neue Allgemeine Deutsche Bibliothek* [*New General German Library*]
NBsWfK	*Neue Bibliothek der schönen Wissenschaften und der freyen Künste* [*New Library for the Fine Sciences and the Free Arts*]
NHGZ	*Neue Hallische Gelehrte Zeitungen* [*New Halle Learned Papers*]
PEGS	*Publications of the English Goethe Society*
TM	*Teutscher Merkur* [*German Mercury*]

Translations in the text are my own unless otherwise stated.

INTRODUCTION

The year 1808 saw the publication of Alexander von Humboldt's *Ansichten der Natur* [*Views of Nature*], part travel narrative, part celebration of the diversity of the natural world. In the foreword, he summarized some of the narrative difficulties confronting the travel writer:

> Die Verbindung eines literarischen und eines rein szientifischen Zweckes, der Wunsch, gleichzeitig die Phantasie zu beschäftigen und durch Vermehrung des Wissens das Leben mit Ideen zu bereichern, machen die Anordnung der einzelnen Teile, und das, was als Einheit der Komposition gefordert wird, schwer zu erreichen.[1]

> [The combination of a literary and a purely scientific aim, the desire to engage the imagination and at the same time to enrich life with new ideas by the increase of knowledge, render the arrangement of the separate parts, and what is required for the unity of composition, difficult to attain.]

The travelogue therefore seemed to negotiate around a series of tensions between scientific accuracy and a 'literary' style, between the need to be instructive and yet to mobilize the imagination, and between the description of separate scenes and the production of a composition that was a unified whole. The twofold aim of his work, he explained, was to increase the reader's enjoyment of the natural scenes he described through vivid representation, while at the same time offering an informative scientific account. This clearly termed manifesto therefore sought to counter what Humboldt perceived as the failure of previous travellers to produce non-fictional travel accounts that engaged the emotions and imagination of the reader.

That same year, Goethe published his *Briefe aus der Schweiz* [*Letters from Switzerland*], based on an account of his travels in Switzerland between October and December 1779. Originally published in a much shorter version in *Die Horen* [*The Horae*] of 1796, the text of 1808 — particularly in its second section — attempted to combine an authentic travel narrative with the sensibilities of the age, articulated through its key literary protagonist, Werther. Presented as having been penned by him, it highlighted the problem of representation in travel writing:

> Ich las auch so viele Beschreibungen dieser Gegenstände, ehe ich sie sah. Gaben sie mir denn ein Bild, oder nur irgend einen Begriff? Vergebens arbeitete meine Einbildungskraft sie hervorzuheben, vergebens mein Geist etwas dabei zu denken. Nun stehe ich und schaue diese Wunder und wie wird mir dabei? ich denke nichts, ich empfinde nichts und möchte so gern etwas dabei denken und empfinden.[2]

> [I also read so many descriptions of these subjects, before I saw them. Did they give me a picture, or just some notion? In vain my imaginative powers worked

at elevating them, in vain my mind tried to think something as I read. Now I stand and observe these wonders and how do I feel? I think nothing, I feel nothing and would so very much wish to think and feel something while I am observing.]

Indeed, as Werther remarked at the end of his letter of 4 November 1779, following a day walking in the foothills of Montblanc, 'Meine Beschreibung fängt an unordentlich und ängstlich zu werden, auch brauchte es eigentlich immer zwei Menschen, einen der's sähe und einen der's beschriebe' [My description is beginning to become disordered and nervous. Moreover it really always required two people, one person who looks and another who describes].[3] These concerns voiced by Goethe — through Werther — and Humboldt were therefore in many ways a reaction to what they both perceived to be a crisis in the representation of the foreign experience through the medium of travel writing.

Their call for the employment of different narrative strategies that would more vividly recreate in the mind's eye of the reader the scenes they had encountered sprang above all from a concern to define their work as different from the writings of previous travellers. Travel narratives produced earlier in the century are traditionally (if rather schematically) seen as falling into two groups: the 'instructive' account and the travel narrative written purely for entertainment.[4] Certainly even beyond mid-century, the modes of representation adopted by 'curious' journals written by navigators and explorers continued to encourage the systematization and tabulation of the new and exotic. German explorers did not necessarily enjoy the same patronage and financial support that the Royal Society could offer their British counterparts. Nevertheless they too aimed to produce recordings of the world in conformity with the dictates of the Royal Society and other Enlightenment scientific institutions. Carsten Niebuhr's voyage to Arabia in the 1760s, recorded in the *Reisebeschreibung nach Arabien und andern umliegenden Ländern* [*Description of a Journey to Arabia and Other Neighbouring Countries*] (1774–78), had essentially aimed to answer a series of scientific questions drawn up by learned figures in Germany prior to departure, and overseen by the orientalist and Hebrew scholar Johann David Michaelis.

At the other end of the spectrum were accounts which were more obviously subjective in orientation and sought to convey the traveller's personal response to the foreign environment. The most pioneering of these was Laurence Sterne's *Sentimental Journey through France and Italy* (1768). It seized public attention both in England and Germany (Johann Joachim Bode's translation appeared the same year) feeding its readership's hungry desire for emotional identification. An immediate bestseller, the *Empfindsame Reise* was into its sixth edition by the end of the century.[5] Disparagingly described by an anonymous critic as having ushered in '[eine] Epoche der übertriebenen Empfindsamkeit oder Empfindeley' [an age of exaggerated sensibility],[6] Sterne's work became a model for a rash of sentimental travel accounts, both fictional and non-fictional, which appeared on the German book market from the 1770s onwards.[7] Its radical rejection of systematic description, its privileging of the emotions, elliptical sentence structure and moments of disjuncture echoed through works such as Johann Georg Jacobi's *Winterreise* and *Sommerreise* [*Winter*

Journey and *Summer Journey*] (1769), Johann Gottlieb Schummel's *Empfindsame Reise durch Deutschland* [*Sentimental Journey through Germany*] (1771), Andreas Georg Friedrich Rebmann's *Empfindsame Reise nach Schilda* [*Sentimental Journey to Schilda*] (1793), or Johann Friedrich Ernst Albrecht's *Empfindsame Reise durch den europäischen Olymp* [*Sentimental Journey through the European Olympus Mountains*] (1800). These were all reflections of the literary and cultural movement known as 'Empfindsamkeit' which reached a peak in Germany in the second half of the eighteenth century, 'empfindsam' denoting both emotional and physical susceptibility as well as one's sensitive response to the feelings of others.

Thus while in the early eighteenth century forms of description in travel writing were used which stabilized and ordered the foreign encounter through reasoned, coherent mechanisms of observation and recording, by the end of the century alternative perspectives were being privileged which withdrew such emphasis on rationality. Whereas the voice of the early eighteenth-century traveller strove to be predominantly disinterested, sober, and analytical, that of his nineteenth-century successor was more concerned (but not exclusively so) to include the expression of passionate, creative, and imaginative forces. The travel account, as Humboldt also observed, should be a narrative which offered a description of the observer's physiological and emotional reactions combined, conveying something of the aesthetic dimension of the foreign environment. As he explained:

> Auf gleiche Weise wirken Naturschilderungen stärker oder schwächer auf uns ein, je nachdem sie mit den Bedürfnissen unserer Empfindung mehr oder minder in Einklang stehen. Denn in dem innersten, empfänglichen Sinn spiegelt lebendig und wahr sich die physische Welt.[8]

> [Descriptions of nature affect us more or less powerfully, according to how much they harmonize with the condition of our own feelings. For the physical world is reflected with animation and truth on the inner susceptible world of the mind.]

An important influence on Humboldt's writing style had come from Georg Forster, his mentor on their travels to the Low Countries, France, and England in 1790. In his *Voyage Round the World* (1777), Georg Forster had already challenged the notion that an individual was capable of purely objective observation. He argued that 'two travellers seldom saw the same object in the same manner, and each reported the fact differently, according to his sensations, and his peculiar mode of thinking'.[9] Moreover, he continued, it 'was necessary to be acquainted with the observer, before any use could be made of his observations'.[10]

The collation of fact, as both Forster and Alexander von Humboldt had insisted, was only one aspect of the travel writer's task: equally important was the complex act of narration that underpinned these findings. In setting themselves against the work of their predecessors, they not only implicitly criticized earlier work for its coldness and dry, scientific reporting of fact, which made false claims to objectivity. They also deplored its lack of animation and its inability to engage with the reader's imagination, its inability to be, in Humboldt's terms, 'lebendig und wahr'. Thus they implied that the account they were engaged in writing would be warm and vibrant, leaving a vivid impression on its readership. They correlated the faithful representation of the foreign, the 'truth' of their accounts, with the vitality of their writing. The claim of travel writers to speak with an authentic voice was therefore closely bound up with the discourses they employed. As Johann Georg Büsch lamented in his highly critical overview of travel writing in 1786, even Cook's account was dull in places. In others, though, it made thoroughly gripping reading:

> Aber wenn Cook erzählt, wie er auf jener Hälfte der Erdkugel, fern von einem Ufer, daß ihm Zuflucht geben konnte, mit seinem Schiffe auf die Spitze eines Corallen-Felsen gestossen sei, und mit welchem Muht und Erfindsamkeit er sich aus dieser fürchterlichen Gefahr gerettet habe, so nimmt jeder Leser [. . .] Anteil daran.[11]

> [But when Cook narrates how in that half of the globe, far from any shore that could offer him refuge, his ship struck the point of a coral reef and with what courage and ingenuity he saved himself from such dreadful peril, every reader feels sympathy for him.]

The ability to engage affectively with the subject by means of imaginative projection was therefore paramount in this creation of a new style of travel writing.

'Sensibilitas' as Johann Heinrich Zedler's *Universal-Lexikon* termed it under the lemma for 'sense', was 'ein Vermögen der Seele, von den Objecten afficiret zu werden, und hierdurch sie zu empfinden' [the ability of the soul to be affected by objects and as a result to be moved by them], therefore relating it to fellow feeling in the broadest sense.[12] By the end of the eighteenth century, a rash of related terms such as 'Sympathie' or 'Simpathie', 'Mitleiden' and 'Mitleidigkeit' had entered circulation. They expressed both the feeling for someone else's suffering (which we now understand as 'sympathy') and the power of understanding and imaginatively entering into another person's feelings (which we now understand as 'empathy'). While the notions of empathy and sympathy are generally associated with negative emotions such as pain and suffering, it is also important to stress that empathy can also create positive feelings of delight, satisfaction, and even elation. The concepts of sympathy and empathy are an integral and important part of how people 'read' and react to each other: it colours relationships and orientations not only towards our acquaintances, but also towards strangers. As Adam Smith remarked in the *Theory of Moral Sentiments* (1759), 'even the greatest ruffian, the most hardened violator of the laws of society' was not altogether without pity and compassion.[13] Sympathy could therefore also mark a dissolution of social difference and aim to reach common ground. As James Engell has argued, sympathy 'becomes that special power of the imagination which permits the self to escape its own confines, to identify with other people, to perceive things in a new way'.[14] Yet for all that sympathy created affiliations, it also set boundaries. Representations of sympathy frequently returned to the social differences that such scenes had sought to discount. Thus while sympathetic engagement seemed to suggest the dissolving of boundaries between self and subject, it in many ways encouraged a self-scrutiny that was more about the identity of the viewer than the viewed. As Smith had also argued, 'as we have no immediate experience of what other men feel, we can form no idea of the manner in which they are affected, but by conceiving what we ourselves should feel in the like situation'.[15]

Scholars have generally associated the imaginative and sentimental concerns of the period lying within the scope of this study not with non-fictional literature such as travel accounts but with the novel.[16] But the boundaries between fictional and non-fictional writing were far from clear — as the inclusion of Sterne's *Sentimental Journey* in Count Leopold Berchtold's *An Essay to Direct and Extend the Inquiries of Patriotic Travellers* (1789) demonstrated.[17] By exploring the impact of sensibility on other non-fictional genres at this time, this study seeks to reconsider conventional generic distinctions and suggests that it is more helpful to see non-fictional travel writing as a cluster of attributes, styles, and approaches overlapping with other forms of fictional and non-fictional narrative. Interdisciplinary research carried out by a range of scholars in the fields of narrative theory, literary history, and psychology, including most recently Suzanne Keen, has focused on how the way in which a story can be told evokes empathy with its characters and cultivates sympathetic actions. They have demonstrated that personal involvement in a text can be influenced by narrative structure, including issues of external and internal narration and point of view, by rhetorical strategies which foster an appreciation of the aesthetic quality of the narrative, as well as by the presence or absence of stylistic devices such as metaphor or irony which defamiliarize conventional conceptions of referents.[18]

This study therefore has two main aims. Firstly, it seeks through close reading to analyse some of the rhetorical practices deployed in late eighteenth- and early nineteenth-century travel writing to demonstrate how the traveller — the moving figure — was also moved by what he or she observed. It asks how a sense of connection between reader and text cultivated an affective response and which characters or objects were deemed appropriate subjects of sympathetic concern. What did these authors seek to achieve by appealing to their readers' sensibilities and what did this focus on the susceptibility to feeling also tell us about how the travellers perceived themselves? Secondly, this study aims to capture something of the range of impulses that travel writing gained from other aesthetic practices (not necessarily literary) for the purposes of sympathetic representation and in so doing to better understand the range of representational devices on which travel writers of this period drew.

One destination which readily lends itself to an analysis of the way in which modes of description changed in travel writing is Britain, and in particular England, the focus of this study.[19] 'Großbritannien', enthused Johann Wilhelm von Archenholtz in 1785, 'diese Königin der Inseln, [. . .] ist so sehr von allen andern Ländern in Europa unterschieden, als wenn diese sonderbare Insel nicht zu unserm Welttheile, sondern zum Südmeer gehörte' [Great Britain, this queen of islands, differs so greatly from all other countries in Europe, that it seems as if this curious island does not belong to our part of the world, but to the South Seas].[20] Archenholtz's comparison between Britain and more exotic corners of the world may have seemed somewhat surprising, but his next claim was even more astonishing. One felt, he continued, as if one had been transported to another planet, since this transformation did not take place gradually, or after a lengthy journey but in a few hours.[21] In the third quarter of the eighteenth century, Germans increasingly crossed the channel in search of the 'English experience', and by the 1780s the trickle of travelogues published on England had grown to a torrent. As the ambassadorial secretary Friedrich Wilhelm von Schütz hesitantly noted in his epistolary travelogue of 1792, 'Es scheint gewagt zu seyn, die Menge der Schriften über England, durch gegenwärtige Briefe noch vermehren zu wollen' [It seems rash to wish to increase further the number of works on England with the present letters].[22] Why was it that Germans were so curious about England? What was it that made it seem so very different that Germans should liken it to another planet, or at the very least the South Seas?

German travellers hailed England as the cradle of liberty, 'public spirit', religious tolerance, and freedom of the press. Wilhelm von Taube enthused in 1774: '*Engländische Freiheit! Das süße Wort, welches in allen Ländern erschallet und doch so wenig bekannt ist*' [*English Liberty! That sweet word which echoes in all countries and yet is so little known*].[23] Britain had also established a reputation as a nation of philosophers — of 'tiefdenkende Engländer', who included John Locke and Edmund Burke. Meanwhile, to the industrialist, it meant progress in the shape of Matthew Boulton's Soho tool factory, Erasmus Darwin's and James Watt's steam engine, Richard Arkwright's spinning jenny, and a host of scientific instruments captured in masterly detail by the Derbyshire painter Joseph Wright. Art connoisseurs found that British Grand Tourists had amassed such an impressive collection of classical art that it seemed as if they had transported half of Italy back to their country.[24] Britain, the land of Shakespeare, Ossian, and Pope, vaunted a literary pedigree second to none. Poets' Corner in Westminster Abbey recorded that it had also been home to Dryden, Butler, Goldsmith, and a host of other writers and poets now conquering German hearts. And for Karl Philipp Moritz, who claimed in his *Reisen eines Deutschen in England im Jahr 1782* [*Travels, chiefly on foot, through several parts of England, in 1782*] (1783) to have departed for the Peak District with just four guineas and a copy of *Paradise Lost* in his pocket, it was the land of Milton.

German travellers were also, of course, delighted to record their countrymen's contribution to British greatness. Christlob Mylius was gratified to note that there was a marble statue of Georg Friedrich Händel in Vauxhall Pleasure Gardens, even if he was disdainful of its aesthetic proportions. The astronomer Wilhelm Herschel, whose 'wonderful improvements which he has made in the telescope' were lauded by Samuel Johnson, provided a welcome watering hole for German travellers to England in the house Herschel shared with his sister in Bath.[25] Gebhard Friedrich August Wendeborn, Pastor of the German community in London, when not busy saving souls, was at work on his magnum opus *Der Zustand des Staats, der Religion, der Gelehrsamkeit und der Kunst in Großbritannien gegen das Ende des achtzehnten Jahrhunderts* [*The Condition of the State, Religion, Learning, and Art in Great Britain at the Close of the Eighteenth Century*] (1785–88), which remained an authoritative reference work on England well into the nineteenth century.

London in particular offered numerous platforms for staging modern ideas and values, nurturing political, literary, and artistic allegiances. As Georg Christoph Lichtenberg enthused in his letters on David Garrick's theatrical performances, London nurtured a multitude of talents in a way few other cities could. The proliferation of clubs, societies, and coffee houses permitted news, novelty, and gossip to circulate in the capital at breakneck speed. Culture as a print-based form of communication served a varied public through journals, newspapers, and belles-lettres. Britain's thriving capital was also home to the British Museum and the Royal Academy, founded in 1753 and 1769 respectively, which provided varied distraction for aspiring aesthetes. Enlightenment in Britain therefore meant more than technological breakthroughs. It was the expression of new intellectual and moral values, new canons of taste, forms of sociability, and views on human nature.

The already substantial corpus of scholarship on German travel to England in the Enlightenment has primarily been given a new impetus by Michael Maurer's pioneering and prescient study *Aufklärung und Anglophilie* (1987).[26] Its thematic regrouping of the information contained in travel accounts under key headings such as 'public spirit' and patriotism, liberty, civil, and national consciousness, as well as its case studies of eight travellers, carefully constructs a picture of how the Germans conceived of the English and how the English conceived of themselves. Research on travel writing has not solely concentrated, though, on the application of historical methodology to narratives of travel. Charles Batten's *Pleasurable Instruction: Form and Convention in Eighteenth-Century Century Travel Literature* (1978) has explored — if in rather polarized terms — the shift from seemingly objective, instructive, accounts written at the start of the eighteenth century, to those of a more subjective nature produced at its end. A deeper analysis of the rhetorical devices at work in travel writing has been made by Percy G. Adams in his *Travel Literature and the Evolution of the Novel* (1983). Parody, satire, and other conventions characteristic of literary writing were also to be found in the travelogue, he argues, while certain character types, actions, and themes in fictional and non-fictional travel writing also showed clear parallels with novels of the period.

Within German scholarship, Manfred Link's survey *Der Reisebericht als literarische Kunstform von Goethe bis Heine* [*The Travel Narrative as Literary Art Form from Goethe to Heine*] (1963) analyses the types of travel literature produced between 1770 and 1830, their typology, and their evolution. But in organising travel literature into four distinct categories, Link pays insufficient attention to the fluidity of the boundaries between 'scientific' and 'literary' travel writing. Peter Brenner's 1990 study *Der Reisebericht in der deutschen Literatur* [*The Travel Narrative in German Literature*] likewise explores the travel narrative as a literary genre and therefore does not focus on its evolution alongside other non-fictional works, nor does it look outside the sphere of literature to ask how it was influenced by modes of representation in other branches of aesthetics. More recently, Tilmann Fischer's *Reiseziel England: Ein Beitrag zur Poetik der Reisebeschreibung und zur Topik der Moderne (1830–1870)* [*Destination England: A Contribution to the Poetics of the Travel Narrative and to the Theme of Modernity*] (2004), while considering travel literature within a historical context, has convincingly explored the rhetorical strategies used by travel writers to authenticate their work, as well as analysed the use of symbolism and recurring thematics in travelogues of the mid to late nineteenth century.[27]

Unlike most research on German travel writing about England, including William Robson-Scott's still masterly piece, this study does not take 1800 as some artificial watershed by which to close off my discussion of German non-fictional travel writing. Instead, it pursues how modes of representation shift up to the point where guides for formalized, tourist travel and viewing radically restructured the ways in which people wrote on travel in the mid-nineteenth century. The advantage in taking this view that crosses the invisible watershed of 1800 is that it can better focus on notions of continuity and change.

Research on extra-European travel writing has traditionally tended to subscribe to the positivist, binary, models of 'self' and 'other' which underlie post-colonial discussions of difference. Nevertheless one should be cautious in suggesting that it is possible to respect the historical peculiarity of the German traveller's encounter with the foreign culture of the British nation by adopting such an approach. The geographical proximity of the German states to England, and the political ties which linked Britain and the House of Hanover, would have meant that the differences perceived by German travellers to England could not have been of the same order as those experienced by travellers to the New World or other distant lands. Indeed it could be more fruitful to argue that the currents of humanism and cultural relativism ushered in by the Enlightenment meant that similarity, rather than difference, was in fact the feature underlying how Europeans perceived each other in the eighteenth century.

Here it is also necessary to acknowledge a few of this work's limitations. Its focus is strictly on German narratives of England which were published as travel accounts. Articles on England or collections of letters not published in the form of a travelogue have therefore not been taken into consideration. This study is also by no means intended as a comprehensive survey of German travel writing on England during the period in question. Rather it traces the role that empathy played in travel writing and the rhetorical means through which it was conveyed. By focusing on six case studies, it seeks to offer a detailed analysis of just a few of the German travel accounts of England in circulation and represent a range of different political, social, and stylistic positions within German culture in this period.

For some of the writers on whom this study focuses, issues of empathetic identification are problematic, while for all of them it is a challenge to find narrative solutions to the problem of how they can create a vivid, emotionally engaging, representation of England. Chapter 1 charts the use of the spoken word and orality in the 1783 account of England published by Karl Philipp Moritz (1756–1793). It explores how direct speech contributed to the creation of a sense of 'affective realism', which invited the reader's emotional involvement in the scenes described. The second chapter focuses on the representational strategies used by women writers and travellers to England, notably Sophie von La Roche (1730–1807). Her account of England, published in 1788, explicitly engages with female practices of viewing and women's articulation of curiosity within the domain of travel. Sensibility is traditionally considered to have facilitated women's entry into the profession of writing, with its alliance to the domestic, to emotional subjectivity and the intimate. Yet the more sober, dispassionate, style of reporting which still dominated travel writing, coupled with persistent doubts about women's capacity to endure the rigours of travel, potentially marginalized women as writers of serious non-fictional travel literature. Chapter 3, which centres on the account by Esther Domeier (née Gad)

(1770?–?) of her travels to England and Portugal in the period between 1801 and 1803, analyses how her use of anecdotal description foregrounded individuals who invited sympathetic concern. It also assesses where the boundaries of appropriate forms of empathy lay and where potentially excessive scenes of compassion and pity might even set up barriers between reader and subject. The fourth chapter focuses on the work of Carl Gottlieb Horstig (1763–1835), whose account of travel to England appeared in 1806. His recourse to the aesthetics of the picturesque, and in particular his treatment of the use of light and the movement of water in the landscape scenes which he described, explored the affective investment that could be made in landscape. Chapter 5, which focuses on the account by Johanna Schopenhauer (1766–1838) of her travels to England and Scotland (1813), analyses the complex relationship between pictorial and textual landscape description. It also examines her use of the *tableau vivant*, the *attitude*, and other devices borrowed from the theatre to construct in the reader's mind a three-dimensional scene. In the final chapter, the 1820 travelogue of August Hermann Niemeyer (1754–1828) explores the inclusion of the rhetoric of sympathy within a more openly instructive piece of writing. Drawing on the lives of British queens — as Schiller and other tragic dramatists had done before — Niemeyer exploits the significance of specific historical sites in London as *Erinnerungsorte* (*lieux de mémoire*) which allow him to reconstruct in the mind's eye of the reader the tragic events that took place at those locations.

This study therefore focuses upon the discursive nature of non-fictional travel writing and aims both implicitly and explicitly to challenge some of our accepted notions of 'literariness'. Readers (and travel writers) of the late eighteenth and early nineteenth centuries ranged in their reading habits across literary and non-literary terrain, and their ordering of experience took in the pictorial, the theatrical, the historical, and more besides. This study seeks to counter the notion that non-fictional travel writing is a poor cousin to 'proper' literature by focusing on the different ways in which, in late eighteenth- and early nineteenth-century German non-fictional travel writing, sympathetic engagement connected with other competing terms in the matrix of aesthetic and ideological debates being held at that time.

Notes to the Introduction

1. Foreword to second edition, Alexander von Humboldt, *Ansichten der Natur*, ed. by Hanno Beck and others, Forschungsunternehmen der Humboldt-Gesellschaft, 40 (Darmstadt: Wissenschaftliche Buch-gesellschaft, 1987), p. xi.
2. *DKV*, I: 16, *Campagne in Frankreich, Belagerung von Mainz, Reiseschriften* (1994), p. 16.
3. Ibid., p. 48.
4. See Charles Batten's *Pleasurable Instruction: Form and Convention in Eighteenth-Century Travel Literature* (Berkeley: University of California Press, 1978).
5. Duncan Large, '"Sterne-Bilder": Sterne in the German-Speaking World', in *The Reception of Laurence Sterne in Europe*, ed. by Peter de Voogd and John Neubauer (Londonand New York: Continuum, 2004), pp. 68–84.
6. Anon., *Das in Deutschland so sehr überhand genommene Uebel der sogenannten Empfindsamkeit oder Empfindeley, nach seinem Ursprung, Kennzeichen und Wirkungen, wie auch die sicherste Verwahrung dagegen. Eine Preisschrift* (Freiberg: [n. publ.], 1782), p. 12, quoted in Gerhard Sauder, *Empfindsamkeit*, 3 vols (Stuttgart: Metzler, 1980), III, 32.

7. See Gerhard Sauder, 'Empfindsame Reisen', in *Reisekultur: Von der Pilgerfahrt zum modernen Tourismus*, ed. by Hermann Bausinger, Klaus Beyrer, and Gottfried Korff (Munich: Beck, 1991), pp. 276–83.

8. Humboldt, *Ansichten*, p. 128.

9. Georg Forster, *A Voyage Round the World, in his Brit. Majesty's Sloop Resolution, commanded by Capt. Cook, during the years 1772, 1773, 1774 and 1775*, 2 vols (London: White, Robinson, Elmsly, Robinson, 1777), I, xi–xii.

10. Ibid.

11. Johann Georg Büsch, *Bemerkungen auf einer Reise durch einen Teil der Vereinigten Niederlande und Englands* (Hamburg: Bohn, 1786), p. 4.

12. Johann Heinrich Zedler, *Grosses vollständiges Universal-Lexicon,* 64 vols (Leipzig: Zedler, 1732–54), XXXVII (1743), col. 1691.

13. Adam Smith, *The Theory of Moral Sentiments* (London: Miller, 1759), p. 2.

14. James Engell, *The Creative Imagination: Enlightenment to Romanticism* (Cambridge, MA: Harvard University Press, 1981), p. 55.

15. Smith, p. 2.

16. Among other important work on sensibility see Sauder, *Empfindsamkeit;* Janet Todd, *Sensibility: An Introduction* (London: Methuen, 1986); G. J. Barker-Benfield, *The Culture of Sensibility: Sex and Society in Eighteenth-Century Britain* (Chicago: University of Chicago Press, 1992).

17. AR (1789), 313–18 (318).

18. See Suzanne Keen, *Empathy and the Novel* (Oxford: Oxford University Press, 2007); Willie van Peer and Henk Pander Maat, 'Perspectivation and Sympathy: Effects of Narrative Point of View', in *Empirical Approaches to Literature and Aesthetics*, ed. by Roger J. Kreuz and Mary Sue MacNealy (Norwood: Ablex, 1996), pp. 143–54; Max Louwerse and Don Kuiken, 'The Effects of Personal Involvement in Narrative Discourse', *Discourse Processes*, 38.2 (2004), 169–72.

19. While this research includes accounts by travellers who passed through England then on to Scotland, it focuses solely on their account covering the area south of the border. For an excellent study of German travellers to Scotland at the start of the nineteenth century, see Alison Hiley's two-volume doctoral thesis, 'German-speaking Travellers in Scotland, 1800–1860, and their Place in the History of European Travel Literature' (University of Edinburgh, 1985).

20. Johann Wilhelm von Archenholtz, *England und Italien*, Nachdr. der dreiteiligen Erstausg. Leipzig 1785, mit Varianten der fünfteiligen Ausg. Leipzig 1787, ed. and notes, Michael Maurer, 3 vols (Leipzig: Dykische Buchhandlung, 1785/1787; repr. Heidelberg: Winter, 1993), I, 1.

21. Ibid.

22. Friedrich Wilhelm von Schütz, *Briefe über London. Ein Gegenstück zu des Herrn von Archenholz England und Italien* (Hamburg: Bachmann and Sundermann, 1792), p. iii.

23. Friedrich Wilhelm von Taube, *Von der Beschaffenheit Englands überhaupt, in Absicht auf die Manufakturen, Handlung und Schiffahrt* (1774), in *O Britannien, von deiner Freiheit einen Hut voll: Deutsche Reiseberichte des 18. Jahrhunderts*, ed. by Michael Maurer (Munich: Beck, 1992), pp. 225–40 (p. 231).

24. Johann Jacob Volkmann, *Neueste Reisen durch England, vorzüglich in Absicht auf die Kunstsammlungen, Naturgeschichte, Oekonomie, Manufakturen und Landsitze der Großen: Aus den besten Nachrichten und neuern Schriften zusammengetragen*, 4 vols (Leipzig: Fritsch, 1781–82), I, Vorbericht, unpaginated.

25. Esther [Hester] Lynch Piozzi, *Letters to and from the Late Samuel Johnson, LL.D. To which are added some poems never before printed*, 2 vols (London: Strahan and Cadell, 1788), II, 356.

26. See Michael Maurer, *Aufklärung und Anglophilie in Deutschland* (Göttingen: Vandenhoeck and Ruprecht, 1987); other useful studies include Horst W. Blanke, *Politische Herrschaft und soziale Ungleichheit im Spiegel der Anderen: Untersuchungen zu den deutschsprachigen Reisebeschreibungen vornehmlich im Zeitalter der Auklärung*, 2 vols (Waltrop: Spenner, 1997). Earlier literature on German travel writing includes W. D. Robson-Scott's *German Travellers in England, 1400–1800* (Oxford: Blackwell, 1953) as well as Robert Elsasser's rather brief *Über die politischen Bildungsreisen der Deutschen nach England vom Anfang des 18. Jahrhunderts bis 1815*, Heidelberger Abhandlungen zur mittleren und neueren Geschichte, 51 (Heidelberg: Winter, 1917).

27. Tilmann Fischer, *Reiseziel England: Ein Beitrag zur Poetik der Reisebeschreibung und zur Topik der Moderne (1830–1870)*, Philologische Studien und Quellen, 184 (Berlin: Schmidt, 2004).

CHAPTER 1

Theatre and Orality in Karl Philipp Moritz's
Reisen eines Deutschen in England im Jahr 1782

In a letter of 3 February 1787, Karl Philipp Moritz confirmed to his publisher, Johann Heinrich Campe, his intention to write an account of his travels through Italy. During the winter he had reflected on how his account would differ from the many travelogues on Italy which were flooding the German book market. His aim, he elaborated, would be to describe a journey that not only allowed him to educate the reader in classical literature, Roman customs, and practices, but also to reconstruct these in the key *loci* of classical antiquity. Moritz therefore sought to create 'eine Art von täuschender Komposition [. . .], worinn di [sic] allgemeinen Bemerkungen immer auf dem gehörigen Fleck lebhaft und anschaulich gemacht würden' [a deceptive kind of composition in which the general comments would always be given in the right place and presented in a lively and visual fashion].[1] Rather than offering the sterile narrative of facts which characterized so many beaten-track accounts of Italy's past glories, he aimed to describe and revivify classical scenes at the places where he paused on his itinerary, making these events 'lebhaft und anschaulich' in the mind's eye of the reader.[2]

Furthermore, Moritz noted to Campe, his account of travel to Italy would be a very different affair from his previous travelogue, the *Reisen eines Deutschen in England im Jahr 1782* (1783). There, he observed:

> Man hat sich di Erzählung einer Reihe von Abentheuern wohl einmal gefallen lassen, und statt solider Bemerkungen, damit vorlieb genommen; man möchte diß aber wohl nicht zum zweitenmale thun.[3]

> [Readers have tolerated the narration of a series of adventures once and instead of sound comments, made done with this; but it would not be advisable to do so a second time.]

His dismissal of this travelogue as nothing more than a series of cheap adventures was undoubtedly the embarrassed acknowledgement by a man who now belonged to Goethe's intellectual circle in Rome that this account was not characterized by great intellectual or factual rigour. Certainly it could not claim the same depth of observation or authority as studies of England which appeared in the years preceding or just after its publication. Wendeborn's handy octavo volume, the *Beyträge zur Kenntniß Grosbritanniens vom Jahr 1779* [*Contributions to Our Knowledge of Great Britain in the Year 1779*] (1780) — a valuable book as Moritz himself acknowledged[4] —

was the work of a man who had been living in Britain for some thirteen years. Johann Jacob Volkmann's four-volume *Neueste Reisen durch England* [*Latest Travels through England*] (1781–82), published two years before Moritz's account, offered a comprehensive description of art, architecture, industry, and manufacture which (while fiercely rebutting accusations of plagiarism) drew on a multitude of existing sources on England. Wendeborn's subsequent four-part work, the *Zustand des Staats, der Religion, der Gelehrsamkeit und Kunst in Großbritannien gegen das Ende des achtzehnten Jahrhunderts* (1785–88) and Archenholtz's multi-volume *England und Italien* [*England and Italy*] (1785) also, by their sheer comprehensiveness, put Moritz's travel account in the shade.

The *Reisen eines Deutschen in England* was, at best, a brief account of a journey conducted through England in the few snatched months between May and August 1782. It consisted of nine letters written from London and five from other towns on his itinerary. These were addressed to Friedrich Gedike, member of the illustrious *Berliner Mittwochsgesellschaft* [*Berlin Wednesday Society*] and co-editor with Johann Erich Biester of the free-thinking *Berlinische Monatsschrift*. Moritz's narrative began aboard a boat on the Thames drawing close to London. It went on to describe in some detail life in the capital and contained separate sections pertaining to London. These included a description of the standard tourist sights: St. James's Park, Vauxhall Pleasure Gardens (then at their heyday), the British Museum, St Paul's Cathedral, Parliament in session, and a parliamentary election. Unlike many of the German travellers to England before him, Moritz then took the unusual course of looking outside London to see what else England had to offer. He headed out of the capital via Richmond and Windsor and went on to Oxford, where he related his encounter with scholars and clerics at the university. He then walked on to Derby and Birmingham before reaching the caves at Castleton in Derbyshire, after which he returned south via Loughborough and Leicester to London. Precisely because he opted for a pedestrian mode of travel (or rather, the impecunious Moritz had little choice but to complete most of the journey on foot), Moritz, the *Fußreisender*, was often taken as a tramp, refused beer and bread by innkeepers on his travels, and his bed for the night was offered to those of less unkempt appearance. Thus he saw life in England from a very different angle from that of his aristocratic predecessors. His account related what could not be seen here in Germany and could be learnt from very few descriptions, the *Neue Hallische Gelehrte Zeitungen* noted in its 1784 review, namely national customs abroad and the spirit of the people, especially among the lower classes.[5] Particularly in this section of the travelogue, readers saw the darker side of English hospitality. But not everyone considered this a productive way of gaining a more accurate and complete picture of life in England. Georg Forster noted in his review which appeared in the *Göttingische Anzeigen von gelehrten Sachen* in May 1784 that the appearance of poverty rarely aroused sympathy in the English, more likely distrust.[6] Indeed, Forster lamented, 'Es ist Schade, daß der Hr. V. bey der Art zu reisen, sich den Zutritt zu den höhern Classen versagte; wo sein Beobachtungsgeist auf eine angenehmere und weit vollkommenere Art befriedigt worden wäre' [It is a shame that the author forewent access to the higher classes by travelling in this manner; where his powers of observation could have been satisfied in a more pleasant and far more comprehensive fashion].[7]

Unlike Forster, the *Critical Review* was much warmer in its praise of his account and enthused about the *Travels, Chiefly on Foot, through Several Parts of England, in 1782*, its English translation published with Robinson in London in 1795. It lauded Moritz's work as a resounding success and considered that its presentation of 'the turns of the human heart in every situation of life' made it highly accessible to a contemporary readership.[8] While recent research on Moritz's travel writing — notably the work of Isabel A. White, Heide Hollmer, and Albert Meier — has focused in particular on landscape description as a means of evoking the reader's sympathetic response towards the travelling subject, the figures whom Moritz encountered in the city have largely been overlooked.[9] Yet Moritz paid considerable attention to the rhetorical practices of a range of individuals, from gypsies to housemaids, innkeepers to politicians.[10] It was precisely this aspect which differentiated his account from those of previous travellers. In these scenes the affective investment is of quite a different order. The subjects are not landscapes onto which the author can project his feelings. Rather, they are figures whom the author seeks to construct rhetorically as individuals with whom the reader is invited to identify or sympathize. Moritz clearly reconstructs the figures whom he describes — including, to a degree, himself — as inhabiting a theatrical space. He peoples the 'stage' constructed in his travel account with public 'performers' such as politicians and preachers, as well as more unassuming subjects. This notion of theatricality is primarily reinforced by Moritz's use of direct speech in his recording of interaction between people in London and Oxford, often given in English and subsequently translated into German. From the cry that goes up at Vauxhall Pleasure Gardens 'take care of your Pockets, nehmt eure Taschen in Acht!', to the calls of 'to Order' in parliamentary session, or the remark overheard by Moritz about himself, 'he is a poor travelling creature! (er ist ein armes herumwanderndes Geschöpf)', Moritz's travelogue of England is punctuated by strikingly vivid, if almost over-emphatic, oral encounters.[11] As Michael Eggers has shown, Moritz's use of the human voice and the spoken word in *Anton Reiser* (1783–90) and *Andreas Hartknopf* (1786) creates a nexus of affective attachments closely allied to notions of self-conception and self-presentation, while also setting up a series of tensions between the representational possibilities of the spoken and the written word.[12]

In what follows I shall complement Eggers's arguments by suggesting that Moritz's use of direct speech in these later works was an important rhetorical strategy for eliciting affective identification which he had already begun to develop in his earlier non-fictional writing, notably his account of travel to England in 1782. This chapter begins by exploring the use of direct speech in four particular scenes. It looks first at the Whig politician Charles James Fox's defence in the House of Commons of his support of Cecil Wray at the Westminster by-election in July 1782, then Wray's speech at this by-election, Fox's resignation on Tuesday 9 July 1782, and, finally, Moritz's theological debate with a group of Oxford clerics. Then it seeks to contextualize Moritz's use of direct speech in prose within the broader framework of late eighteenth-century narrative practice. What 'added value' did theorists of the time consider that it brought to a text? How, both in historical writing and in the novel, could the medium of voice create a sense of presence and evince readerly identification? Finally, the chapter locates theatrical sensibility within the dramatic theory of the period, focusing particularly on the acutely problematic nature of theatricality at this time and its attendant claims to authenticity. Thus, by pursuing theatrical concerns in a text (and genre) which might at first sight seem wholly unrelated to theatre, this chapter aims to reposition the non-fictional travel account within an aesthetic programme which points up not only the possibilities but also the limits of affective involvement in Moritz's account of England.[13]

The Theatre of Parliament: 'the whole of the British nation assembled in its representatives'

'Bald hätte ich vergessen', wrote Moritz in the fifth letter of his *Reisen eines Deutschen in England*, 'Ihnen zu sagen, daß ich schon im Parlament gewesen bin, und doch ist dies das Wichtigste' [I had almost forgotten to tell you that I have already been inside Parliament, and yet this is of the utmost importance].[14] The year 1782 was an eventful one in British politics. The independence of the American colonies and their freedom from British taxation, wrangles in the cabinet over economic reform, and the discussion of whether Ireland should be separated from the English crown — all these made the Strangers' Gallery a particularly exciting window on British politics. Nevertheless, and paradoxical as it might seem, Moritz professed to show no great interest in politics itself. Indeed, what attracted him to London's political scene was less the *content* of the debate than the rhetorical *skill* of those speaking. Even during his brief stay in England, he saw some of Britain's finest political orators — Charles James Fox, Edmund Burke, and William Pitt the Younger — take centre stage. Three incidents in particular caught Moritz's attention as he watched events in the British Parliament in those few weeks in July and August 1782. Extracts from these were published in 'Ein Brief aus London' [A Letter from London] in the *Berlinische Monatsschrift* of March the following year, prior to the publication of the *Reisen eines Deutschen in England*.[15] Moritz's first visit to Parliament came shortly after a by-election in Westminster, Charles Fox's constituency. Admiral Rodney had just been elevated to a peerage, thereby leaving one of the two seats for Westminster vacant. Sir Cecil Wray had won the by-election for Westminster the previous Tuesday, supported by Charles James Fox (then first Foreign Secretary under the Rockingham government), who had acted as chairman for his committee. Fox, on the day Moritz visited the House, was defending the fact that he had acted as a private individual rather than as statesman in supporting Wray against the other candidate, Admiral Hood. The second scene, 'Eine Parlamentswahl' [A Parliamentary Election], following on from this speech of defence, detailed the election itself. It described the hustings in Covent Garden where Wray addressed the listening crowd. The third scene recorded the debate in Parliament following Rockingham's death on 1 July 1782, at which Fox was called upon to justify his resignation of 4 July, while Burke and Pitt also addressed the House.

Moritz's opening description of the House of Commons suggested important similarities with a church interior which already emphasized the analogy in his own mind between the oratorical skill of the preacher and that of the politician:

> Und nun sah ich also zum erstenmal in einem ziemlich unansehnlichen Gebäude, das einer Kapelle sehr ähnlich sieht, die ganze Englische Nation in ihren Repräsentanten versammelt: der Sprecher, ein ältlicher Mann, mit einer ungeheuren Allongenperücke, in einem schwarzen Mantel, den Hut auf dem Kopfe, mir gerade gegenüber auf einem erhabenen Stuhle, der mit einer kleinen Kanzel viel Ähnlichkeit hat, nur daß vorn das Pulpet daran fehlt; vor diesem Stuhle ein Tisch, der wie ein Altar aussieht.[16]

> [And thus I now, for the first time, saw the whole of the British nation assembled in its representatives in rather an unattractive-looking building, which resembles to a great degree a chapel: the Speaker, an elderly man, with an enormous wig with two knotted tresses and a black cloak, his hat on his head, sat opposite me on a lofty chair which was not unlike a small pulpit, save only that in front of it there was no lectern. Before the Speaker's chair stands a table, which looks like an altar.]

Moritz therefore wasted few words on the architectural features of the 'unansehnliche[s] Gebäude' in which the House of Commons met at that time, likening it simply to a chapel. Rather, he drew the reader's attention to the Speaker whose chair seemed like a pulpit, the table before him an altar. Beneath the public gallery were the seats for the Members of Parliament:

> An den Seiten des Hauses rund umher unter der Galerie sind die Bänke für die Parliamentsglieder, mit grünem Tuch ausgeschlagen, immer eine höher, als die andre, wie unsre Chöre in den Kirchen, damit derjenige, welcher redet, immer über die vor ihm sitzenden wegsehen kann.[17]

> [All around the sides of the House under the gallery are benches for the members, covered with green cloth, always one above the other, like our choirs in churches, in order that he who is speaking may see over those who sit in front of him.]

Such analogies were perhaps only intended to facilitate the German reader's visualization of the scene, but Moritz sustained the metaphor of the church by commenting that a politician speaking was like a priest conducting a sermon: the former would only occasionally draw 'eine Art von Konzept aus der Tasche, [. . .] wie ein Kandidat, der in der Predigt stecken bleibt' [a kind of memorandum from their pocket, like a novice priest who is at a loss in his sermon].[18]

Moritz is quick to note that while a certain tradition and ceremony underlies the politicians' modes of speech, this should not be interpreted as the empty rhetoric of display:

> Das Reden geschiehet ohne alle Feierlichkeit: einer steht bloß von seinem Sitze auf, nimmt seinen Hut ab, wendet sich gegen den Sprecher, an den alle Reden gerichtet sind, behält Hut und Stock in einer Hand, und mit der andern macht er seine Gesten.[19]

> [Speeches occur without great gravity. Speakers simply stand up, take off their hat, turn to the Speaker, to whom all speeches are addressed, hold hat and stick in one hand and with the other make their gestures.]

FIG. 1.1. Charles James Fox as Demosthenes
History of the Westminster Election (London: Debrett, 1784)
reproduced by permission of Cambridge University Library

Public speaking in the House of Commons was not obviously characterized by the use of artificial rhetorical codes, but rather by the direct, seemingly authentic, expression of one's thoughts and feelings. Public speaking was by no means a monologic undertaking:

> Sobald hingegen einer gut und zweckmäßig redet, so herrscht die äußerste Stille, und einer nach dem andern gibt seinen Beifall dadurch zu erkennen, daß er "hear him!" hört ihn! ruft, welches [. . .] verursacht, daß der Redende wiederum durch eben dieses "hear him!" oft unterbrochen wird. Demohngeachtet ist dieser Zuruf immer eine große Aufmunterung, und ich habe oft bemerkt, daß einer, der mit einiger Furchtsamkeit oder Kälte zu reden anfängt, am Ende dadurch, in ein solches Feuer gesetzt wird, daß er mit einem Strome von Beredsamkeit spricht.[20]

> [On the contrary, when a member speaks well and to the point, the most perfect silence reigns, and one after the other the listeners show their approval by calling 'hear him!', which means that the speaker is often interrupted by this 'hear him!'. Nevertheless, this calling out is always considered a great encouragement and I have often observed that those who begin with some diffidence and even coldness by the end have become so animated that they speak with a torrent of eloquence.]

The speaker's performance was under constant threat from the listening crowd who at intervals broke their silence with 'hear him! hört ihn!'. There was a constant tension between approving silence and the audience's desire to turn the communicative act of public speaking into a form of dialogue. Yet this tension was productive to the extent that, as Moritz hastens to explain, the comments made by an appreciative audience energized and enhanced the speaker's performance by inspiring greater confidence in him. Thus a communicative reciprocity informed public speaking that encouraged affective identification.

Charles James Fox's speech in defence of his support of Cecil Wray at the Westminster by-election gave Moritz a chance to see British oratory at its best. Fox was one of the most distinguished political orators of his day. Fiery and vehement, he was a master of the impromptu speech, sometimes repetitive and over-excited, but capable of sweeping the audience along on what Sir James Mackintosh described as 'torrents of impetuous and irresistible eloquence', keeping them hanging upon his every word for the best part of two hours at a time.[21] The sheer vigour of his ideas, breadth of information, retentiveness of memory, and exuberance of invention made his speeches magnetizing performances. Fox's speeches were traditionally off-the-cuff, seemingly unprepared affairs; the day before an important speech, he could be found at the Newmarket races; the night before, drinking and gambling with friends at Hockerel.[22] One political print of the time described Fox's style as 'Demosthenean' (Fig. 1.1). A satire upon the great classical orator-statesman, it showed Fox in his accustomed attitude of speaking, legs bent, with his hat in his left hand and his chubby right hand on his heart, his considerable girth bursting his waistcoat buttons asunder.

As Moritz was well aware, Fox was a consummate actor, drawing not only on all the arts of rhetoric, but creating a powerful interplay of speech and movement:

> Fox hatte seinen Platz zur rechten Seite des Sprechers, nicht weit von dem Tische, worauf der vergoldete Szepter liegt, nun nahm er seine Stellung so nahe an diesem Tische, daß er ihn mit der Hand erreichen, und manchen herzhaften Schlag darauf tun konnte, nachdem es der Affekt seiner Rede erforderte.[23]

> [Fox was sitting to the right of the Speaker, not far from the table on which the gilt sceptre lay. He now took his place so near this table that he could reach it with his hand, and, thus placed, he gave it many a hearty thump, depending on when the emotional force of his speech required it.]

Fox therefore availed himself of the rich possibilities of movement and action literally to thump a point home on the table at his side. In Moritz's casting of him, it was primarily Fox's oratorical skill that brought the listening members to heel:

und mit welchem Feuer und hinreißender Beredsamkeit er sprach, und wie
der Sprecher auf dem Stuhle aus seiner Wolkenperücke ihm unaufhörlich
Beifall zunickte, und alles 'hear him!' rief, und 'Speak yet!' wenn es schien,
als wollte er aufhören zu reden; und er auf diese Weise beinahe zwei Stunden
nacheinander sprach, das kann ich Ihnen nicht beschreiben.[24]

[It is impossible for me to describe with what fire and persuasive eloquence he
spoke and how the Speaker in the chair incessantly nodded approbation from
under his curly wig, and everyone called 'hear him!' and 'Speak yet!' when it
seemed as if he wanted to stop speaking; and so he continued to speak in this
manner for nearly two hours continuously.]

Intriguingly, what Moritz again does not do is give the reader a taste of the speech
itself. Rather, he shows the effect that Fox's speech has on its audience, through the
response of the Speaker, reduced to nodding agreement, and the other members of
the house calling in unison 'Hear him!' and 'Speak yet!'. The rhetorical power of
the speech appears to quell resistance or discord into these two unifying utterances.
But Fox's rhetorical strength is conveyed less through the fact that his speech lasted
two hours than that it literally silenced Moritz: he cannot describe the effect that it
had upon him it in its entirety and must concede that he has reached the limits of
narrative representation. The written word is therefore incapable of describing fully
the very power that the spoken word has over the listener, the emotional energy
which is conveyed through the speaker's oratorical skill. Here Moritz gives primacy
to the spoken over the written word: the reverse in fact of the relationship that he
would later point to in his *Versuch einer deutschen Prosodie* [*Essay on German Prosody*]
(1786) in which speech could no longer capture with clarity the thought processes
being articulated.[25] As Eggers argues with respect to *Anton Reiser* in particular and
to Moritz's work in general:

So bildet sich schließlich ein Wandel in der Sprachauffassung ab: Ist diese
zunächst an einem Ideal des wahren, weil vom Geist beseelten Sprechens
orientiert, [. . .] so kommt schließlich dem Schreiben eine zunehmende
Bedeutung zu.[26]

[Thus in the end a change in the perception of language takes place. If this is
initially oriented towards an ideal of speech which is true because it is inspired
by the mind, in the end writing becomes increasingly important.]

In the passage from Moritz's account quoted above, it is, paradoxically, Moritz's
inability to record what was said that is proof that he was there, and that his record
of these events is authentic.

What drew Moritz to the figure of Fox was certainly not his physical appearance.
As Moritz himself was compelled to admit, Fox was 'schwärzlich, klein, untersetzt,
gemeinhin schlecht frisiert, hat ein etwas jüdisches Ansehen' [swarthy, short,
stocky, hair generally unkempt and with a somewhat Jewish appearance].[27] That
also meant, though, that he was not an aristocratic dandy. Quite the contrary,
he was a politician who liked to present himself as a man of the people, a grand
commoner.[28] Not for nothing was it Fox who was illustrated in a political cartoon
of 1782 entitled 'Vox Populi', portraying him in declamatory stance, fist aloft,
hand on hip, ramming his point home with his sheer physical bulk as much as

with his rhetorical force. Moritz too was keen to represent himself as a man of the people. In the *Reisen eines Deutschen in England* Moritz had likewise sought to examine and represent what life was like for ordinary tradespeople. True, he had arrived in England with the requisite sheaf of letters of recommendation and socialized with the likes of Baron Grothaus while in London, but his account is unusual precisely because it addresses issues of literacy and of national identity in the lower classes. Had Moritz been at Westminster Hall on Friday 17 July, the day after Parliament had gone into summer recess, he would have heard Fox address the electors of Westminster. Moritz would undoubtedly have approved of the spirit in which the British politician spoke. Fox's speech vehemently opposed the sovereign's right to exercise 'his Majesty's negative', whereby the sovereign could interpose his prerogative in affairs of state, despite these having already received the consent of two other parts of legislature. '[T]he time approaches', Fox had declared, 'when the House of Commons will become, in fact, the representation of the people, and when their language will be the genuine voice of the people'.[29]

Cecil Wray and 'der niedrigste Pöbel'

Like Fox, Moritz seemed to seek some degree of affiliation with the lower classes. His treatment of them in crowd scenes therefore merits particularly close examination. As Peter Brenner has remarked, even until the end of the nineteenth century, crowded streets and crowds themselves were a phenomenon less characteristic of German and Austrian cities than of London or Paris.[30] Although Moritz described the crowd as a still and homogeneous mass of people, not an amorphous coming and going of individuals, the representation of it was still a challenging descriptive undertaking for a German travel writer. Ann Rigney has explored in her analysis of the presentation of crowd scenes in accounts of the French Revolution the decisions which the historian makes about how to represent collective actors. She discusses which figures are selected by writers as representative of the crowd as a whole and whether and how they identify them as individuals in their own right.[31] An examination of this second political scene, where Wray is elected second Member of Parliament for Westminster following a hustings in Covent Garden, shows how Moritz's representation and our interpretation of the crowd scene are directly related to decisions concerning which individuals are allowed to 'speak'.

Moritz sets the scene in such a way that the marketplace at Covent Garden is made to resemble a *Freilichtbühne*, with those people who have the right to vote seated in their red robes on a rather makeshift wooden stage.[32] On mats laid in front of this stage those hoping to convince undecided voters 'perform' to the crowd of people who have gathered. This crowd is described as 'eine Menge Volks und größtenteils der niedrigste Pöbel versammelt' [a multitude of people and largely riffraff of the lowest order].[33] This distinction between 'Volk' and 'Pöbel', which Moritz already makes so early on in this scene, signals two types of actor in the throng of spectators — 'the people' who listen attentively to the speakers and evaluate their words, and those who belong to 'the mob', unthinking and violent.[34] In this rather grotesque performance, candidates for Member of Parliament act subserviently even to this latter category of spectator:

> Die Redner bückten sich tief vor diesem Haufen, und redeten ihn allezeit mit dem Titel '"Gentlemen" (edle Bürger!)' an. Herr Cecil Wray mußte hervortreten und diesen Gentlemen mit Hand und Mund versprechen, seine Pflichten, als ihr Repräsentant im Parlament, auf das getreuste zu erfüllen. Auch entschuldigte er sich mit seiner Reise und Kränklichkeit, daß er nicht einem jeden unter ihnen, wie es sich gebühre, seine Aufwartung gemacht habe.[35]

> [To this crowd, the speakers bowed low and always addressed them with the title of 'Gentleman'. Cecil Wray was obliged to step forward and promise these gentlemen with hand and heart that he would most faithfully fulfil his duties as their representative in Parliament. He also apologized that because of his journey and his ill health, he had not been able to pay a call on them, as was appropriate, at each of their houses.]

This creates an absurd reorganization of the social hierarchy in which the mob are now addressed directly as 'Gentlemen' by their social superiors and whose pardon is craved for illness or absence. In this brief moment, the 'high' theatre of Parliament represented by the rousing skill of Fox is debased to make it become the theatre of fools. It is reminiscent of the lament made by the seventeenth-century author Anton Reiser (who had inspired Moritz's own *Anton Reiser*) in his *Theatronamia*:

> Wir sind ein Schauspiel worden | ja wir sind Narren | das ist wie sonsten die Welt keine Aktion vor hat | es muß ein oder mehr Narren dabey seyn | denen Zusehern ein Gelächter zu machen | aber müssen wir uns von der klugen Welt vor Narren gebrauchen werden | ihnen eine Kurzweil vorzustellen.[36]

> [We have become a theatre act, verily we are fools, it is as if the world undertook no activities or one or more fools should be present, to make the audience laugh, but we must allow ourselves to be taken as fools, in order to afford them entertainment.]

Only once Cecil Wray stands to address the crowd is some kind of order restored, social hierarchy is righted, the crowd settles 'wie das tobende Meer, wenn der Sturm sich gelegt hat' [like the raging sea after a storm], and silence ensues.[37] The response to his speech given in unison by the crowd, 'hear him! hear him!', echoes the calls of the members of Parliament in response to Fox's address. It posits a link between these communicative acts, affirming the continuity between the debates held in Parliament and the people's engagement in politics.

Once Wray has formally been voted in, he is then introduced to the crowd by an eloquent speaker, eliciting the following reaction from a bystander in the crowd: 'Dieser Mann hatte eine gute Ausrede: "he speaks very well!" sagte ein Karren-schieber der neben mir stand' ['This man has a good turn of phrase: he speaks very well', said a carter, who stood next to me.][38] The fact that the opinion of someone as apparently lowly as a *Karrenschieber* is recorded in direct speech and that this figure is given a 'voice' suggests that Moritz is allowing a kind of textual democracy to be played out. Not only are politicians like Fox, Wray, Pitt, and Burke allowed to speak but also the 'lesser' individuals whom other travellers ignored. By including the carter's comment, Moritz fleshes out the identity of one of the individuals in the crowd, thereby making the *Volk* as a whole seem less anonymous. They are people impressed by the artistry of the eloquent speaker, unlike the mob, who, once the speakers have finished, tear the matting into strips, triumphantly encircling the politicians as they process through the streets.[39] Later the carter stands synecdochally for the rest of the *Volk*, becoming a figurative focus of our attention. In what follows, Moritz's remarks gain emotive force precisely because he had accorded the *Karrenschieber* the opportunity to 'speak' earlier:

> O lieber Freund, wenn man hier siehet, wie der geringste Karrenschieber an dem was vorgeht seine Teilnehmung bezeigt, wie die kleinsten Kinder schon in den Geist des Volks mit einstimmen, wie ein jeder sein Gefühl zu erkennen gibt, daß er auch ein Mensch und ein Engländer sei, so gut wie sein König und sein Minister, dabei wird einem doch ganz anders zu Mute, als wenn wir bei uns in Berlin die Soldaten exerzieren sehen.[40]

> [O dear friend, when you see how the lowest carter demonstrates his interest in what is taking place here, how the smallest children contribute to the spirit of the people, how each person can declare his feelings at being a man and an Englishman just as much as his King or his Ministers, one feels very different when one sees our soldiers parading in Berlin.]

The carter now appears to lose his individual status, becoming the generic 'geringste[r] Karrenschieber'. He therefore blends back into the crowd, but because he was singled out for individual treatment earlier and spoke directly to the reader, we relate to what follows with greater affective involvement. The humblest of carters, and children too, are involved in the theatre of politics. They can also voice their feelings of national pride, of a sense of belonging, in a city where — in contrast to Moritz's Berlin — order is upheld by the word rather than the sword.

The scene closes with the arrival of Fox, who is greeted with a cry from the crowd:

> zuletzt nachdem der Aktus beinah vorbei war, fiel es dem Volke ein, ihn reden zu hören, und alles schrie: Fox! Fox! ich rief selber mit, und er mußte auftreten und reden, weil wir ihn hören wollten. Er trat denn auf und bekräftigte nochmals vor dem Volke, daß er schlechterdings nicht als Staatsminister, sondern nur als Privatmann bei dieser Wahl Einfluß gehabt habe.[41]

> [At length, when it was nearly over, the people took it into their heads to hear him speak and everyone cried 'Fox! Fox!' and I also shouted with them and he was obliged to come forward and speak, as we wanted to hear him. He then got up and confirmed again in the presence of the people that he had by no means any influence as a minister in this election, but only as a private person.]

The shouts of 'Fox! Fox!' are striking because they reinforce the immediacy of the action. They are also a pivotal point in the scene at which Moritz seems to suspend his role as foreign onlooker. He becomes drawn into the crowd, combining his voice with theirs ('ich rief selber mit'). Indeed, he becomes rhetorically so involved with the shouting subjects that the description shifts from the first-person singular to the plural 'wir'. This is, admittedly, merely a fleeting moment of alliance with those in the crowd around him, as they shift back to being identified as the *Volk* in the next breath. But it is a moment in which the writer could don a narrative *Tarnkappe*, seemingly eradicating his presence by dissolving into a larger body of onlookers, becoming part of them and empathizing with their interests and concerns.

Moritz's decision to assume the persona of a member of the crowd — akin to Fox's adoption of the role of private individual rather than statesman in the election campaign — is also inherently theatrical. As Eckehard Catholy has observed, Moritz's desire to be an actor was founded upon the need to be part of a group, and a group whose community was founded on struggle. Catholy politicizes it in these terms: '[w]irkliche Gemeinschaft liegt nur in den Klassen, die noch vor dem Kampf um Geltung und um Gleichberechtigung stehen' [true community can only be found in those classes who have still to fight for standing and equality].[42] It is true that Moritz gains a sense of companionship through keeping company with the lower classes, not only in this scene, but also elsewhere. If, however, as Catholy continues, '[i]n den gehobenen Schichten der Zeit [. . .] nur noch Individuen [existieren], da diese ihr Ziel erreicht haben und der massierten Stoßkraft nicht mehr bedürfen' [in the elevated classes of the time only individuals exist since they have attained their goal and no longer need the impetus of the masses], this would suggest that Moritz held a certain disrespect for great political orators such as Fox and Burke. Yet the success of their speeches depends precisely on harnessing the massed powers of the people, on gaining their trust, their empathy, and their understanding through the power of the spoken word.

Fox's Resignation Speech: 'für den Zuhörer rührend und erschütternd'

Moritz's letter of 14 July 1782 in his travel account of England details events that day in Parliament which one contemporary observer of British politics described rather exaggeratedly as a 'debate universally allowed to be the most important one that ever happened in the House of Commons'.[43] Two motions were being discussed at this session: the granting of a pension of £3,200 per annum to Colonel Isaac Barré, a pension approved by Fox; and the reasons for Fox's own resignation. The latter was a matter for discussion, given that one of Fox's opponents, General Conway, had implied that Fox had left the administration on account of personal enmity against the new appointee, the Earl of Shelburne. To save face, it was Fox's task to convince the House that he had intended to resign before the Marquis of Rockingham's death and the cabinet reshuffle that followed.

Moritz presents this speech in a way which stages Fox as an individual speaking to the group of collective actors in Parliament representing 'the nation':

> Am Dienstage war eine der wichtigsten Debatten im Parlamente. *Fox* war aufgefordert, seine Gründe der Nation darzulegen, warum er resigniert habe. Um elf Uhr war das Haus von Zuschauern schon so voll, daß niemand mehr darin Platz finden konnte.[44]

> [On Tuesday there was one of the most important debates in Parliament. *Fox* was called on to explain to the nation the reasons for his resignation. At eleven o'clock the visitors' gallery was already so full that no-one else could find a seat.]

The prolonged delay, which Moritz emphasizes, suggests parallels with an expectant audience waiting for the rise of the curtain at the theatre. When Fox finally arrives, it is the delivery of his speech on which Moritz focuses first:

> Gegen vier Uhr kam Fox. Alles war voll Erwartung. Er sprach mit großer Heftigkeit, ließ es aber dennoch merken, wie sehr er diese Heftigkeit mäßige, und als er nun den Schritt den er getan, mit allen Gründen verteidigt hatte, und nun sagte: ›now I stand here again, poor as I was etc.‹ nun stehe ich hier wieder, arm wie ich war! usw. so war dies wirklich für den Zuhörer rührend und erschütternd.[45]

> [Fox came at about four. Everyone was full of expectation. He spoke with great vehemence at first, but allowed it to become clear how he gradually became more moderate and when at length he had defended the step he had taken with all his reasons, he then said 'now I stand here again, poor as I was etc.'. It was truly impossible for the audience not to be moved and shaken by it.]

Once again, the content of the speech itself does not really feature in Moritz's résumé of events. Rather it is Fox's moving words 'now I stand here again, poor as I was', and the reaction of the spectators to them, that become the focus of attention. But the quotation which Moritz gives in direct speech from Fox's appeal to the nation is not — if the note-takers employed by the publishers Debret, Stockdale and Axtell are to be believed — an accurate transcription of any part of his address.[46] Indeed Moritz's brief snatch of text is in noticeably faltering English while the 'official' account more credibly captures the fiery flow of Fox's defence. This is not to doubt Moritz's presence at the debate. Indeed the line he gives could well be a condensation of two aspects of the 9 July speech which particularly sought to appeal to the audience, namely the opening:

> Never did I rise under such a pressure of mind as at this moment. The peculiar situation in which I stand, would certainly overwhelm me, were it not for two considerations which I have to resort to within myself.[47]

and the close:

> It is, therefore, I have returned, whence I was taken; here it is I can still exert my endeavours in their cause, and here they shall be exerted while I retain the power and confidence of being their servant.[48]

But if Moritz appeared to play rather fast and loose with the notion of accuracy (both here and perhaps elsewhere), this revealed his concern to place in the subject's mouth statements which would have been in character, even if they were not the words actually spoken. Thus the appropriation of direct speech as a rhetorical device which serves to create a sense of immediacy and to underscore the account's authenticity is here unmasked.

FIG. 1.2. 'Freylich ist es das!', artist Daniel Chodowiecki, engraver Daniel Berger
Karl Philipp Moritz, *Reisen eines Deutsche in England im Jahr 1782*, 2nd edn
(Berlin: Maurer, 1785)
Reproduced by permission of the Universitätsbibliothek Leipzig, Hist.Brit.370

'Ich bin auch ein Mann der Predigt'

An arresting addition to the second edition of the *Reisen eines Deutschen in England* of 1785 was the engraved frontispiece by none other than the renowned engraver and key illustrator of the age Daniel Chodowiecki (Fig. 1.2). It showed the scene in which Moritz entered into theological debate with a group of Oxford clerics. This engraving reaffirmed the strong human interest element of Moritz's account: in the first edition the reader's eye had instead been caught with an engraving depicting the sublime horror of the caves at Castleton in Derbyshire. It also carried certain Pietist overtones — the importance of reading aloud from the Bible and debating the interpretation of its content.

The scene at Oxford is one in which it is Moritz's turn to take centre stage. He thereby creates for himself the opportunity to allow the reader to hear his own voice directly in a piece otherwise constructed from his 'inner' voice and from reported speech. The role he was playing on this occasion was not that of the bystander in the crowd associating with tradespeople, but rather that of the preacher rubbing shoulders with Oxford clerics. 'Ich bin auch ein Mann der Predigt' [I also am a preacher] he answers in response to the enquiry of his travelling companion whom he has met on the way from Nettlebed to London, and thus defines the role he will play and his oratorical status for events to come.[49] Two clerics singled out by name, Mr Modd, who had been Moritz's travelling companion as he approached Oxford, and Mr Caern, attempt to uphold the credibility of the Bible against two assertions made about God by the secular free-thinker Mr Clerk. The power of the spoken word to cause offence is here brought into sharp focus. The first of these statements is 'Gott sei ein Weintrinker' [God is a drinker of wine].[50] Modd becomes outraged at this, suggesting that it is unlikely that such a statement could be found in the Bible. Caern likewise thinks it improbable and the matter is settled by Clerk calling for a Bible:

> 'Waiter! fetch a Bible!' (Aufwärter, holet eine Bibel!) rief Mr. Clerk, und es wurde eine große Hausbibel gebracht, und mitten auf dem Tische unter allen den Alekrügen aufgeschlagen.[51]

> ['Waiter! Fetch a Bible', called Mr. Clerk, and a great family Bible was brought in, and opened in the middle of the table amongst all the ale jugs.]

Without much ado, he turns up the passage in Judges 9. 13 which bears out his claim that wine 'rejoices the Heart of God and Man'. The clerics sit stunned and there is a silence lasting a few minutes. Silence here plays a rhetorically important role in a situation where otherwise so many voices are heard. No longer the sign of appreciative agreement, as in the Parliament scenes, it covers a pause in which brains are racked to counter such an irreverent assertion:

> und es herrschte eine Stille von einigen Minuten, als auf einmal der Geist der Exegese über mich kam, und ich sagte: 'Gentlemen! that is an allegorical Expression!' (Meine Herrn, das ist ein allegorischer Ausdruck,) denn, fuhr ich fort, wie oft werden die Könige der Erden in der Bibel Götter genannt?[52]

> [A silence of some minutes prevailed, when all at once the spirit of revelation

seemed to come upon me and I said, 'Gentlemen! That is an allegorical expression!' How often in the Bible are the kings of the earth called gods?]

The spotlight therefore then turns on Moritz, who breaks the silence with a reply made as if another voice were speaking through him. The 'spirit of exegesis', he argues, has cast its power over him as he declares that Clerk has failed to see the symbolic value of the statement. This is a modest assertion on Moritz's part that in fact it was less his individual voice speaking than that of that pastor, trained to use his powers of critical interpretation in such situations. Ironically what we do not see (or hear) in Moritz's use of direct speech is a spontaneous representation of his own ideas. Rather, it is the observation of someone who now assumes his professional role and adopts this language and stance accordingly.

On a second occasion, Clerk tries to test the clerics with the assertion 'Gott sei ein Bartscherer' [God is a barber]. Modd almost loses his temper at this point, while Clerk tries to find a place in Ezekiel to support his claim. Again, it is Moritz who breaks the embarrassed silence:

> Ich brach das Stillschweigen aufs neue, und sagte: Gentlemen! dies ist ja ebenfalls ein allegorischer Ausdruck! — Freilich ist es das! fielen mir Mr. Modd und Mr. Caern ins Wort, und schlugen dazu auf den Tisch.[53]

> [I broke the silence a second time and said, 'Gentlemen! This is likewise an allegorical expression!' — 'To be sure it is!' rejoined Mr. Modd and Mr. Caern and rapped on the table their agreement.]

This time, Moritz is less shy in suggesting that he has the explanation for this strange assertion. The passage from Ezekiel should not be interpreted as meaning that God would shave the beards of the stubborn Jews, Moritz argued, but that God would make them prisoners of those who would shave off their beards. The immediate agreement on the part of Modd and Caern was obviously to cover up their own intellectual shortcomings. As Moritz had noted at the end of the previous paragraph, 'hier ließ selbst den Mr. Caern sein Bruder, der schon vierzig Jahr im Amt war, ganz im Stiche' [here even Mr Caern's brother who had been in the office forty years left him in the lurch], since Caern did not have an answer for the free-thinking Clerk. He follows this mischievously at the end of the next paragraph with 'und Mr. Caern setzte hinzu, sein Bruder, der vierzig Jahr im Amte wäre, erklärte es eben so' [and my brother, rejoined Mr. Caern, who has been forty years in the office explains it just as this gentleman does] to point up the basic untruths which often underlay what was so emphatically affirmed.[54]

The last words we hear from Mr. Modd are 'damm [sic] me! I must read Prayers in all Souls College!' as, in the first light of morning, he leaves the house where he has been drinking with Moritz and the rest of the company through the night. Moritz is quick to explain that although 'damm me!' is an abbreviation of 'God damm me! Gott verdamme mich!', it does not mean more than 'Ei zum Henker! oder Potztausend!'.[55] These words nevertheless sit ill on a cleric's lips, particularly as he is about to read prayers. In this scene we therefore see the actor off-stage, before he has assumed the persona of the learned cleric, the role that he has to perform, and are confronted with the disparity between the vocabulary used and our expectations of the character he portrays. Nevertheless, we feel, despite (or precisely because of) the roughness of the language, that we have gained an authentic picture of the figure of Mr. Modd.

Transposing Narration into Action

Although spoken dialogue was obviously an established form in literary texts, how did eighteenth-century narrative theorists consider that orality in prose texts could encourage a sense of the speaker's presence in non-fictional writing? In what way could this strengthen the reader's sympathetic engagement with the narrative? Moritz was one of the earliest German travel writers on England to recognize the value of direct speech in rendering description 'lebhaft und anschaulich'. But German literary theorists had acknowledged this several decades before. As early as 1740, Johann Jakob Breitinger had argued in his *Critische Dichtkunst* [*Critical Poetry*] that poetic narrative should not consist of simply narration, but rather should aspire to conjure up events in a lively and visual fashion.[56] The powers of the imagination could therefore be usefully employed in constructing as vividly as possible a (fictional) narrative. Although Breitinger did not underestimate the importance of appealing to the reader's visual faculties, he was also aware of the aural immediacy which direct speech — mediated through written text — lent to the imaginative construction of a particular scene.

   Some three decades later, Johann Christoph Gatterer, professor of history at Göttingen, rose to the challenge of legitimizing the performative potential of narrative for the genre of historical writing. His essay 'Von der Evidenz in der Geschichtkunde' [*Of Proof in Historiography*] (1767), published as the preface to a general historical compendium, wholeheartedly endorsed Breitinger's pronouncement that the sterile rehearsal of fact would now no longer suffice, even, and particularly, in the genre of historical writing:

> Man berathschlägt sich über Krieg und Frieden: es gehen Unterhandlungen vor: man belagert Städte, man liefert Schlachten [. . .] Dis [sic] sind lauter wichtige Begebenheiten. Der Geschichtschreiber soll sie erzählen. Sagt er mir sie so trocken weg: so weiß ich wol ungefähr, was vorgegangen ist; allein ich will noch mehr haben: ich will gerührt, ich will bis zur Evidenz überzeugt seyn.[57]

> [Discussions concerning war and peace are conducted; negotiations take place; towns are occupied, battles fought. These are of course important occurrences. The historian should narrate them. If he tells me them in a dry fashion, I know approximately what happened; but I want to have more; I want to be moved, I want to be convinced to the point of certainty.]

Gatterer therefore appeared to dispense with traditional notions that historical description should be solely allied to factual reportage. Rather, the historian should ensure through rhetorical artistry that his account of events deceived the reader into thinking that they seemed immediate.

   Gatterer's essay, which gave German historical narrative a vital new impulse, openly acknowledged a debt to the work of the British empiricists, most notably Henry Home, Lord Kames.[58] Kames's *Elements of Criticism* (1762) offered German aestheticians particular food for thought in its discussion of the faculties of imagination and memory, and the significant role played by language in raising ideas and emotions.[59] Kames's most important contribution to this debate concerned the faculty of memory, in which he distinguished two different forms of recollection: 'reflective remembrance' and 'ideal presence'. In the former, we 'barely recall the idea and think of an event as past, without forming any image' of it in our minds.[60] But in the latter, where the reader 'perceives every thing as passing before him and hath a consciousness of a presence similar to that of a spectator,' he then falls imperceptibly into a state of 'ideal presence [which] may be termed a *waking dream*'.[61] Ideal presence therefore constituted a form of mental illusion in which past action was revivified and re-enacted on the stage that we constructed in our mind. Skilled representation — be it speech, writing or painting — could conjure up in the mind's eye of the reader 'ideas no less distinct than if I had originally been an eye-witness'.[62] Through 'ideal presence' we therefore have seemingly unmediated access to actions which have actually formed part of another individual's experience, allowing us to apprehend events which lie outside our own. Certainly Kames, like Breitinger, did not consider that notions developed with respect to poetic writing also held for factual narrative such as historical writing. 'In history,' argued Kames, 'the reflections ought to be chaste and solid; for while the mind is intent on truth, it is little disposed to the operations of the imagination'.[63] However, while 'ideal presence' did not necessarily enhance the authenticity of historical claims, 'even genuine history has no command over our passions but by ideal presence only'.[64] Indeed, he continued, 'even real events, entitled to our belief must be conceived present and passing in our sight before they can move us'.[65]

Eight years before Moritz's journey to England, two tracts by the theoreticians Friedrich von Blanckenburg and Johann Jakob Engel appeared which showed their debt to Kames. Both published in 1774, each work added new impetus to the discussion surrounding the imaginative powers of narration. Blanckenburg's weighty *Versuch über den Roman* [*Essay on the Novel*] was an important milestone in German narrative theory. It gestured towards the development of the novel in one particular direction: that of the theatre. Blanckenburg placed the emphasis on the ability of text to describe scenes dramatically, to convey action as it developed, rather than to present it in stasis: 'wir werden durch alles in Bewegung gesetzt, was selbst in Bewegung ist' [we are moved by everything which is in itself in movement].[66] Expanding upon this, he echoed in many ways the comments of previous theorists, but placed renewed emphasis on the overlap between the description of action in prose text and performance on stage:

> Der Eindruck ist sehr verschieden, den es macht, wenn wir eine Wirkung vor unsern Augen erfolgen sehen, oder wenn wir sie erzählt hören. Und diesen flachen, kahlen Eindruck, den die bloße *Erzählung* der Begebenheit macht, und der unsre Leidenschaften gar nicht erregt, kann nun der Romanendichter vermeiden, wenn er diese Erzählung in Handlung zu verwandeln weis.[67]

> [Whether we see an action in our mind's eye or hear it narrated makes a very different impression upon us. And this flat, cold impression, which the simple *narration* of an event gives us and does not excite our passions, is something the novelist can avoid if he knows how to turn narration into action.]

The sensory impression engendered in us if we are eye-witnesses to a scene which happens apparently in 'real time' is very different from that which we might have gained simply through the narration of fact:

> Jeder Mensch von einigem Nachdenken muß gemerkt haben, daß ein Vorfall einen weit stärkern Eindruck auf einen Augenzeugen macht, als auf dieselbe Person, wenn sie von einem dritten ihn erst erfährt. Scribenten von Genie, welche wissen, daß das der beste Zugang zum Herzen ist, stellen jedes Ding so vor, als ob es vor unsern Augen vorgienge, und verwandeln uns gleichsam aus Lesern und Zuhörern in Zuschauer. Ein geschickter Scribent verbirgt sich und läßt nur seine Personen sehen; mit einem Wort, alles wird dramatisch, so sehr es nur immer möglich ist.[68]

> [Every person of a reflecting mind must have noticed that an incident has a far stronger impression on an eye-witness than on the person who only hears it from a third person. Writers of genius, who know that this is the best access to the heart, present every event as if it occurred before our eyes and transform us at the same time from readers and listeners into onlookers; a skilful writer conceals himself and only allows his characters to be seen; in a word, everything becomes dramatic only to the extent that this is possible.]

The theatre metaphor is also extrapolated further. The talented writer, Blanckenburg argues, hides in the wings, 'off-stage', thus giving the figures in the description the opportunity to 'perform', seemingly without the narrator's interference or mediation.

Johann Jakob Engel's article 'Ueber Handlung, Gespräch und Erzehlung' [On Plot, Dialogue and Narration] was — as its title suggests — closely concerned with the significance of the spoken word in narrative. In his discussion of the notion of 'ideal presence', he singled out the position of the narrator for particularly close treatment.[69] The traces of the past, Engel argued, could not be expunged from a narrative even when the narrator spoke and wrote in the present tense.[70] He would still have to talk of others in the third person to situate them in his text. For as long as he maintained his position as narrator, it would fall to him to weave them into the larger context of his own work, thereby reinforcing the temporal disparities that he had hoped to present as unified. However:

> Führt er sie selbstredend ein; ja führt er seine eigne Person so ein, indem er sich aus der gegenwärtigen Zeit in die vergangne zurücksetzt: so ist er nicht mehr Erzehler; er wird auf diesen Augenblick dramatischer Schriftsteller.[71]

> [If he introduces them speaking themselves, indeed if he introduces his own character in such a way that he transports himself from the current time into the past, then he is no longer a narrator; in that instance he becomes a dramatic author.]

Once he transplants himself into the past, and allows all the figures to speak for themselves in that past time that he is now in, he has become more of a dramatic author than a narrator, relinquishing his role as co-ordinator or narrator of events. Even then, though, his powers are limited:

> Der Erzehler kann also zwar der Gegenwart durch verschiedene Stufen näher rücken; er kann der Imagination, durch Verwechslung der Zeitfälle, in ihrem Bestreben nach Gegenwart und Anschauen zu Hülfe kommen; aber so ganz

kann er sie doch nie in die Wirklichkeit hineinsetzen, als der Dialogist, bey welchem alles Gegenwart, alles jetziger Augenblick ist.[72]

[The narrator can admittedly draw closer to the present by taking different steps; he can aid the imagination in its striving for the present and the vivid by changing the tenses. But he cannot locate it wholly in the present, as the dialogist can, for whom everything is the present, everything the current moment.]

Engel acknowledges that the narrator can manipulate temporal levels in text, and by appealing to readers' imaginative powers can exploit their willingness to be 'transported' to the past. But Engel also bursts the illusory bubble constructed through the notion of 'ideal presence' which suggests that they might gain privileged proximity to the situation described. Only the work of the dialogist, he concludes, has that elusive capacity to capture through the written word the present action of the speaking voice.

   Late eighteenth-century narrative practices in Germany therefore encouraged experimentation that endorsed the yielding of critical distance to emotional proximity. Through the suspension of disbelief, events narrated would take on a certain immediacy and transparency, imaginatively transporting the reader of the historical text into the past, and, by analogy, the reader of the travelogue to foreign shores. Readers could therefore willingly lose themselves in the 'spectacle' of the scene conjured up in the text before them. The metaphor of the mind as a stage had become a commonplace which rendered the experience of reading the same as, or at least similar to, the experience of being the observer of a moving spectacle. But despite the claims made by narrative theorists for the power of orality in both fictional and non-fictional prose, they remained acutely aware that the creation of sympathy was bound fast to notions of display and appearance. The theatrical nature of this sensibility into which writers of prose narrative now tapped was of an order which, as the next section seeks to show, their contemporaries working within the field of drama found infinitely more troubling.

Theatrical Sensibility and Moritz's *Anton Reiser*

Schiller, in his lecture of June 1784 entitled 'Was kann eine gute stehende Schaubühne eigentlich wirken?' [What can a well-established stage actually achieve?] also recognized the efficacy of theatre in providing moral action: 'So gewiß sichtbare Darstellung mächtiger wirkt, als toder Buchstabe und kalte Erzählung, so gewiß wirkt die Schaubühne tiefer und daurender als Moral und Geseze' [As surely as visual representation is more compelling than the mute word or cold narration, it is equally certain that the theater wields a more profound, more lasting influence than either morality or laws].[73] Theatre could call up onto the stage the crimes of past criminals and show contemporary audiences how they should and should not behave. But the power of theatrical representation went beyond simply didactic aims. As Schiller declared: 'Die Schaubühne ist mehr als jede andere öffentliche Anstalt des Staats eine Schule der praktischen Weisheit, ein Wegweiser durch das bürgerliche Leben, ein unfehlbarer Schlüssel zu den geheimsten Zugängen der menschlichen Seele' [The stage is, more than any other public institution, a school of practical wisdom, a guide through our daily lives, an infallible key to the most secret points of access of the human soul].[74] Through the medium of drama, the spectator could see directly into the protagonist's mind and heart, understanding the motivations which caused individuals to act as they did. Schiller therefore endorsed theatrical sensibility as a means to promote a sense of identification and affective projection.

Moritz's vitriolic reviews of Schiller's *Kabale und Liebe* [*Intrigue and Love*] which appeared in the *Vossische Zeitung* [*Vossian Newspaper*] in July and September of 1784 might have suggested that his theatrical agenda was poles apart from that of the young playwright. His attack on Schiller's work primarily revolved around the fact that it was unclear why figures such as Franz Moor had become such outlaws. 'Wozu nützt es denn, die Einbildungskraft mit solchen Bildern anzufüllen, wodurch wahrlich weder der Verstand noch das Herz gebessert wird?' [What is the purpose of supplementing the imagination with such pictures, when neither reason nor the heart are improved?], he queried testily.[75] But his most vicious criticism was reserved for Schiller's style, which he condemned as failing to belong to the language of the heart and nature.[76] It was the language of a man, he concluded, who sought to impress through 'falsche[r] Schimmer' [false lustre], hoping to equal the talent of Lessing and others by the cheapest of means. Regardless of whether Moritz's assessment of Schiller's work in such negative terms was legitimate or not, he clearly had little time for the artificial representation of emotion which rendered theatrical sensibility purely an issue of display, divorcing it from any notions of true sentiment.

Moritz's autobiographical novel *Anton Reiser*, which he started to publish in the same year as his travel account of England, exemplified his own stance towards theatrical sensibility, imaginative 'transport', and the evocation of sympathy. *Anton Reiser* shows how, from Moritz's earliest days as a schoolboy in Hanover, he was inspired by watching the greatest actors of his time, such as Hans Konrad Ekhof, Konrad Ernst Ackermann, Sophie Charlotte Schröder and Friedrich Ludwig Schröder. But the 'performances' which Moritz cast in the most positive light were not those of conventional 'actors' at all. In his description of the preacher at Braunschweig, Moritz shows most clearly how he was impressed by the rhetorical potential of a sermon to create a sense of collective emotional excitement, if not sheer frenzy.[77] Pastor P...'s voice, pacing, and expression hold the young Moritz enthralled. The sheer electricity of the tension and excitement which Pastor P... creates when he preaches is evident not just in his oratorical skill but in his very movements and body:

> So wie er inniger in seine Materie eindrang, so fing das Feuer der Beredsamkeit in seinen Augen zu blitzen, aus seiner Brust an zu atmen, und bis in seine Fingerspitzen Funken zu sprühen. Alles war an ihm in Bewegung; sein Ausdruck durch Mienen, Stellung und Gebärden überschritt alle Regeln der Kunst und war doch natürlich, schön und unwiderstehlich mit sich fortreißend.[78]

> [The deeper he went into his subject matter, the more the fire of eloquence began to flash in his eyes, to breathe from his chest and to spray sparks right down to the very tips of his fingers. Everything about him was in movement, his expression through his look, position, and gestures violated all the rules of art and yet was natural, beautiful, and irresistibly enrapturing.]

He preached for some three-and-a-half hours, captivating his congregation, but also reducing them to melancholy and tears on each occasion that he exhorted them to beg God for mercy. In the silences too, the congregation is also transported into a state of frenzy, panic-stricken as they wrestle with their consciences and consider their past.[79] Even in the pauses between such energetic pleas for soul-searching, the listening congregation is still capable of exploiting its own fertile imagination to cast itself into a state of fear and panic. Thus the power of the Pietist sermon to 'transport' its listeners lay less in its appeal to reason and to the power of thought, than to sensibility and to the formidable forces of affective identification — which marked a radical break with the dry, dogmatic teaching of the church. Here Moritz also stressed the importance of a pastor's task as a 'calling' — inspired by religious commitment rather than professional (financial) rewards.

Theatre likewise occupies an ambivalent status in *Anton Reiser*. It allowed Reiser to construct an environment for himself in which he could assume different personae, interact with a series of fictional interlocutors, and gain access to worlds previously closed to him:

> der *Dialog* auf dem Theater bekam mehr Reize für ihn, als der immerwährende *Monolog* auf der Kanzel — Und dann konnte er auf dem Theater alles sein, wozu er in der wirklichen Welt nie Gelegenheit hatte — und was er doch so oft zu sein wünschte — großmütig, wohltätig, edel, standhaft, über alles Demütigende und Erniedrigende erhaben.[80]

> [the *dialogue* in the theatre gained more appeal for him than the continuous *monologue* in the pulpit — And then in the theatre he could be everything that in the real world he had not had the opportunity to be — and what he so often wished to be — magnanimous, charitable, noble, steadfast, rising above everything humiliating and degrading.]

This projection of himself into these new roles recast him as magnanimous, steadfast, and charitable, thereby freeing him from the humiliation that he otherwise felt in everyday life. But it also enabled him to represent himself as a wholly different character and, as Rousseau argued in his criticism of the theatre, to 'forget' his real self in the process.[81] The notions of theatre and theatricality in *Anton Reiser* are therefore founded less upon sympathy and theatrical sensibility, than upon a need to flee reality.

In the *Reisen eines Deutschen in England im Jahr 1782* (1783), by contrast, theatrical performance is less a site of spiritual self-discovery and more an institutional matter, since what Moritz sees played out before his eyes is the articulation of democratic principles through open debate, free and public voting, and the apparent dissolution of hierarchies between aristocracy and the lower classes. In short, this is the very performance of what Jürgen Habermas has termed a structural change of the public sphere. It would seem, therefore, that Moritz meant his account to be a form of didactic and identificatory reading — that there were lessons to be learned by his German audience about what it was that their society lacked. As Robert S. Bledsoe has emphasized, however, Moritz also argued that identificatory reading carried certain dangers with it. In an article published in the *Deutsches Museum* of 1782, the very same year that he was in England, he lamented that the desire to be solely

imitative, which characterized contemporary German society, hindered readers'
development as individuals: 'Die Nachahmungssucht erstreckt sich gar so weit, daß
man Ideale aus Büchern in sein Leben hinüber trägt. Ja nichts macht die Menschen
wohl mehr unwahr, als eben die vielen Bücher' [The addiction to imitation does in
fact extend so far that people transfer ideals gained from books into their lives. Indeed
nothing makes people more false as precisely these many books].[82] The maturity
for which Moritz strives in his readers is therefore in itself jeopardized by the very
works which they consume. Anton Reiser's reading of *Werther* is a case in point:

> Indes fühlte er sich durch die Lektüre des Werthers ebenso wie durch den
> Shakespeare, sooft er ihn las, über alle seine Verhältnisse erhaben; das verstärkte
> Gefühl seines isolierten Daseins, indem er sich als ein Wesen dachte, worin
> Himmel und Erde sich wie in einem Spiegel darstellt, ließ ihn, stolz auf seine
> Menschheit, nicht mehr ein unbedeutendes weggeworfenes Wesen sein.[83]

> [However, each time after reading Werther he felt just as he had done after
> reading Shakespeare, sublime above all his current circumstances; the intensified
> feeling of his isolated existence, in which he thought of himself as a being in
> which heaven and earth were represented as if in a mirror, permitted him,
> proud of his humanity, no longer to be an insignificant, discarded being.]

As Bledsoe argues, reading in *Anton Reiser* compensates for the lack of satisfaction
which Reiser gains from his personal relationships by making him feel as if he is
more than merely some insignificant being, but remains a solution of only limited
value.[84] Character identification in this example leads only to a greater sense of
isolation and an increased inability to engage with the real world.

How, then, should we understand the empathetic engagement which Moritz seeks
to construct in the *Reise eines Deutschen nach England*? Is the level of identification
we detect there also fleetingly compensatory and does it serve only to isolate the
central figure still more? In terms of Moritz's biography, perhaps this was indeed the
case, since his imminent return to Germany also signalled a return to those forms
of rule which did not display that same degree of democracy he felt sure he had
witnessed in England. Suzanne Keen has argued for fictional works that readers'
perception of a text's fictionality increases the likelihood of their empathy through
the suspension of disbelief.[85] But in the case of Moritz's *Reise eines Deutschen nach
England*, it was precisely the non-fictionality of it — the very real possibility of
the regulation of the public sphere by the people themselves — which was what
enthralled him. This sense of excitement at witnessing a range of scenes in London
was also far from isolating: quite the contrary, one feels that Moritz energetically
allowed himself to be drawn into the action, if only later to stand critically on the
margins as he watched the soldiers in Berlin demonstrating military might.

Moritz's travel account of England therefore exemplifies the shift in the second half
of the eighteenth century from the traditional emphasis on instruction and mimetic
representation towards the newly articulated powers of evocation, presence, and
identification. Tensions between objective and subjective description, between
dispassionate and affective engagement, are articulated in this highly productive
generic redefinition. While it is clear that the various theatrical, rhetorical strategies

on which this redefinition now drew departed from the traditionally sanctioned
narrative forms deployed in travel writing, it is harder to argue that they were
necessarily innovative within a broader narrative context. Indeed, what this chapter
has suggested is that they were deeply characteristic of the literary and dramatic
culture of the period. The 'staging' in his travel narrative of certain scenes as if
they were theatrical performances offered Moritz the opportunity to adopt different
personae in new surroundings. In a letter to Jean Paul two years after Moritz's
death, his brother Johann Christian Conrad Moritz had reflected, 'Von seinen
Freunden sich trennen, um sich ihnen in einer interessantern Gestalt aufs Neue
wiederzugeben, das war das größte Vergnügen, was er sich bei seinen Reisen dachte'
[Separating himself from his friends in order to *present* himself to them anew in a
more interesting form was the greatest pleasure which he gained from his travels].[86]
Thus travel allowed him to see himself in a different light and to test himself in
various situations. In the course of his account he is the travelling gentleman, the
tramp, the German minister, the cleric, and the intellectual. His constant reflection
on his outward appearance, the state of his dress, and the way in which he is treated,
point up the importance of 'costume' and display in determining the role which one
must assume. For Moritz, travel and performance had become closely entwined. If
he conceived of himself as an actor, performing a host of walk-on parts, so too were
the politicians who engaged in parliamentary debate or the Oxford clerics fiercely
defending the scriptures.

   In investigating the rhetorical function of direct speech in Moritz's travelogue,
it is just as crucial to explore *who* is allowed to speak as *what* they are permitted
to say. Orality was not simply a tool to convey more effectively the emotions of
the characters encountered or to attempt to persuade the reader that this was an
unmediated account of the foreign. Moritz's inclusion of direct speech by all members
of the social hierarchy, from the politician Charles James Fox down to the carter or
maid, was explicitly all-encompassing. It emphasized the work's clearly collective,
social bias. But it was precisely in such scenes that variation in affective proximity and
detachment created a double engagement with the text. For while the foreign could
be figured as close and we might project ourselves imaginatively into scenes eliciting
our compassion, at the same time this emotional proximity suggested that a form
of self-recognition was at work. Moritz, in spirit and in word, felt a powerful bond
with the carter and those like him who were upholding the democratic process of
election that characterized British politics. But this was engendered precisely because
the inclusion of the people in political decision-making was something which Moritz
saw to be lacking at that time in the German states. Thus for all that such seemingly
immediate, transparent scenes strove to maintain the illusion that Moritz was
offering an unmediated account of his encounters in England, his voice continued
to pervade the text. Indeed, a narrative play of hide-and-seek seems at times to be
at work in his travelogue which encourages a highly productive play of proximity
and distance, which in turn points up the multivocality of the author himself.

Notes to Chapter 1

1. Karl Philipp Moritz, *Werke*, ed. by Horst Günther, 3 vols (Frankfurt a.M.: Insel, 1993), II, 865–66. All quotations are given using the orthography and punctuation in this edited work, which reproduces Moritz's (somewhat erratic) spelling as found in the 1792–93 edition.

2. See also his earlier letter of 18 November 1786 to the Director of the Gymnasium zum Grauen Kloster in Berlin, Anton Friedrich Büsching, in which he proposed that his travel account of Italy would be 'ein Werk über die klassischen Schriftsteller der Römer [. . .], wodurch der Leser beständig an Ort und Stelle, wo sich die Begebenheiten ereignet haben, hingeführet, ihm alles vors Auge gebracht [. . .] wird' [a work on the classical Roman authors, in which the reader is continually led to the very spot where the events took place and in which everything is presented in a visual fashion] (*Werke*, II, 862). In choosing to orient his travels towards the work of classical authors, Moritz was following in the footsteps of Joseph Addison, whose *Remarks on Several Parts of Italy, &c In the Years 1701, 1702, 1703* (1705) drew on the work of Virgil, Horace, Martial, and other classical writers.

3. Moritz, *Werke*, II, 865.

4. Ibid., p. 20.

5. *NHGZ*, 5–8 January 1784, p. 13.

6. *GAgS*, 76 (1784), pp. 765–66.

7. Ibid., p. 765.

8. *CR*, February 1796, p. 156.

9. See Isabel A. White, '"Die zu oft wiederholte Lektüre des Werthers": Responses to Sentimentality in Moritz's *Anton Reiser*', *Lessing Yearbook*, 26 (1994), 93–112. See also Mark Boulby, *Karl Philipp Moritz: At the Fringe of Genius* (Toronto: University of Toronto Press, 1979), pp. 106–07. Heide Hollmer and Albert Meier, '"Die Erde ist nicht überall einerlei!" Landschaftsbeschreibungen in Karl Philipp Moritz' Reiseberichten aus England und Italien', in *Erschriebene Natur: Internationale Perspektiven auf Texte des 18. Jahrhunderts*, ed. by Michael Scheffel and Dietmar Götsch, Jahrbuch für Internationale Germanistik, Reihe A: 66 (Berlin: Lang, 2001), pp. 263–88.

10. For a detailed examination of Moritz's *Erfahrungsseelenreise* in his account of England, see Alexander Košenina, *Karl Philipp Moritz. Literarische Experimente auf dem Weg zum psychologischen Roman* (Göttingen: Wallstein, 2006), pp. 73–90, particularly p. 77.

11. Moritz, *Werke*, II, 24; 31; 111–12.

12. Michael Eggers, *Texte, die alles sagen: Erzählende Literatur des 18. und 19. Jahrhunderts und Theorien der Stimme*, Reihe Kulturpoetiken, 1 (Würzburg: Königshausen and Neumann, 2003), particularly part 1, section 4 (pp. 67–83). See also Anke Gilleir's 'Die Vielstimmigkeit der Aufklärung: Georg Forsters *Ansichten vom Niederrhein*', *Das achtzehnte Jahrhundert*, 27 (2003), 171–88, which offers a Bakhtinian reading of the notion of 'voice' in travel writing. Gilleir argues that the polyphonic structure of Forster's account of the revolt of Brabant reveals his awareness of other 'social languages' in circulation at the time.

13. In taking this approach I have not only been informed by David Marshall's work on sympathy but also Michael Fried's *Absorption and Theatricality: Painting and Beholder in the Age of Diderot* (Los Angeles: University of California Press, 1980).

14. Moritz, *Werke*, II, 28.

15. 'Ein Brief aus London', *BM*, 1783.1, 298–305.

16. Moritz, *Werke*, II, 29–30.

17. Ibid., p. 30.

18. Ibid., p. 31.

19. Ibid.

20. Ibid.

21. See John W. Derry, *Charles James Fox* (London: Batsford, 1972), p. 120; also Loren Reid, *Charles James Fox* (London: Longmans, 1969) and more recently Penelope J. Corfield, Edmund M. Green, and Charles Harvey, 'Westminster Man: Charles James Fox and his Electorate, 1780–1806', *Parliamentary History*, 20 (2001), 157–85.

22. Loren D. Reid, 'Did Charles Fox Prepare his Speeches?', *Quarterly Journal of Speech*, 24 (1968), 17–26 (p. 17).

23. Moritz, *Werke*, II, 31.

24. Ibid., p.32.

25. Moritz, *Werke*, III, 486: 'Doch hierüber will ich Ihnen meine Gedanken lieber schriftlich mitteilen; denn unsre Materie fängt an, für die mündliche Unterredung *zu voll* zu werden', quoted in Eggers, p. 81.

26. Eggers, p. 82.

27. Moritz, *Werke*, II, 32.

28. See Derry, p. 161.

29. Anon., *The Speech of the Right Honourable Charles James Fox, At a General Meeting of the Electors of Westminster, Assembled in Westminster-Hall, July 17, 1782, In Which are Accurately Given the Reasons for Withdrawing Himself from the Cabinet, Taken in Short-hand by W. Blanchard of Dean-Street, Fetter Lane* (Dublin: Mills, 1782), p. 11.

30. Peter J. Brenner, *Reisen in die Neue Welt: Die Erfahrung Nordamerikas in deutschen Reise- und Auswandererberichten des 19. Jahrhunderts*, Studien und Texte zur Sozialgeschichte der Literatur, 35 (Tübingen: Niemeyer, 1991), p. 277.

31. See Ann Rigney, *The Rhetoric of Historical Representation: Three Narrative Histories of the French Revolution* (Cambridge: Cambridge University Press, 1990), esp. chs 3 and 4 on 'The configuration of actors'.

32. Moritz, *Werke*, II, 34.

33. Ibid.

34. As early as 1741, Zedler's *Universal-Lexicon* records this distinction: 'Pöbel-Volck, oder der Pöbel heisset die gemeine Menge niederträchtiger und aller höhern Achtbarkeit beraubter Leute' [The mob denotes the general crowd of despicable people who are bereft of any greater worthiness.] (XXVIII (1741), col. 948); the notion 'Volck' can be either positively or negatively charged, 'Denn es ist entweder eine Gesellschaft, so aus verschiedenen kleinern Gesellschaften bestanden, [. . .] Oder es ist nur eine Rotte oder ein Hauffen zusammen gelauffenes Gesindels, so sich anfangs zusammen rottirt, auf Rauben und plündern auszugehen' [For it is either a group which comprises different smaller groups or it is simply a pack or a crowd of riff-raff who have collected and initially go around together with the intention of robbery and plundering.] (L (1746), cols 362–75 (col. 362)).

35. Moritz, *Werke*, II, 34–35.

36. Anton Reiser, *Theatromania; oder, Die Wercke der Finsterniß, in denen öffentlichen Schau-Spielen von den alten Kirchen-Vätern verdammet, welches aus ihren Schrifften zu getreuer Warnung kürzlich entworffen* (Ratzeburg: Nissen, 1681), p. 5.

37. Moritz, *Werke*, II, 35.

38. Ibid.

39. Ibid., p. 36.

40. Ibid., p. 35.

41. Ibid.

42. Eckehard Catholy, 'Karl Philipp Moritz: Ein Beitrag zur "Theatromanie" der Goethezeit', *Euphorion*, 45 (1950), 100–23 (p. 103).

43. Anon., *A Complete and Accurate Account of the Very Important Debate in the House of Commons, on Tuesday, July 9, 1782. In Which the Cause of Mr Fox's Resignation, and the Great Question of AMERICAN INDEPENDENCE came under Consideration*, 3rd edn (London: Stockdale and Axtell, 1782), Preface (unpaginated).

44. Moritz, *Werke*, II, 119 (Moritz's emphasis).

45. Ibid.

46. See Anon., *The Speech of the Right Honourable Charles James Fox, in the House of Commons, on Tuesday the 9th Instant* [July 1782], *in Defence of his Resignation, A New Edition Corrected* (London: Debret and Stockdale, 1782). The anonymously authored *A Complete and Accurate Account of the Very Important Debate in the House of Commons, on Tuesday, July 9, 1782*, 3rd edn (London: J. Stockdale and Axtell, 1782) also reported the speeches of the day, but in the third person. Compare likewise: Anon., *The Speeches of the Right Honourable Charles James Fox, in the House of Commons*, 6 vols (London: Longman, Hurst, Reed, Rees, Orne, and Brown, 1815), II, 71–92, for Fox's resignation speech, again in the third person.

47. *Speech of the Right Honourable Charles James Fox*, p. 1.

48. Ibid., p. 30.

49. Moritz, *Werke*, II, 77.

50. Ibid., p. 79.

51. Ibid.

52. Ibid.

53. Moritz, *Werke*, II, 81.

54. Ibid.

55. Ibid.

56. Johann Jacob Breitinger, *Critische Dichtkunst worinnen die Poetische Mahlerey in Absicht auf die Erfindung im Grunde untersuchet und mit Beyspielen aus den berühmtesten Alten und Neuern erläutert wird*, 2 vols (Zurich: Orell, 1740) I, 32.

57. Johann Christoph Gatterer, 'Von der Evidenz in der Geschichtkunde', in *Die Allgemeine Welthistorie die in England durch eine Gesellschaft von Gelehrten ausgefertiget worden. In einem vollständigen und pragmatsichen Auszuge*, ed. by Friedrich Eberhard Boysen, 37 vols (Halle: Gebauer, 1767–90), I (1767), 1–38 (pp. 13–14).

58. For a detailed account of Kames's position within German aestheticism, see Nicholas Saul, *History and Poetry in Novalis and in the Tradition of the German Enlightenment,* Bithell Series of Dissertations, 8 (London: Institute of Germanic Studies, 1984), pp. 15–31.

59. The first volumes of Johann Nicolaus Meinhard's translation of the *Elements of Criticism*, the *Grundsätze der Critik*, which began appearing one year after the publication of the original, were completed in 1766 and then reissued in 1772, 1785, 1790, and 1791. Herder and Lessing certainly knew of Kames' work, as did Christian Friedrich von Blanckenburg, Johann Joachim Eschenburg, and Johann Christoph Adelung. Its influence even extended to Christian Hirschfeld's *Theorie der Gartenkunst* (1779–85). See Leroy R. Shaw, 'Henry Home of Kames: Precursor of Herder', *Germanic Review*, 35 (1960), 16–27; Norbert Bachleitner, 'Die Rezeption von Henry Homes *Elements of Criticism* in Deutschland 1763–1793', *arcadia*, 20 (1985), 115–33.

60. Henry Home [Lord Kames], *Elements of Criticism. With the Author's Last Corrections and Additions*, 6th edn, 2 vols (Edinburgh: Bell, Creech, Cadell, and Robinson, 1785), I, 34.

61. Ibid., p. 91 (Home's emphasis).

62. Ibid., p. 35.

63. Home, *Elements*, II, 325–26.

64. Home, *Elements*, I, 36.

65. Ibid., p. 37.

66. Friedrich von Blanckenburg, *Versuch über den Roman* (Leipzig: David Siegers Witwe, 1774), pp. 24–25.

67. Ibid., p. 494 (Blanckenburg's emphasis).

68. Ibid., pp. 499–500.

69. Johann Jakob Engel, 'Ueber Handlung, Gespräch und Erzehlung', *NBsWfK*, 16 (1774), 177–256 (pp. 231–32).

70. Ibid., p. 232.

71. Ibid.

72. Ibid., pp. 232–33.

73. Friedrich Schiller, *Werke. Nationalausgabe*, ed. by Julius Petersen and others, 43 vols (Weimar: Hermann Böhlaus Nachfolger, 1943-), XX (1962), 93.

74. Ibid., p. 95.

75. Karl Philipp Moritz, 'Noch etwas über das Schiller'sche Trauerspiel: Kabale und Liebe', in *Schriften zur Ästhetik und Poetik*, ed. by Hans Joachim Schrimpf (Tübingen: Niemeyer, 1962), pp. 301–06 (p. 302).

76. Ibid., p. 303.

77. See Lothar Müller, 'Die Erziehung der Gefühle im 18. Jahrhundert: Kanzel, Buch und Bühne in Karl Philipp Moritz' "Anton Reiser" (1785–1790)', *Der Deutschunterricht*, 48.2 (1996), 5–20 (p. 9).

78. Moritz, *Werke*, I, 86.

79. Ibid., p. 89.

80. Ibid., p. 173 (Moritz's emphasis).

81. Qu'est-ce que le talent du comédien? L'art de se contrefaire, de revêtir un autre caractère que le sien, de paroître différent de ce qu'on pense, aussi naturellement que si l'on le pense réellement, et d'oublier enfin sa propre place à force de prendre celle d'autrui. [What is the comedian's talent? The art of counterfeiting oneself, taking on a different character than one's own, appearing different from what one thinks, as naturally as if one really thinks it, and finally forgetting one's own place by dint of assuming that of another.] (Jean-Jacques Rousseau, *Du Contrat Social et autres œuvres politiques*, introduced by Jean Ehrard (Paris: Garnier, 1975), p. 186)

82. Karl Philipp Moritz, 'Vorschlag zu einem Magazin einer Erfahrungs-Seelenkunde', *DM*, 1782: 1, 485–503 (p. 497). See also Robert S. Bledsoe, 'Empathetic Reading and Identity Formation', *Lessing Yearbook*, 33 (2001), 201–31 (p. 203).

83. Moritz, *Werke*, III, 247.

84. Bledsoe, p. 205.

85. Keen, pp. 88, 170.

86. Letter of 1 August 1795, in Hugo Eybisch, *Anton Reiser: Untersuchungen zur Lebensgeschichte von K. Ph. Moritz und zur Kritik seiner Autobiographie* (Leipzig: Voigtländer, 1909), p. 268 (J. C. Moritz's emphasis).

CHAPTER 2

Female Enquiry and the Ordering of Knowledge: Sophie von La Roche and the Problem of Sensibility

'Es giebt unstreitig eine Art der Belehrung durch Reisende, die uns am vollständigsten und zweckmäßigsten aus einer weiblichen Feder zufließt' [There is indisputably a form of instruction by travellers which in its most comprehensive and expedient form comes to us from a female pen], wrote Georg Forster in his preface to the 1790 translation of Hester Lynch Piozzi's travel account of France, Italy, and Germany.[1] Arguably one of the first in Germany to pay women's travel writing its full due, Georg Forster applauded women's superior powers of observation and description in a variety of ways. Their curiosity caused them, he elaborated, to direct their interests towards details 'über die das männliche Auge sorglos hingleitet oder wohl gar mit Geringschätzung wegblickt' [over which the male eye passes unconcernedly or indeed even looks away from with contempt].[2] Moreover, these tender beings, he added, were receptive to the many passing impressions that they saw on their travels, which gave them a keener sense of the singularities of the environment around them. Forster's arguments were therefore an endorsement of women travellers' ability to produce more detailed and more sensitive narratives of travel. They were also a tacit acceptance that women could lay claim to the educated process of viewing and recording — hitherto exclusively within the male domain — that had underpinned the composition of travel accounts. Thus, by a rhetorical sleight of hand, Forster had made narrative strengths of what contemporaries such as Schiller and Wilhelm von Humboldt condemned as the particularized, sentimentalized discourse characteristic of women's writing in the last decades of the eighteenth century.[3]

That Forster argued the cause of female travel writing in such superlative terms suggests that, in that period, women's travelogues still occupied a precarious, liminal position. The publishing market was in any case flooded with accounts written by travellers returning from destinations sometimes exotic, more often quite ordinary, who sought an easy means to get their name in print.[4] Indeed, as an anonymous contributor to the *Berlinische Monatsschrift* testily noted in 1784, 'Kinder und Unmündige, Weiber und Jungfrauen, Unwissende und Unstudierte, Menschen ohne Kopf und Sinn und Kenntniß und Beobachtungsgeist, lassen Reise-beschreibungen drucken' [children and minors, women and young girls, the ignorant and the uneducated, people without reason and sense and knowledge and powers of observation are having their travel accounts printed].[5]

Travel writing presented female authors with a variety of difficulties, despite the fact that, in two crucial respects, it was essentially a genre well suited to appropriation by women in the last quarter of the eighteenth century. Firstly, the influence of sensibility on travel writing encouraged accounts which allowed travellers to respond to the foreign environment more obviously with their heart than with their head. This personal, more subjectively styled tone which emerged in both fictional and non-fictional literature of the late eighteenth century is considered to have served the interests and the capabilities of the female writer well.[6] As Cheryl Turner argues, sentimentality offered eighteenth-century women valuable opportunities for self-expression and encouraged the emergence of the female writer as a public persona.[7] Secondly, the epistolary mode in which travel narratives were increasingly written, in the wake of Richardson's *Clarissa*, Rousseau's *Emile*, and above all, Goethe's *Werther*, was a rhetorical device that could be easily appropriated by women.[8] Epistolarity, closely associated with the private, domestic sphere, offered a spontaneity, intimacy, and immediacy which was invaluable in travel narratives, since it created a vivid sense of place and reinforced the notion that the account was indeed authentic.

However, it was precisely the 'culture of sensibility', to use G. J. Barker-Benfield's phrase, which made the aesthetics of gender highly complex and the production of travel writing by women so very ambiguous.[9] Certainly, sensibility stressed those qualities of 'intuitive sympathy, susceptibility, emotionalism and passivity' which were considered feminine by the sexual psychology of the time.[10] Within the conventional polarities of the period, women were seen as creatures of the body, of sensation and responsiveness, while men were governed by the *ratio*, the mind. Thus the orientation towards a greater display of sensibility testified to the 'feminization' of culture as the century drew to a close. But, as Ann Jessie Van Sant observes, sensibility predominantly defined a new *male* rather than a *female* character type: the man with an intensified capacity for refined feeling.[11] While women were indeed considered to be creatures of greater sensibility, they were also thought to lack a man's emotional balance and self-command. Theodor Gottlieb von Hippel's *Ueber die bürgerliche Verbesserung der Weiber* [*On Improving the Status of Women*] (1792) gives some indication of the prejudices which women at that time were fighting:

> Die große Lebhaftigkeit weiblicher Empfindungen und weiblicher Einbild-ungskraft, das zu reizbare Nervensystem soll indeß Schuld an der Unbeständigkeit und dem bloß flüchtigen Feuer bei Gegenständen des Nachdenkens in Hinsicht der Weiber seyn; auch sollen sie für große Gegenstände des menschlichen Wissens nur selten ein wahres Interesse fühlen.

> [The great vividness of female emotions and the female imagination, their overly sensitive nervous system, is said to be responsible for the inconstancy and the mere fleeting fervour of women with regard to subjects of contemplation; they are also rarely considered to show a true interest in the key objects of human knowledge.][12]

The wild fancy and overwrought sensibility attributed to women as an innate part of their physiological make-up was believed to render them incapable of measured judgement or the ability to engage with serious debates of the time. As Franz Posselt's *Apodemik oder die Kunst zu Reisen* [*Apodemic or the Art of Travel*] (1795) pointedly queried, considering the vivid nature of women's imagination and feelings, together with the lack of firmness of character, should women be encouraged to travel at all?[13]

Thus if women were deemed particularly unsuitable as travelling subjects and relegated to the sphere of domestic affection, it was men who were considered capable of acting as public figures, the embodiment of reason. Within this concept of 'separate spheres', the very practice of travel — by definition the negation of domesticity — was therefore potentially highly transgressive for women. Yet although this public–private dichotomy is helpful in enabling us to categorize and to gender these spaces, it does not really reflect the reality of female travel in the eighteenth century, headed as it was by respected women such as Lady Mary Wortley Montagu. The feminist re-enactment of the exclusion of women from public roles, positions of power and influence, does, as Amanda Vickery observes for women in eighteenth-century England, need to be treated with a certain amount of scepticism.[14] Parallel arguments could be made for the role of women in the life and letters of the German states. By the time that Sophie von La Roche came to publish her travelogue of England in 1788, she had already established a public profile, most notably through the immense success of her sentimental novel the *Geschichte des Fräuleins von Sternheim* [*History of Lady Sophia Sternheim*] (1771). The identity of women in print was therefore not such a strange one. Moreover, as the eighteenth century drew to a close, salons increasingly became a serious way for women to enter and maintain a presence in the public sphere, and one in which they acted centrally as discursive mediators. The systematic use of 'separate spheres' as an organizing concept does not therefore fully accommodate the reality that women were not immured in a private sphere but also occupied a surprisingly active role in the public sphere. Thus to a certain degree women were accustomed to being objects of the public gaze and more sophisticated arguments must be applied than those previously encountered to understand how a woman like Sophie von La Roche could construct an account of herself as a travelling (public) subject.

Indeed, by the end of the century Posselt's reservations about women travelling could be seen as something of a rearguard action, suggesting that the reality of female travel had overwhelmed male condemnation of it. Performing something of a volte-face, he conceded that there were exemplary models of travel accounts written by women.[15] These were La Roche's descriptions of travel to Switzerland, France, the Netherlands, and to England. This chapter will examine the rhetorical strategies used in her *Tagebuch einer Reise durch Holland und England* [*Diary of a Journey through Holland and England*] (1788) against the gendered parameters established in Forster's preface. As she was credited with being the first German woman to publish an account of travel to England, her travelogue thus marks the inception of a new phase in travel writing on this country. This travel narrative was long seen as adhering to the excesses of sentimental writing, namely that of *Schwärmerey*.[16] It is only more recently that Monika Nenon has argued that the sheer amount of factual information which La Roche's account contains aligns it within a statistical tradition and that it is 'noch älteren Vorbildern verpflichtet [. . .] als den empfindsamen' [owes more to older models than those of the age of sensibility].[17] Margrit Langner has also suggested that La Roche's narratives of travel to France, Switzerland, England, and Holland have a highly informative, pedagogic content which underlies the empirical nature of certain aspects of her undertaking.[18]

While these statements go some way to acknowledging the more dispassionate, 'male' discourses in La Roche's travel writing, they do not offer a detailed examination of the rhetorical devices she used to represent England to a German-speaking audience in her *Tagebuch einer Reise durch Holland und England* (1788). Nor do they ask how these strategies negotiated around prejudices held at that time concerning female enquiry and overly sentimental, 'female' modes of writing. Forster's endorsement of the validity of the female viewpoint continued to reinforce the notion that the genre of travel literature was predicated on authentic observation, relayed through representation to third parties. If the gaze therefore functioned as an ordering and legitimating principle, it also laid claim to the articulation of various forms of knowledge. But it was itself constrained by conditions of production and reception. In the following discussion, Sophie von La Roche's positioning with regard to the politics and poetics of observation within travel writing will be explored in some detail.

The *Tagebuch einer Reise durch Holland und England* was published a year after La Roche's two-and-a-half-month journey through the Netherlands to England, and reprinted in 1791. The third of her travelogues — she had published her *Tagebuch einer Reise durch die Schweiz* [*Diary of a Journey through Switzerland*] and the *Tagebuch einer Reise durch Frankreich* [*Diary of a Journey through France*] one year earlier — described her travels, in the company of her adult son Carl and a female friend of hers. Over 700 pages in length, it essentially recorded a journey through England that was even shorter than Moritz's. Setting off from Adernheim in the Pfalz region of Germany on 9 August 1787, La Roche travelled via Bingen to Berlin, where she met her son Carl, and the rest of the journey was then continued in his company. By mid-August they had visited Coblenz, Cologne, and Düsseldorf and on 18 August they were in Nijmegen in the Netherlands. Late August saw them in The Hague, Amsterdam, and Leiden, and at the very end of the month they boarded the ship at Hellevoetssluis which was to take them to England. On 4 September, after a miserable 48-hour Channel crossing during which La Roche was, she lamented, the first on board to start being sea-sick and the last to stop, they set foot in Harwich. Bowling up to London through Suffolk by coach, they arrived at the 'German Hotel' on 5 September. Having unpacked (and remarked on how slow the servants were to rise in England) she then set to examining life in England bit by bit.[19] Her letter of 7 September included an itemization of all the articles in the newspaper that day.[20] In the course of the following week she had marvelled at Sir Ashton Lever's collection, ticked off the standard sights of Westminster Abbey and Parliament, drooled over a Wedgewood tea service that (had she had the space and money) would have well sufficed as her souvenir of England, attended a Quaker meeting, and paid the Forsters a visit in Covent Garden. The next fortnight saw her steeling herself to observe the inmates in Bedlam, as well as apply herself to the less unpleasant task of taking tea with Fanny Burney, visiting Mrs Fielding, the Count and Countess Reventlow, and the Hastings at Beaumont Lodge. On 12 October, barely a month after she had landed in England, she was departing for Germany and on 25 October she was back in Speyer.

Her itinerary was therefore very much the standard one, with an emphasis placed on sites of cultural and social interest in London, although she also made excursions to Windsor, Eton, and Slough before returning to Dover via Canterbury. In contrast to the heavier political and economic content of accounts such as Wendeborn's *Zustand des Staats* or Archenholtz's *England und Italien*, her account attempted to occupy a position somewhere between the serious and the trivial and to balance sentimental reflection with empirical narrative and description. The sheer length of her account (almost 400 pages of which were devoted to England) was due to the fact that she made detailed entries on a near daily basis. The title of the account characterized its format as that of a journal and indeed its style was highly personal, but it was not necessarily characterized by privacy. Indeed La Roche's musings on life in England were frequently interrupted by exclamations to her implied readers, notably her daughters. As she was on the point of departure, for example, she wrote, 'Ihr denkt wohl, liebe Töchter! daß ich noch überall mich umsah; noch in mich schlürfte, was ich fassen konnte' [You will imagine, dear daughters, that I still looked about me everywhere, sucked in all that I could].[21]

This chapter will first examine how visual perception determined what it was 'proper' for one to see, how this shaped travellers' presentation of themselves as 'curious' individuals and how this influenced the organization of knowledge presented in their accounts. The second section discusses the ways in which women themselves approached the notion of education and the representation of themselves as intellectually enquiring subjects. It seeks not only to understand how they constructed an image of themselves as educators and as educated. It also aims to tackle the difficult question of how women dealt with the distinctly troubled problem of sensibility. The third section then offers a detailed analysis of how La Roche employed a variety of rhetorical devices, both sentimental and empirical, to locate her account within the shifting modes of representation in use in travel writing at the close of the eighteenth century. It examines the rhetorical strategies which she uses to lay claim to a field of knowledge and to modes of description defined as exclusively masculine in this period. It also focuses on how women whom Sophie von La Roche mentions in her writings, such as Marie Anne du Boccage (1710–1802), presented knowledge and the forms of curiosity they articulated. Finally, this chapter will reflect on the audience whom La Roche was addressing, asking whether she was in fact writing primarily for a female or a male readership and what their differing expectations and demands might be. By asking these questions, this chapter seeks to explore La Roche's negotiation of what Sigrid Weigel has called 'der schielende Blick' [the squinting look] appropriated by female writers at that time: 'sich mit einem (bebrillten) Auge im Alltag zurecht zu finden, und in dem anderen (freien) Auge ihre Träume und Wünsche zu entwerfen' [to manage in everyday life by looking through one (spectacled) eye and with the other (free) eye formulate their dreams and wishes].[22]

Travel and the Articulation of Curiosity: Between the 'lasterhafft' and the 'nützlich'

'[W]enn eine Reisebeschreibung angekündigt wird, [. . .] was soll die edelste Wißbegierde eines gebildeten Weltmanns und eines strebenden Jünglings, eines aufgeklärten Gelehrten und eines im Stillen thätigen Patrioten sehnlicher erwarten?' [When a travel account is announced, [. . .] what should the noblest curiosity of a learned man of the world or an aspiring youth, an enlightened intellectual and a quietly active patriot await more enthusiastically], mused a critic of the *Berlinische Monatsschrift* of 1784.[23] Travel legitimized the spectatorial pleasures of curiosity, and tourism of the type that was increasingly practised in the final quarter of the eighteenth century equated it with education in art, nature, and science. But what exactly was it legitimate for one to see? What did the concept of 'curiosity' connote in German in the eighteenth century? As the definitions given in Zedler's *Grosses vollständiges Universal-Lexikon aller Wissenschaften und Künste* [*Large Comprehensive Universal Dictionary of All the Sciences and Arts*] show, the conceptual and semantic fields which it was seen to cover were morally charged.[24] The positive valency of curiosity was most clearly articulated in Zedler's definition of *Wißbegierde*, being:

> ein von dem allweisen Schöpfer in die menschliche Seele gelegter Trieb und Grund-Begierde, nöthige und nützliche Wahrheiten zu erkennen [. . .] die gute und löbliche Wiß-Begierde ist eine Tugend, unbekannte Dinge in göttlicher Ordnung und nach dem Willen des höchsten Gesetzgebers zu erforschen.[25]

> [an impulse and basic desire placed by the omniscient creator in the human soul to recognize essential and useful truths [. . .] the good and praiseworthy form of curiosity is a virtue which entails the study of unknown things in their god-given order and according to the will of the highest legislator.]

This mode of curiosity was therefore understood as an innate desire to seek out useful information with the aim of attaining truth and of maintaining the current systems of order. Part of the entry for *Neugierigkeit* which appeared eight years earlier, and which focused on 'gelehrte Curiosität', made similar claims regarding the utility of curiosity:

> So ist hinwiederum die gelehrte Curiosität [. . .] vornehmlich iedem Gelehrten anzupreisen. Sie erwecket Nachdencken; Nachdencken bringet scharffsinnige Wahrheiten hervor; diese zeigen einen vielfältigen zuvor unerkannten Nutzen der Dinge. Und eben die Erwegung dieses Nutzens bekräfftiget und rechtfertiget die Curiosität derer, die mit gutem Fortgange nachdencken, und scharffsinnige Wahrheiten zu erfinden trachten.[26]

> [By contrast learned curiosity is principally to be recommended to every learned person. It inspires contemplation; contemplation arrives at discerning truths; these reveal the manifold and previously unrecognized benefit of things. And precisely this mention of benefit reinforces and justifies the curiosity of those who make good progress in their reflections and attempt to uncover discerning truths.]

Here, however, Zedler seemed to argue that only academics — or, more broadly, the well-educated — were capable of performing the 'right' kind of enquiry.

Learned curiosity was therefore associated with rigorous intellectual thought and empirical study, thereby positing an implicit social and gender distinction between those who were deemed suitable to exercise curiosity and those who were not.

While he afforded relatively little space to the morally and intellectually beneficial characteristics of curiosity, Zedler was far more expansive in his discussion of its negative valencies. His entry for *Neugierde*, almost exclusively oriented towards such illustrations, defined it as:

> eine Art der Wollust, da man nach neuen und ungewöhnlichen Sachen begierig ist, um sich dadurch zu belustigen, und die Zeit hinzubringen. Auf solche Weise gehöret *die* Curiosität mitunter die Schwachheiten des menschlichen Willens, weil das Absehen auf eine blosse Belustigung und Veränderung gehet.[27]

> [a form of lust, since one is hungry for new and unusual things, in order to amuse oneself and pass the time with them. Thus *this* curiosity belongs among the weaknesses of the human will, since the act of looking is based on mere amusement and change.]

This ascribed pejorative associations to the new and the unusual, associating curiosity with an unhealthy interest in what was novel as a form of 'Belustigung', of idle amusement. In contrast to its learned counterpart, this 'gemeine Curiosität' emphasized the weaknesses in human nature which craved change for change's sake and sought spectacle as cheap entertainment. It therefore showed a disregard for the distinction between the valuable and the valueless. But it was the illegitimate nature of the 'lasterhaffte Curiosität' described under the entry for *Wißbegierde* which perhaps represented the most damaging form of negative curiosity:

> Die lasterhaffte Curiosität ist ein Laster, unbekannte Sachen wider GOttes Ordnung und Willen Wissen zu wollen [. . .] und daher jene, weil er die in der Heiligen Schrifft geoffenbarten Seligkeiten nicht lebhafft kennt, über alle geistliche und ewige Güter erhebet und schätzet, wodurch er die in seiner Seele bereits eingewurtzelte Welt-Liebe mehr stärcket, zu seiner zeitlichen und ewigen Unseligkeit.[28]

> [Wicked curiosity is the vice of wanting to know unknown things against the divine order and God's will [. . .] and therefore raises up and treasures those possessions above all holy and everlasting things, because that person does not know vividly the salvation revealed in the Holy Scripture, as a result of which he strengthens that love of the world in his soul which has already taken root, to his temporary and everlasting damnation.]

It signalled an enquiry into those things which went beyond what it was appropriate for any individual to know. This was a greed for knowledge bordering on the profane. While the desire to extend any type of knowledge implicitly overstepped current boundaries, this was transgressive in the more current pejorative sense in that it contravened divine order. Curiosity was therefore conceived of as the desire to know more than one already knew and to see further than one could already see. Hence intellectuals and travellers alike aspired to that same elusive goal of total, comprehensive understanding. The eighteenth-century traveller sought not only to leave no stone unturned but also to offer an account of travel which was in some way 'complete'. These two elements — the desire to discover the unexplored and the totality of representation — are essential notions underlying the concept of curiosity as it was expressed in travel literature at that time.[29]

Hans Blumenberg has shown that curiosity occupied a central position in the 'Umkehrung' that the sciences underwent in the seventeenth century as they struggled free from under the thumb of theology.[30] But the narrative of emancipation which he constructs fails to acknowledge that while the concept of curiosity was figured for men as intellectually positive, the topos of female enquiry was necessarily allied with its negative pole. While curiosity was about the attribution of *value* to what one saw, women were considered incapable of making the right judgements regarding a subject's relative *importance*. If curiosity was a trademark for progress, it signified precisely the reverse within the context of women's emancipation. Gottlieb Sigmund Corvinus's *Nutzbares, galantes und curiöses Frauenzimmer-Lexicon* [*Useful, Gallant and Curious Women's Dictionary*] (1715) was more concerned to instruct women in the finer points of making crab sausage or the art of producing perfect laundry. It placed the woman fairly and squarely within the realm of the domestic — indeed, it had no entry for 'Reise' but, tellingly, one for the 'Reisekappe' to protect women in their peregrinations between domestic spaces.[31] Stéphanie de Genlis's later *Handbuch für Reisende zur Conversation* [*Conversational Dictionary for Travellers*] (1814) was designed primarily to enable the travelling woman to create a sense of domestic stability in each of the establishments where she lodged with her husband and children. While the reading of travel accounts was an acceptable pastime for the woman seeking instructive amusement, to undertake travel herself remained at the very limits of propriety.

Just how bold an act was La Roche's traversing of gender boundaries? How did she construct a rhetorical position for herself that endorsed her role as a travelling 'curious' woman? La Roche's travel writing was self-conscious to a degree rarely found in accounts by her male counterparts. Her account of travel to England adopted a structure of telling in which the form of narration was in places, and certainly in its opening, highly personal:

> Ja es werden Alle staunen, daß eine Frau, in meinen Jahren, die Gelegenheit und den Willen hat, solche Reisen zu machen, welche sonst allein die Sache der Jugend, des Reichthums, der Freiheit und der Geschäfte sind. *Yorik* setzte noch zwei Arten Reisende hinzu: *Kranke*, die eine Hülfsquelle aufsuchen, — und *Wißbegierige*, welche sich, auch ausser ihrem Wohnort, nach der Erde und ihren Kindern umsehen.[32]

> [Indeed, everyone will be astonished that a woman at my age has the opportunity and the desire to undertake such journeys which are otherwise reserved solely for the young, those with money or freedom and those on business. *Yorick* added two other forms of traveller: the *sick*, who seek a source of help, — and the *curious* who want outside of their home town to see the world and their children.]

She therefore immediately sought to associate her account with travel for health purposes, thereby neatly and quickly allying it to the domestic through the implication that she was travelling primarily to visit her daughters. For 'legitimate' reasons such as these, women were thus not necessarily reduced to stasis.[33] La Roche was swift to ward off criticism of the idea that she should undertake a journey, disarming it in two ways. She pre-empted external disapproval by admitting that a 57-year-old woman travelling was an unusual spectacle. By couching her reasons for travel in terms which explicitly echoed the taxonomy that Sterne had memorably compiled in his *Sentimental Journey*, she also therefore sought to justify her journeys according to a rhetoric amply legitimized by the success of Sterne's work.

But in terming herself a 'Wißbegierige', La Roche clearly looked beyond the relative safety of the domestic as a motivation for travel. She was positioning herself within the 'male' domain of scientific enquiry which had established a tradition of recording knowledge dispassionately, keeping sentimentalized judgement or description at bay. The dangers to her own status and credibility as a writer should she appear to be a woman articulating 'female' curiosity were all too clear to her. The contents of her library, which she itemized for the benefit of her readership in *Mein Schreibetisch* [*My Desk*] (1799), included the:

> *Memoires secrets* par Gorani, wollte ich kennen, nicht wie Sie vielleicht sehr schnell vermuthen werden, weil Geheimnisse stets für eine Frau sehr lockend sind, sondern weil ich ihn einige Male sprach, und wußte, daß die Gemahlin seines Bruders in Mailand, eine Schwester von den zwey *Comnenen* ist, welche ich 1785 in *Versailles* sah.[34]

> [I wanted to know about Gorani's *Mémoires secrets* not, as you might hasten to presume, because secrets are always most tempting to a woman, but because I spoke with him on a few occasions and knew that the wife of his brothers in Milan is a sister of the two *Comnene* whom I saw in *Versailles* in 1785.]

Thus she was quick to distance herself from the assumption that her interest in this particular work might in some way be prurient, 'lasterhafft', and trivial. Rather, she was concerned to see how Giuseppe Gorani's work enabled her to situate better the author within certain social or literary networks. La Roche was also aware of the dangers that curiosity could entail in its desire to possess. In her library she also stumbled across a copy of the *Lady's Magazine*, which the innkeeper's wife in Dover gave her:

> als sie das Vergnügen bemerkte, welches ich an den schon zerrissenen Blättern fand, die mir aber sehr gefährlich wurden, indem ich von da an der Begierde nicht widerstehen konnte, diese Monatsschrift selbst zu besitzen.[35]

> [when she noticed the pleasure which I gained from the torn leaves, which became most dangerous for me, since from then on I could not resist the desire to possess this monthly magazine myself.]

This suggests that she was all too aware of the uncontrollable forces associated with curiosity, which could almost wholly overtake the observer, interested more in the act of possessing information than in its content itself.

'Die rühmliche Wißbegierde eines Frauenzimmers'

'Die Französischen Frauenzimmer waren [. . .] schon lange glücklicher als wir' [The women of France have long been happier than we], observed La Roche rather sweepingly in *Pomona für Teutschlands Töchter* [*Pomona for Germany's Daughters*], the monthly review which she wrote and published between 1783 and 1784.[36] The reason for their happiness, she argued, lay in their explicit inclusion in decisions made in matters of taste and style. In France, she noted enviously, women's opinion was actively sought by artists and writers who valued the attribute of good judgement which women 'naturally' possessed and in the exchange of opinion which followed, could valuably inject their work with innovative ideas and approaches. My women readers will realize, La Roche reflected, what a great advantage and relief this is for a praiseworthy lady's curiosity.[37] Indeed, she argued, it was the prime reason why France could boast so many learned women and why the German states, by contrast, in this respect lagged sadly behind. Thus La Roche was concerned to link the public endorsement of women's learned curiosity and desire for knowledge with notions of cultural production, progress, and taste. Certainly her own interest in travel was very closely bound up with the desire to meet precisely this type of woman: intellectually enquiring, publicly respected, and, above all, an active participator in the cultural life of her country. It was therefore unsurprising that her meetings with 'Madame Fielding'[38] and Fanny Burney[39] numbered amongst the highpoints of her journey to England.

La Roche was also concerned to promote travel and travel writing as the articulation of female enquiry — in part, perhaps, to legitimate her own undertakings. In *Mein Schreibetisch* (1799) she gives a detailed account of the travelogues which she has read. These include Joseph Addison's *Remarks on Several Parts of Italy, &c. in the Years 1701, 1702, 1703* (1705), Henry Swinburne's *Travels in the Two Sicilies in the Years 1777, 1778, 1779 and 1780* (1783–85), and she would go on to read James Bruce's *An Interesting Narrative of the Travels of James Bruce Esq.; into Abyssinia* (1790) and Mungo Park's *Travels in the Interior District of Africa* (1799) after she had completed her narrative of England.[40] But she particularly emphasized her reading of accounts by women. These included Lady Wortley Montagu's *Letters of the Right Honourable Lady M — y W — y M — e: Written during her Travels in Europe, Asia and Africa to Persons of Distinction* (1763–67). Marie Anne Fiquet du Boccage's *Lettres de Madame du Boccage: Contenant ses voyages en France, en Angleterre, en Hollande et en Italie, faits pendant les années 1750. 1757. & 1758.* [*Letters by Madame du Boccage, Containing her Voyages in France, England, Holland, and Italy, Undertaken during the Years 1750. 1757. & 1758*] (1771) was also a must, given that few women had written accounts of travel to England before Sophie von La Roche.[41] The letters of women such as the Countess of Nesselrodt on Portugal and Madame Morikäfer on Turkey and Egypt had, she noted in *Pomona*, also given her great pleasure.[42] Her lament that women from other countries did not publish their travel correspondence expressed her concern to raise public awareness for women's travel writing and to encourage other women to assume authorship more openly.

But while she strongly endorsed women's enquiry and learning, the means by which she felt that she had herself achieved the status of an educated woman did not necessarily show her to be the product of a traditional female education. Indeed, La Roche's brief autobiographical description in the May 1783 edition of *Pomona* is instructive in understanding her attempt to cross gendered boundaries:

> Als Tochter eines Gelehrten, hörte ich von Jugend auf von dem Werth der Wissenschaften [. . .] aber Umstände verhinderten die Erfüllung meines

Wunsches, daß ich *als Knabe erzogen werden möchte, um ordentlich gelehrt zu werden.* Die Hauptsache meines Stolzes war also verlohren; aber die Wißbegierde und der Geschmack an Kenntnissen blieben in meiner Seele, und vereinigten sich mit den Empfindungen der ersten Freuden meines Herzens.[43]

[As the daughter of a learned man, I heard from my youth of the value of the sciences [. . .] but circumstances prevented the fulfilment of my wish that I *should be educated as a boy, in order to be taught properly.* The main object of my pride was thus lost; but the curiosity and taste for knowledge remained in my soul and combined themselves with the sensations of the first joys of my heart.]

The sciences, with which she associates the learned conversation of men such as her father, a successful doctor who had studied medicine under Boerhaave, are therefore placed within the domain of male knowledge. Her access to this world, she reasoned, would be through receiving education of the type offered to her male counterparts. That she was not given access to this type of learning throughout her schooling, did not, however, appear to blunt her curiosity towards matters scientific. 'Ich sitze wirklich zwischen einer Menge Bücher [. . .] Naturgeschichte und Reisebeschreibungen, die Berliner Bibliothek, die Werke des Abbe Reynal, Rousseau, Litleton [sic]' [I am sitting here between veritable mountains of books [. . .] natural history and travel accounts, the Berlin Library, the works of the Abbé Reynal, of Rousseau, Littleton], recounted La Roche, in the virtual tour of her library she gave for the benefit of readers of the May 1783 edition of *Pomona*.[44] Indeed her collection of books included works of reference such as Valmont de Bomare's *Dictionnaire raisonné universel* [*Reasoned, Universal Dictionary*] (1768) and Lavater's *Physiognomische Fragmente* [*Physiognomical Fragments*] (1775–78). If an individual's library was a metaphor for the knowledge that he or she 'possessed', then La Roche was clearly concerned to demonstrate more than a passing interest in scientific study. The holdings which she lists show a library markedly different from that of Lady Mary Wortley Montagu, who, although the owner of an original work by Isaac Newton himself, only had ten scientific works in her library of some 465 titles. Indeed, the greater weight (approximately one quarter) of Wortley Montagu's collection lay in fiction.[45] La Roche's library also demonstrated the pursuit of learning that went well beyond the titles of her youth. This intellectual independence cultivated in her adult years was the product of a careful primary education that La Roche enjoyed from her father, a man of strong Pietist beliefs, who therefore considered that girls should be educated, initially at least, in the same fashion as boys. He was thus keen to see his daughter acquire not just the necessary social graces that should be at a woman's employ, but also a broader understanding of the world, which included a knowledge of natural science and history.[46] As such it pointed towards aspirations to attain a level of education beyond the bounds of 'pleasurable instruction'.

The achievements of Maria Sybilla Merian (1647–1717) undoubtedly bridged the divide between the fine arts and the sciences. A master in the art of drawing insects and flowers, as La Roche described her in her account of travel to England, in her lifetime she eclipsed her male contemporaries to achieve international acclaim for her drawings.[47] Born into a Frankfurt family of naturalists, Merian initially made her name with close studies of flowers and fruit, very much in the style of Dutch still-life painting, and with entomological studies of the finest detail. Her fame owed itself not only to the thorough training she had received in her father's workshop, but also to her botanical subject matter. While botany was an accepted female scientific practice, few women had published in this field, but those bold enough to do so, like Merian, faced little competition from men.[48] However, the pioneering nature of the work which Merian undertook owed much more to her spirit of scientific enquiry than simply to the accuracy of hand and eye. Her lavishly illustrated *Der Raupen wunderbare Verwandelung* [*The Marvellous Transformation of Caterpillars*] (1679) attempted to record as many species of insect in the local habitat that she could find, showing them not just in their adult form, but in the four stages of their life cycle: as egg, caterpillar, pupa, and then as moth, butterfly, or fly. But what really brought about the culmination of her talents in the aesthetic masterpiece, the *Metamorphosis Insectorum Surinamensium* [*Metamorphosis of the Insects of Surinam*] (1705), was Merian's curiosity about the insect and plant life that lay beyond the flat wetlands of her adopted Dutch home. In 1698 she set sail from Amsterdam with her daughter for the Dutch colony of Surinam. The drawings she made there captured in brilliant colour and astonishing detail hitherto unknown insects, amphibians, and flowers. All these studies were made in the spirit of scientific endeavour without the slightest hint of 'female' squeamishness. The opening plate of the *Metamorphosis* greeted the reader with uncomfortably large cockroaches on a pineapple plant, while plate XVIII was still less appealing. It depicted a guava tree crawling with a host of ants and spiders, including a couple of tarantulas, one of which was pictured sucking the juices out of a dead hummingbird.

For an artist to embark on scientific exploration was uncommon enough at that time, but rarer still for a woman and her daughter to head unchaperoned to parts as exotic and dangerous. However, as Natalie Zemon Davis rightly remarks, the topos that best describes Merian's activities might be more than just that of going 'beyond her sex'.[49] While her work was pioneering in that it crossed boundaries of education and gender, its concern with the very nature of metamorphosis in the natural world brought her close to laying bare God's mysterious powers. She saw her work as sanctified by God, as the depiction of divine creativity in nature. But as Zemon Davis also notes, her descriptions of organic nature were both beautiful and dangerous, showing not only creation but destruction.[50] Indeed, her work was in many ways a far cry from the depiction of enchanting blooms which young ladies were encouraged to make the subject of botanical study. It was 'unfeminine' both in the range of subject matter it covered and in Merian's own pursuit of publication possibilities.

For all that La Roche endorsed women's enquiry into the sciences, she stressed in her travel account on England that there was an essential balance to be maintained. In adopting too scientific a line of enquiry and in viewing the world from a highly dis-passionate perspective, the observer failed to engage the reader's emotion. Certainly La Roche greatly respected Merian's artistic achievements, exclaiming at the end of the detailed biography which she gives of this artist in her travel account on England:

> Welch ein Beweis ist nicht unsre *Merian*, daß auch Frauenzimmer, wenn ihre Talente angebaut werden, in dem Gebiete männlicher Wissenschaften sich

Kenntnisse, Ruhm und Verdienste zu erwerben fähig sind, die selbst Männer beneiden und sich wünschen würden![51]

[What proof *Merian* is to us that women too, when their talents are developed, are capable of acquiring knowledge, fame, and merit in the domain of the male sciences, which even men would envy and wish for themselves!]

Yet Merian's task to view and to record accurately, according to principles of botanical observation, was in many ways not so difficult an undertaking, La Roche implied:

Wie glücklich war *Sybilla Merian*, da sie ihr großes Talent zum genauen Zeichnen und Mahlen allein der Naturgeschichte widmete; ihr scharfes Auge und feines Gefühl allein mit den wundervollen Gestalten und Schönheiten der Pflanzenwelt beschäftigte; denn bei diesen, und bei den Insekten, hatte ihre Seele bei der Beobachtung nicht so viel zu leiden, als der Historienmahler, welche allen Zügen der menschlichen Leidenschaften nachspüren muß.[52]

[How fortunate *Sybilla Merian* was, since she devoted her great talent only to the precise drawing and painting of natural history; only busied her sharp eye and fine feeling with the wonderous forms and beauties of the plant world; since in the observation of these subjects and of the insects, her soul did not have to suffer as much as the historical painter, who must trace all the expressions of human suffering.]

By viewing the world through this lens, Merian did not need to engage her own sympathies in her work. Thus, while scientific modes of enquiry, observation, and representation were to be applauded as means by which women could be seen to enter the 'male' sphere, they failed to achieve that balance between head and heart which La Roche implied in her travel narrative on England was ultimately her goal.

'Ausbrüche einer sehr lebhaften Empfindsamkeit'

Certainly in La Roche's account of travel to England sentimental passages and somewhat lachrymose scenes are not rare. She wipes away a tear at seeing Pope's bust in the grounds of his house at Twickenham. Walking through the grounds of the house, she imagines herself to be near him in spirit. Looking down into the water of the Thames flowing through the gardens, she calls to mind the last poem that he wrote before his death. She fancies that she stands at the spot where he composed his poem 'To Mrs. M. B. on her Birth-Day'.[53] Concerned not to bestow gifts upon his friend that are but 'Toys the female world admire', Pope wishes his friend 'Long health, long youth, long pleasure'.[54] But if the poem is about a birthday, it also refers to the subject's death, reminding her that at some point she will 'wake to raptures in a Life to come'.[55] It is this sense of mourning within celebration that brings La Roche to tears:

Ihr glaubt wohl, meine geliebte Töchter, daß ich mit einer Thräne im Aug, noch auf Popens Brustbild und auf die Stelle sah wo er vielleicht dieses schöne Gedichte schrieb.[56]

> [You may indeed believe, my beloved daughters, that I looked upon Pope's
> bust and the spot where he perhaps wrote this beautiful poem with a tear in
> my eye.]

That this might lack factual accuracy is something she concedes ('wo er vielleicht
dieses schöne Gedichte schrieb'). But by giving herself a certain poetic licence, she
could make the scene more vivid and thus appeal more directly to the emotions.
Sentimentality thus functioned as a means by which to move the reader through its
reference to the loss of past greatness.

It was not only literary stimuli that underpinned her tearful outbursts. Her
preoccupation with mortality was also evident in her visit to William Hamilton's
collection in London. The Greek and Roman funerary urns which she sees there
are embodiments for her of an imperiousness which has destroyed the well-being
and peace of all known corners of the earth.[57] In many ways they represented the
same arbitrary and violent use of force that was illustrated by fragments of rock
from Vesuvius or Etna, she argued. It was not just these human remains that evoked
feelings of sadness at human loss:

> Mit was für Empfindung nimmt man einen bei Capua ausgegrabenen Helm der
> Carthaginenser, — Hausgeräthe aus dem vorzweitausend Jahren verschütterten
> Herkulaneum, — Thränengläser aus den Gräbern von Großgriechenland in
> die Hände![58]

> [With what kind of a feeling does one take up in one's hand a Cartheginian
> helmet excavated near Capua, — household artefacts from Herculaneum, buried
> two thousand years ago, — tear glasses from the graves of Greater Greece.]

Thus it was not only the traditional military museum pieces such as helmets which
conjured up in her a sense of affective identification with this past civilization, but
also the more domestic items excavated. Included among the items found in the
graves of Roman ladies was a mirror which La Roche takes up in her hand, musing:

> Mag wohl der Zufall unter diesen Ueberresten einen Theil des Staubes der
> schönen Augen einer Griechin oder Römerin aufbehalten haben, welche vor
> so vielen Jahrhunderten in diesem Spiegel sich betrachtete, vielleicht aus ihm
> forschte: ob das Ohrgehänge und das Halsband, welche vor mir liegen, ihr gut
> stünden.[59]

> [It may be that chance has preserved the remains of a part of the dust of the fair
> eyes of a Greek or Roman woman who looked at herself in this mirror many
> centuries ago, or enquired of it whether this earring or this necklace, which lie
> before me, suited her.]

She therefore makes the mirror function as an object that 'transports' her to the
time that it was last used, and by looking in it she tries to forge some imaginative
link between herself and its previous user. Macabre as this might seem to modern
sensibilities, it was the contents of the urn that most invited her affective engagement. Gripped by curiosity, she took the ashes and earth between her fingers and
played with them in her hand:

> Der Gedanke: 'Du getrennter, Ich noch zusammenhängender Staub!' — bewegte
> mich sehr; und ich glaubte am Ende, daß es Sympathie war, welche mich unter

so vielen Aschenkrügen den wählen machte, dessen Asche einst von einer guten gefühlvollen Seele belebt war.[60]

[The thought: '*You dispersed, I still intact dust!*' — moved me greatly and I believed in the end that it was sympathy which made me choose from among so many jars of ashes that one in which the ashes were once animated by a good, sensitive soul.]

The tangible qualities of these remains were what stimulated in her the desire to engage affectively with the figure whom she imagined to be associated with them. Thus these museum exhibits were less significant to her because they informed her about death rituals in Roman times or pointed up differences between her civilization and the one to which they belonged, than because they allowed her to identify with the figures whom she had conjured up in her mind as relating to them. She even draws parallels between her experience of touching the ashes and the deceased being taken by the hand:

Diese Idee wirkte auf mich; ich drückte das bißchen Staub noch sanft mit meinen Fingern, wie einst ihre beste Freundin ihr die Hand gedrückt haben mag, wenn sie ihr klagte, daß ihre Güte übel belohnt, oder ihre besten Gesinnungen mißdeutet würden.[61]

[This idea had an effect on me; I pressed the small amount of dust gently with my fingers, just as once her best friend may have held her hand, when she complained to her that her goodness had been poorly rewarded or her best intentions misinterpreted.]

Thus La Roche constructs a strange intimacy between herself and the dead woman, which she then sustains by wishing that she could take away the urn with her to bury and therefore ensure — somewhat ironically, it must be said — that its contents are henceforth undisturbed.

However her concern is not just with the mortality of past figures. The suffering and tribulation of the destitute in her own time was also of concern to La Roche. In the opening pages, she relates how as they start their journey they encounter a poor but most tidily dressed woman who is working in the field.[62] On enquiring whether this land belongs to her, she is told that she has been given permission to farm it as a way of gaining some income now that her husband is too ill to work. This scene of humble diligence, presented as aesthetically pleasing (the woman is not in rags, but seeks to present herself to the world as decently as she can), evokes La Roche's sympathy:

O wie rührte mich diese einfache Erzählung, und der Gedanke, daß diese Leute nichts über ihre Gesundheit denken und wünschen, als Arbeit — oder Tod.[63]

[Oh, how much this simple story moved me, and the thought that these people do not think about their health or wish for more than work — or death.]

La Roche dramatizes the scene somewhat by reducing this woman's life to an existence between the two poles of 'Arbeit' and 'Tod', even if this does also gesture realistically towards the harshness of her fate. Pressures of time curtail the conversation and La Roche records that she 'gab ihr, was ich konnte, an etwas Geld, und eine Thräne voll Mitleiden und Achtung, für das so einfach redliche Herz' [gave her what I could, in the way of a little money, and a tear of sympathy and respect for the simply so honest heart].[64] Here her sympathy contains elements both of sisterhood and of charity. Thus her sentimental investment in the scene is couched in highly feminine terms, reflecting a preoccupation with the domestic as well as the spiritual well-being of this 'Tochter des Schicksals' [daughter of fate].

Family concerns also underlie another tearful scene. While journeying through Amsterdam they happen across a friend of Carl's with whom he studied in Berlin. The friend is overjoyed to see him and calls his mother over saying, that this was Carl La Roche, about whom he had told her so much. She embraces Carl tenderly:

> dankte ihm für seine Freundschaft gegen ihren geliebten Sohn; wünschte mir Glück, Mutter dieses Carls zu seyn, und umarmte mich mit Freudenthränen mit dem Ausruf: 'Daß gewiß in langer Zeit nicht zwei so glückliche Mütter zusammentrafen!'[65]

> [thanked him for the friendship he had shown towards her dear son; wished me happiness at being the mother of this Carl, and embraced me with tears of joy and the exclamation: 'That certainly two such happy mothers had not met in a long time!']

This form of sentimentalism reinforces the biographical nature of La Roche's travel account, overtly injecting it with a highly personalized content. It also interweaves the foreign experience with the maternal and the intimately familial. In so doing it further legitimates La Roche's travels as the peregrination between domestic spaces.

La Roche's sentimentalism could also border on breathless effusiveness, however. The gardens at Romford came in for such treatment:

> Und Romford [. . .] wie niedlich! [. . .] vor jedem Haus, gegen die Straße zu, ein zehen Schritte langes Gärtchen; — nicht kindisch mit Schnecken und Muscheln, oder geschnittenem Buchs; nein![66]

> [And Romford [. . .] how sweet! [. . .] in front of every house running down to the road a garden ten paces long; — not childishly decorated with snails and shells or cut box hedges; no!]

La Roche appeared to include such outbursts of rather excessively emotive language as a rhetorical means to reinforce the apparent spontaneity of her work. Indeed, the paragraph continues in the same breathless fashion, using enumeration and snatched, incomplete sentences to reinforce how overwhelmed she was by what she saw.[67] But it was precisely this language which Duchess Anna Amalia von Sachsen-Weimar had satirized in response to a letter in 1779 from Johann Heinrich Merck relating that he had visited Sophie:

> Lieber Merck, Sie könnten nicht glauben, wie unendlich Sie mich dadurch verbindlich gemacht haben, daß Sie nach allen Fatiguen und Abentheuern dennoch die Feder ergreifen um uns zu überzeugen daß Sie nach Ettersburg denken; ich fühl's — doch nicht à la Roche, es liegt tiefer in meinem Herzen. Sie haben die theure Sophie gesehen! — Gesprochen! — O Merck, Merck! — eine Empfindsame Reise![68]

> [Dear Merck, you cannot believe how much you have obliged me, that you still

reached for the pen after all your fatigue and adventures, to convince us that
you thought of Ettersburg; I sense it — not *à la Roche*, of course, it lies deeper
in my heart. You have seen our dear *Sophie*! Spoken to her! Oh Merck, Merck!
— a sentimental journey!]

The identification of La Roche's style as overly sentimentalized and superficial,
particularly by another woman, demonstrates the extent to which her earlier work
was also seen to be transgressive in another way, overstepping the boundaries of the
sentient and veering towards the overly sentimental. It suggests that when she came
to write her account of travel to England, La Roche's style held trappings of that
form of overwrought sentimentalism condemned by Anna Amalia.

    Was all of La Roche's contemporary critical audience quite so unforgiving about
her travel account published almost one and a half decades after *Sternheim*? The
public reception of the *Tagebuch einer Reise durch England und Schottland* in journal
reviews offered a more sympathetic analysis of the tension between sentimental
and empirical description. The *Allgemeine Deutsche Bibliothek* tempered its initial
enthusiasm towards what it termed La Roche's 'angenehmes Geschenk für das
Publikum' [pleasant gift to the public], by indicating that it contained few new
and really important observations.[69] It therefore assessed its content in terms of the
conventional expectations of factual novelty. Harsher criticism was reserved for the
prolixity of the account, which stretched over as many as 740 pages:

> Hätte es der würdigen Frau gefallen, nur das niederzuschreiben, was sie
> gesehen, und nicht alles, was sie dabey gedacht, empfunden, gesprochen, oder
> was ihr sonst bey den mancherley Gegenständen eingefallen; so würden statt 2
> Alphabete wenige Bogen hinreichend gewesen seyn.[70]

> [If it had pleased the worthy lady to write down only what she had seen and
> not everything that she thought, felt, said, or whatever else came to her mind
> on seeing a number of objects; then instead of two alphabets just a few sheets
> would have been sufficient.]

The reviewer clearly cared little for the sentimental reflections in her work,
preferring a piece that was concise and informative, very much in the established
tradition of travel writing on England. The *Allgemeine Literatur-Zeitung* likewise noted
the inclusion of 'freylich zum Theil kleine und bekannte Umstände' [admittedly
in part minor and already known facts], but saw the author's particularity and
indiscriminate collecting and viewing as characteristic of her unique style.[71] The
diary-epistolary format offered her a freedom, it added, to include the anecdotal,
as well as asides to her family and friends and extracts from other writers, which
collectively encouraged 'Ausbrüche einer sehr lebhaften Empfindsamkeit' [outbursts
of a most vivid sensibility]. Its focus on La Roche's departure from the sustained
masculine discourse of soberly impartial description and on her inclusion of
references to private relationships outside the narrative demonstrates the extent to
which it judged the writing of Madame *de la Roche*, known for her fine feelings,
within conventional parameters of female discourse. That it should compare her
work with that of Wendeborn and find much in hers that was new, implies also,
though, that women's travel writing was set on a par with that produced by men
and judged accordingly.

Indeed, while it is clear that there was a strong sentimental slant to her approach, she also exercised a curiosity that seemed to take a dispassionate stance and articulate 'male' forms of enquiry. Her conversation with an innkeeper at a hostelry near Bingen about his division of income — expenditure on oxen, outlay for the milling of his grain, the cost of slaughtering a pig — demonstrates a precision with which La Roche is often minded to record fact.[72] Likewise, the amount of food consumed in London is given with numerical exactitude:

> Man sagte uns: daß in London jährlich 2 Millionen 957 tausend Scheffel Weizenmehl, hunderttausend Ochsen, 700 tausend Schaafe und Lämmer, 195 tausend Kälber, 238 tausend Schweine, 115 tausend Scheffel Austern [. . .] verzehrt werden[73]

> [We were told that in London each year 2 million 957 thousand bushels of wheatflour, one hundred thousand oxen, 700 thousand sheep and lambs, 195 thousand calves, 238 thousand pigs, 115 thousand bushels of oysters [. . .] are consumed]

While the figures mentioned here are too overwhelmingly large to be imagined, the sheer optical impact of nearly one page's worth of such enumeration is impressive, as indeed is its implicit claim to scientific accuracy. La Roche's refusal to abandon inclusiveness suggests a desire on one level to position herself within the empirical tradition.

In terms of the selection of the sights she wishes to visit, La Roche is rather indiscriminate. Hers is no handbook to London that covers all that the enquiring tourist might wish to know or see. However, in her descriptions of monuments in London, she has recourse to the conventional device of listing their dimensions which created a sense of totality and satisfied those readers expecting factual accuracy. Her account of Westminster Abbey opens with the standard account of its measurements, as '360 Fuß in die Länge, und in dem Kreuz, nach dessen Form sie gebauet ist, 190 in die Breite' [360 foot long, and at the central point of the cross, the shape in which it is built, 190 wide].[74] She attempted to give a notion of size by taking recourse to the scientifically disinterested systems of classification proposed within the tradition of apodemic literature. She did not, interestingly, adopt the approach taken by Moritz some five years earlier, whose account she had read before departing on her travels. Arguably the first German travel writer on England to dispense with the recreation of size by giving dimensions, Moritz preferred to convey the height of St Paul's Cathedral by describing the view looking upwards into the dome.[75] Unlike Moritz, La Roche does not dwell on this aspect: her interest is more in revivifying the individuals whose memorials stand there than in the building itself. Indeed, her account, while covering most of the sights of London, finds imperatives of inclusion more in individuals than in places. While she was aware of the importance of impartial description in aligning her account within the established tradition of travel writing, her curiosity also remained clearly focused on individuals' lives and achievements, thereby alternating elements of 'female' interest with those of 'male' discourse.

That is not to say that 'curiosities' themselves did not invite enquiry on La Roche's part. The art of collection also held a tireless fascination for her. Sir Ashton Lever's museum in Leicester Square, Forster's cabinet of curiosities, or the British Museum were all examined with wonder. In its desire for precision and accuracy, La Roche's description of the exhibits held at this last institution seemed to consume her completely. It demonstrated an (improper) desire to achieve a totality of description, or in her terms, 'Alles zu betrachten, die Wißbegierde, welche in meiner Seele glüht' [to see everything, that form of curiosity which burns in my soul]:

> Alte und neue Münzen und Medaillen, 23 tausend; Cameos und alte Sigill, 968; Gefäße von Agat, Jaspis u. a. m. 2256; Metalle und Mineralien, 2725; Crystalle, Spathe u. a. m. 1864; Fossilien, Marmor, Talk und andre Steine, 1663; Erdarten und Salze, 1035; Harze, Schwefel, Bernsteine, 399 . . .[76]

> [Old and new coins and medals, 23 thousand; cameos and old seals, 968; vessels of agate, jasper, etc. 2256; metals and minerals, 2725; crystals, spars, etc., 1864; fossils, marble, talc and other stones, 1663; types of soil and salts, 1035; resin, sulphur, amber, 399 . . .]

Far from avoiding detail, she rather enjoyed occupying a position where she could be informative in the most disinterested way possible. Her concluding statement that she would make Forster director of the collection, had she the choice, 'damit eine gute Wahl und Ordnung in den Reichthum eingeführt würde' [so that a good selection and order is introduced into the abundance of specimens], is further indicative of a desire figured as particularly unfeminine to bring order and reason into what she has seen.

Occasionally, though, as at their viewing of Forster's collection, it is her son Carl who is permitted to exercise greater curiosity than she, and it seems that certain aspects of the male curiosity articulated in her account are not voiced by her but through him. The exterior and interior seating arrangements of the coach which they take to Colchester, appropriately enough called a 'Colchester Maschine', is described by La Roche herself. However, it is Carl who is called upon to examine its construction further, and thus the agency of curiosity passes from her to him.[77] Similarly, Carl's conversation with Count Reventlow in which he shows his interest in the 'Feuermaschine' (presumably a type of furnace to power a steam engine), allows La Roche to include a brief comment on the output of the steam-powered mills along the Thames compared with wind-driven ones.[78] Thus La Roche's account includes not only a multiplicity of voices but also a range of angles of viewing that suggests her concern to present an account that records her travels from more perspectives than simply those of the female traveller and writer.

The influence of Madame du Boccage's travel account on the *Tagebuch einer Reise durch Holland und England* is instructive in enabling us to understand how La Roche aligned herself with or diverged from previous women's travel writing on England. Du Boccage was a woman of letters who had collected memberships from a variety of academies, including Lyons, Bologna, Rome, and Padua. Her play *Amazones* had been performed in Paris in 1749 and she had translated Pope. She had met and corresponded with Lady Wortley Montagu. That La Roche takes a section wholesale from the French original of du Boccage's work and incorporates it into her own account is proof enough of the deference she paid to this *grande dame* and the value she accorded to the latter's writing. This inclusion was, however, made with the qualifier that La Roche did not fully agree with the French traveller's assessment of the relative merits of one of the cultural highlights of a visit to London, namely Ranelagh.[79] Du Boccage's brief prose description, followed by a passage of rhymed verse, saw Ranelagh as uniting Händel's brilliant harmonies with the entertainments of Ancient Rome, recasting it as an exotic location.[80] But La Roche's footnoted intervention in the verse section to explain one particular line is an unwelcome disturbance which jars with the mood created by the poetry. It demonstrates rather directly that La Roche prizes comprehension, clarity and accuracy of communication above poetic artistry. Strangely, she does not attempt to sustain the atmosphere created by this verse in her own prose that follows, but pauses simply to add in cold admiration, 'Ich glaube jetzo nichts mehr sagen zu dürfen, als daß dieses Bild noch jetzo wahr ist' [I believe that I am not currently able to say more than that this picture is currently true].[81] Her subsequent, abrupt, change of tack to refer to Carl's visit to inspect another furnace at Chelsea seems intent on destroying any lingering lyricism. While she grants space to the poetic, she is concerned to control and limit it, perhaps to stave off criticism that her work might come across as affected or insufficiently informative.

Certainly, La Roche's handling of scenic description in this account of England is highly ambivalent. Her refusal to offer descriptions of landscape or of natural beauty of her own that go beyond brief bouts of breathless effusiveness shows a marked deference to previous accounts. However, while inclusion in her travel account of du Boccage's text, covering some five pages, implicitly pays her a great compliment, there is no subsequent appreciation of it. Likewise, the few lines she uses to sketch in the scenic landscape around Richmond are, she acknowledges, nothing in comparison with the descriptions in Moritz's account, Archenholtz's *England und Italien*, or Heinrich von Watzdorf's *Briefe zur Charakteristik von England gehörig: geschrieben auf einer Reise im Jahre 1784* [*Letters concerning the Characteristics of England: Written on a Journey in the Year 1784*] (1786). She does not, however, give any intimation of what these earlier travellers actually said.[82] While the inclusion of picturesque scenes was to a degree already at odds with La Roche's larger project to describe individuals past and present connected with her travels, it might also be that she felt her strengths lay elsewhere in ensuring the acceptability of her account.

The preface to the English translation of Boccage's narrative is instructive in summarizing how the (male?) translator-editor wished the text to be received. He announced that the account was 'penned with an artless simplicity, free from the least appearance of affectation or study', which suggested that he was trying to market it as a female travelogue which might nevertheless interest male readers.[83] In a bold refutation of the ideology of separate spheres, he added that '[s]he seems to have had no intention of entering into a circumstantial detail, but only of drawing such sketches of the grand objects', thus scorning the particularity of female discourse.[84] What is more, he claimed, this would 'ever do honour to her judgement and impartiality'. Given her propensity to offer some descriptions in verse, this seemed difficult to ally with his comment that it was 'concise and expressive'. However, this work was generally exact and methodical and far less indiscriminate than La Roche's account, with still more scientific detail applied to descriptions of architectural features.[85] Certainly in its description of the ceremony of afternoon tea in English houses, or the influence of French fashions on English dress, it accommodated feminine interest. But in her narration of a meeting in Leiden with the Dutch physicist Pieter van Musschenbroek, inventor of the Leiden jar for storing electrical charge, or of her encounter with Professor Lallemand, who demonstrated 'the new artificial loadstone, whose force is equal to that of a real magnet', du Boccage also negotiated a position for herself which was authenticated and informed according to principles of male disinterest.[86]

La Roche's Readership and her Literary Salon

'This sensibillity [sic] which oft you praise | Serves but to plague me in unusual ways', wrote Lady Wortley Montagu in a poem of October 1736.[87] La Roche's fine sensibilities, and indeed her alliance with the cult of *Empfindsamkeit* through the *Geschichte des Fräuleins von Sternheim*, likewise brought her a catalogue of difficulties. If this work catapulted her to fame, it later arguably also served to bring about her marginalization. The quintessential novel of sentimentalism, it has been suggested that it was a valuable antecedent to Goethe's *Werther*, which may have had some influence on this work.[88] Goethe's response to *Sternheim*, penned by the woman whom then, at least, he affectionately called 'liebe Mama', was immediately positive. Indeed he robustly defended it in the *Frankfurter Gelehrte Anzeigen* of 14 February 1771 against its (male) critics: 'Allein alle die Herren irren sich, wenn sie glauben sie beurtheilen ein Buch — es ist eine *Menschenseele*' [But the gentlemen are wrong in thinking that they are judging a book — it is a *human soul*].[89] He noted in particular that the scene at the lead mines, inspired by John Macky's *A Journey through Scotland. In Familiar Letters from a Gentleman here, to his Friend Abroad* (1723), was 'für uns die Ergießung des edelsten Herzens in den Tagen des Kummers; und es scheint uns der Augenpunct zu sein, woraus die Verfasserin ihr ganzes System [. . .] wünscht betrachtet zu sehen' [for us the outpouring of the noblest heart in days of sorrow; and it seems to us to be the point of view from which the author wishes her whole system to be considered].[90] But his endorsement of La Roche's work was not to remain unwavering throughout their acquaintance. In 1798 he commented that the good-natured sentimentality which could still at least be endured thirty years ago was now quite out of season.[91] In a letter to Schiller in July the next year, he complained that La Roche belonged to those people who sought to have a levelling influence on things, raising the general to the particular and reducing the excellent to the mundane.[92] As part of Goethe's attack on *Empfindsamkeit*, he now fiercely rejected the brand of sentimentalism which he felt that La Roche continued to peddle, failing to move with the spirit of the time. Certainly, not all had been quite so forgiving of La Roche's sentimentality at earlier points in her career. Well before the publication of her account of travel to England, Lavater had noted in a letter to Goethe of 10 August 1782, 'Sie schien mir, seit ich sie sah, größer gewachsen. Ihre harmlose Zuthulichkeit behagte mir; jedoch nicht soviel, als mir ihre sentimentale Preziosität schenant war' [She seemed to me to have grown in stature since I saw her last. Her harmless friendliness pleased me; but not to the same extent that her sentimental preciousness embarrassed me.][93] Johann Heinrich Merck's judgement upon her was harsher still. He saw her sentimentalism as nothing but a façade: 'Elle prend son masque d'insensibilité comme elle veut, elle sait aussi le déposer, quand elle veut' [She picks up her mask of insensibility when she wants to and also knows how to put it down when she wants to], he wrote acerbically to his wife in the autumn of 1771.[94]

The association of Sternheim with her creator was something that La Roche would find difficult to shake off. The tendency to draw parallels between her life and that of her literary creation was one that observers could not resist. Caroline Herder was disappointed that La Roche was not the 'simple erhabene Sternheim' [simple sublime Sternheim] that she had expected.[95] Fanny Burney's diary account of her meeting with La Roche was altogether more positive, but it still cast her within a literary setting: 'I could scarcely believe that I was not actually listening to a Clelia or Cassandre, recounting the stories of her youth'.[96] As Silvia Bovenschen has argued, the success of the *Geschichte des Fräuleins von Sternheim* typecast La Roche as the sentimental female writer, and as such she was identified with this image in salons across Europe.[97]

If La Roche was indeed concerned to include the scientific and the sentimental in her travel writing, was her goal simply to encourage other female readers and writers to bridge this same divide? Or was she trying to score a point against her male critics, and if so, did this not suggest that she also had a male audience in mind? If, as Silke Schlichtmann has argued, women did not in practice read differently from men, even if the stereotypes of female and male reading implied that they did, how indeed can we make any attempt to determine the audience for whom La Roche was writing?[98] The argument that the *Tagebuch einer Reise durch Holland und England* comes from the pen of a 'traveling woman writing for women' is certainly not entirely convincing.[99] Admittedly La Roche had made the modest claim that her account was put in the shade by those of Archenholtz, Wendeborn, Watzdorf, or Moritz, and had continued:[100]

> [I]ch mache keine Prätension, als daß ich bei dem Erzählen dessen, was ich sah und dachte, meinen Töchtern eine kleine Unterhaltung, mir aber eine Erneuerung angenehmer Tage verschaffen will.[101]

> [I make no pretence of the fact that in the narration of what I saw and thought I wanted to create for my daughters a little entertainment but for myself the revival of pleasant days.]

But the assertions that she was writing only for her daughters could simply be a rhetorical device to ensure that she was not judged so harshly by (male) literary critics. As Langner notes with regard to La Roche's other travel accounts, they were not oriented towards a female audience in the same way that *Pomona* or the *Briefe an Lina* [*Letters to Lina*] more obviously were.[102] Indeed, La Roche had originally intended to dedicate her *Tagebuch einer Reise durch die Schweiz* to her grandfather Georg Friedrich Gutermann, rather than to her daughters Maximiliane Brentano and Louise Möhn.[103] Moreover, the fact that she was trying to earn money from her own pen suggests that she could not afford to aim solely at a female audience. Even in the late eighteenth century, it was principally men who held the purchasing power and sway concerning which books would be bought in a household, particularly with regard to non-fictional writing and travelogues.[104]

Moreover, La Roche's salon, which was not solely a gathering of like-minded women, would have been the environment in which she tested out her travel account. Peter Seibert's work on the literary salon in Germany between the Enlightenment and the *Vormärz* is a useful starting point in assessing the wider implications of social connections on the production of travel writing.[105] Emphasizing the oral narrative practices which often underpinned their creation, he suggests that the fact that Georg Forster read his account of Cook's navigation around the world aloud to an interested but non-specialist public in the salons of Berlin and Vienna may have influenced the style or content of the final version.[106] Similarly Moritz regaled his friends with reports of his voyage to England prior to the publication of his account, while Johanna Schopenhauer, one of the most noted female travellers of the early nineteenth century, would often recount a few experiences during her travels to her Weimar salon.[107] It is likely that La Roche also narrated details of her travels through England to an audience which included Merck and other faithful habitués such as Goethe and Georg Forster. Their own approach to the articulation of sentiment, and particularly its application in travel literature, would surely also have left some lasting impressions on the way in which La Roche angled her travel writing.

La Roche's cordial friendship with Georg Forster undoubtedly encouraged her fascination for travel and her enthusiasm for travel literature. The *Voyage Round the World* (1777) was a seminal piece in establishing those principles which were to underlie the practice of non-fiction travel writing as it made the transition to the Romantic period. It was a parallel account written by Georg Forster, aged just twenty-three, of the voyage round the world undertaken by himself, his father, Johann Reinhold Forster, and Captain Cook. In an open expression of *Empfindsamkeit*, Georg Forster admitted that his emotional response to his surroundings was another factor which relativized the objectivity of his accounts:

> I have sometimes obeyed the powerful dictates of my heart, and given voice to my feelings; for, as I do not pretend to be free from the weaknesses common to my fellow-creatures, it was necessary for every reader to know the colour of the glass through which I looked.[108]

Sentimentality and affective realism of the kind which he endorsed were beginning to demand the reorientation of enquiry away from the purely factual towards the lives and histories of others. La Roche was not always skilful at combining objectively styled scientific accuracy with her appeals to the reader's emotions. Yet she was aware that it was the uniqueness of the individual response which was vital in satisfying (or perhaps stimulating) the reader's emotional curiosity.

Goethe's relationship to the cult of sentiment was, as we have seen, arguably a less tolerant one. In an anonymous review of Johhann Gottlieb Schummel's *Empfindsame Reisen durch Deutschland* in the *Frankfurter Gelehrte Anzeigen* of 1772, attributed to him, he sarcastically dismissed the second instalment of Schummel's work. While this travelogue had clearly intended to imitate the sentimental Sterne, Goethe as self-appointed 'Policeybediente[r] des Litteraturgerichts' [policeman of the court of literature] was of another opinion, sentencing Schummel, if he had his way, to a spell in a workhouse for useless and chattering writers.[109] Goethe scorned what he judged to be the strategy of crude sentimentalism in Schummel's work, remarking that 'Yorick empfand, und dieser setzt sich hin zu empfinden' [Yorick was moved, and this author sits down to be moved].[110] The extracts from Schummel's work which Goethe published in his review were indeed radical examples of the unsystematic nature of sentimental travel writing, its unlinear narrative, and its use of elliptical constructions, all of which more scientific travellers despised.[111] Johann Heinrich Jung-Stilling, another of La Roche's wide circle of correspondents, also deplored the excessive and false sentiment of literature in the late 1770s and early 1780s. Like La Roche's father, he was a devout Pietist and a medical man; like Goethe, he had little time for overwrought sentimentalism. As he complained in a letter to La Roche of 4 July 1779:

> Ich kan des Klagens nicht satt werden, wenn ich so überschaue, wie viel die Schriften Vieler unserer Modeschriftsteller Verdorben haben; eine gränzenlose Empfindeley ohne Empfindsamkeit gegen das Wahre, Gute und Schöne, ohne Ueberwindungskraft gegen das Falsche, hat sich der Herzen der Jünglinge durchgehends bemeistert.[112]

> [I cannot complain enough when I see how much the writings of many of our fashionable writers have ruined; a boundless sentimentalism without real sentiment for the true, the good, and the beautiful, without the power to convince over the false, has thoroughly won over the hearts of the young.]

It is hard to say whether his fervent antipathy towards 'Empfindeley' had abated when he complimented La Roche some nine years later on the publication of *Tagebuch einer Reise durch die Schweiz* and the *Tagebuch einer Reise durch Frankreich*. That these books were the crowning works in her oeuvre and made her immortal in this life tended a little to the superlative, but it implied at least that in his eyes La Roche had not succumbed to 'gränzenlose Empfindeley'.[113]

Sophie von La Roche's *Tagebuch einer Reise durch Holland und England* was therefore a fierce rebuttal of the sort of 'separate spheres' limitations to which Forster had referred in his preface to Piozzi's travelogue. While she did, undeniably, have recourse to a discourse of moral improvement which selected female figures from English history and literature to promote the cause of women, she also at times drew on recent scientific inventions and discoveries, noted either by herself or her travelling companions, which could be styled as masculine in approach. For reasons of acceptability, the rhetoric she used partly legitimized her life as a woman who operated within the limitations of the domestic sphere. At the same time, though, her 'schielender Blick' invited her to act more boldly, spurred on by the work of both male and female counterparts. Other rhetorical devices bear witness to an impartiality, a distinct lack of *Empfindelei*, and an encyclopedism figured as male. In comparison with Moritz's travelogue, one senses that La Roche had no consistent strategy of observation or (self-)representation. Parts of her account had overt recourse to a scientific mode of description that revelled in factual detail, while others emphasized her own sympathetic engagement with the people and the objects — through association — which La Roche encountered in England. With regard to her own positioning, on the one hand she carefully negotiated a place in a previously exclusively male domain of German travel writing on England by creating some sense of continuity with previous accounts by male travellers. On the other, however, she also remained defiantly aware of her 'curious' position as a travelling female, while also attempting to transcend the gendered strictures of permitted and prohibited enquiry.

The gender dichotomy of public and private spheres is undoubtedly helpful in understanding the practices of travel in the eighteenth century. Yet I have sought to show that a tradition of female travel writing was beginning to develop that did not necessarily adhere to the sentimental, particularized, and indiscriminate discourse considered by some male critics of the time to underpin how women viewed and described the world around them. La Roche was therefore involved in the practice and representation of travel at a time when received ideas about travel writing were undergoing a radical revision. Crucially aware of the possibilities available to her but also the limitations, La Roche provided a lively, memorable, and detailed account of life in England that stressed the importance of private experience in narrations of travel whilst also seeking at other junctures to be soberly informative. For all its moments of disruption and disjunction, the *Tagebuch einer Reise durch Holland und England* played a vital role in giving German travel writing a commanding and distinctive female voice.

Notes to Chapter 2

1. Esther [Hester] Lynch Piozzi, *Bemerkungen auf der Reise durch Frankreich, Italien und Deutschland*, trans. by M. Forkel, preface by Georg Forster, 2 vols (Frankfurt a.M.: Barrentrapp and Wenner, 1790), I, x.

2. Ibid., p. xii.

3. See Judith Purver, 'Revolution, Romanticism, Restoration (1789–1830)', in *A History of Women's Writing in Germany, Austria and Switzerland*, ed. by Jo Catling (Cambridge: Cambridge University Press, 2000), pp. 68–87 (p. 69).

4. For statistics on the growth of travel writing as a proportion of the output of German publications at that time, see Uwe Hentschel, 'Goethe und die Reiseliteratur am Ende des achtzehnten Jahrhunderts', *Jahrbuch des Freien Deutschen Hochstifts* (1993), 93–127 (p. 93). See also Arthur R. Schultz's 'Goethe and the Literature of Travel', *Journal of English and Germanic Philology*, 48 (1949), 445–68, for a detailed analysis of the influence of travel literature on Goethe's (early) work.

5. Anon., 'Ueber die vielen Reisebeschreibungen in unsern Tagen', *BM*, 4 (1784), 319–32 (p. 321).

6. Linda Kraus Worley, 'Sophie von La Roche's Reisejournale: Reflections of a Traveling Subject', in *The Enlightenment and its Legacy: Studies in German Literature in Honor of Helga Slessarev*, ed. by Sara Friedrichsmeyer and Barbara Becker-Cantarino (Bonn: Bouvier, 1991), pp. 91–103 (p. 92).

7. Cheryl Turner, *Living by the Pen: Women Writers in the Eighteenth Century* (London: Routledge, 1992), p. 10.

8. Judith Purver, '"Zufrieden mit stillerem Ruhme"? Reflections on the Place of Women Writers in the Literary Spectrum of the Late Eighteenth and Early Nineteenth Centuries', *PEGS*, 64–65 (1993–95), 72–93 (p. 89); also Ute Frevert, 'Bürgerliche Meisterdenker und das Geschlechterverhältnis: Konzepte, Erfahrungen, Visionen an der Wende vom 18. zum 19. Jahrhundert', in *Bürgerinnen und Bürger: Geschlechterverhältnisse im 19. Jahrhundert*, ed. by Ute Frevert, Kritische Studien zur Geschichtswissenschaft, 77 (Göttingen: Vandenhoeck and Ruprecht, 1988), pp. 17–48.

9. See G. J. Barker-Benfield, *The Culture of Sensibility: Sex and Society in Eighteenth-Century Britain* (Chicago: University of Chicago Press, 1992); also Elizabeth Bohls, *Women Travel Writers and the Language of Aesthetics, 1716–1818*, Cambridge Studies in Romanticism, 13 (Cambridge: Cambridge University Press, 1995).

10. Janet Todd, *Sensibility: An Introduction* (London: Methuen, 1986), p. 110.

11. Ann Jessie Van Sant, *Eighteenth-Century Sensibility and the Novel: The Senses in Social Context* (Cambridge: Cambridge University Press, 1993), p. 115.

12. Theodore von Hippel, *Sämmtliche Werke*, 14 vols (Berlin: Reimer, 1827–39), VI: *Ueber die bürgerliche Verbesserung der Weiber* (1828), p. 235.

13. Franz Posselt, *Apodemik oder die Kunst zu reisen. Ein systematischer Versuch zum Gebrauch junger Reisenden aus den gebildeten Ständen überhaupt und angehender Gelehrten und Künstler insbesondere*, 2 vols (Leipzig: Breitkopf, 1795) I, 733. See for a discussion of Posselt's section on female travellers Annegret Pelz, '"Ob und wie Frauenzimmer reisen sollen?"' Das "reisende Frauenzimmer" als eine Entdeckung des 18. Jahrhunderts', in *Sehen und Beschreiben: Europäische Reisen im 18. und frühen 19. Jahrhundert*, ed. by Wolfgang Griep, Eutiner Forschungen, 1 (Heide: Westholsteinische Verlagsanstalt Boyens, 1991), pp. 125–35.

14. See Amanda Vickery, 'Golden Age to Separate Spheres? A Review of the Categories and Chronology of English Women's History', *The Historical Journal*, 36 (1993), 383–414.

15. Posselt, I, 173.

16. W. D. Robson-Scott, *German Travellers in England, 1400–1800* (Oxford: Blackwell, 1953), p. 184.

17. Monika Nenon, *Autorschaft und Frauenbildung: Das Beispiel Sophie von La Roche* (Würzburg: Königshausen and Neumann, 1988), p. 171. See also Linda Kraus Worley's comment that 'La Roche [. . .] includes a broad range of information, at times a truly encyclopedic compendium of cultural, social, agricultural and historical facts' (p. 95). Peter Petschauer approaches this tension in her work from a largely historical perspective, seeing it as the product of a period of transition, between Enlightenment educational ideals and the more Romantic pulls of the heart. See his article 'Sophie von LaRoche [sic], Novelist between Reason and Emotion', *The Germanic Review*, 57 (1982), 70–77.

18. See Margrit Langner, *Sophie von La Roche: Die empfindsame Realistin*, Beiträge zur Literatur-, Sprach- und Medienwissenschaft, 126 (Heidelberg: Winter, 1995), esp. pp. 169–70 and pp. 204–05.

19. Sophie von La Roche, *Tagebuch einer Reise durch Holland und England von der Verfasserin von Rosaliens Briefen* (Offenbach a.M.: Weiß und Brede, 1788; repr. Karben: Wald, 1997), p. 200.

20. Ibid., pp. 211–17.

21. Ibid., p. 555.

22. Sigrid Weigel, 'Der schielende Blick: Thesen zur Geschichte weiblicher Schreibpraxis', in *Die verborgene Frau: Sechs Beiträge zu einer feministischen Literaturwissenschaft*, ed. by Inge Stephan and Sigrid Weigel (Berlin: Argument, 1983), pp. 83–137 (p. 130).

23. *BM*, IV (1784), 319–32 (p. 323).

24. For a comparative discussion of the behaviour of the term 'curiosity' in Latin, French, English, and German, see Neil Kenny, *Curiosity in Early Modern Europe: Word Histories*, Wolfenbütteler Forschungen, 81 (Wiesbaden: Harrasowitz, 1998).

25. Zedler, LVII (1748), cols 1334–35 (col. 1334).

26. Zedler, XXIV (1740), cols 172–74 (cols 173–74).

27. Ibid., col. 172 (Zedler's emphasis).

28. Zedler, LVII, col. 1335.

29. See Krzysztof Pomian, *Collectors and Curiosities: Paris and Venice, 1500–1800*, trans. by Elizabeth Wiles-Porter (Cambridge: Polity Press, 1990), pp. 58–59.

30. Hans Blumenberg, 'Der Prozeß der theoretischen Neugierde', in Hans Blumenberg, *Die Legitimität der Neuzeit*, 3rd edn (Frankfurt a.M.: Suhrkamp, 1997), pp. 263–528.

31. Amaranthes [Gottlieb Sigmund Corvinus], *Nutzbares, galantes und curiöses Frauenzimmer-Lexicon* (Leipzig: Gleditsch, 1715), p. 1603.

32. La Roche, *Tagebuch*, unpaginated (La Roche's emphasis).

33. See Annegret Pelz, 'Reisen Frauen anders? Von Entdeckerinnen und reisenden Frauenzimmern', in *Reisekultur: Von der Pilgerfahrt zum modernen Tourismus*, ed. by Hermann Bausinger, Klaus Beyrer, and Gottfried Korff (Munich: Beck, 1991), pp. 174–78.

34. Sophie von La Roche, *Mein Schreibetisch*, 2 vols (Leipzig: Gräff, 1799; repr. Karben: Wald, 1996), I, 180–81 (La Roche's emphasis).

35. Ibid., p. 21.

36. Sophie von La Roche, *Pomona für Teutschlands Töchter*, 4 vols (Speyer: Enderische Schriften, 1783–84; repr. Munich: Saur, 1987), 2. Heft (February 1783), p. 135.

37. Ibid.

38. La Roche, *Tagebuch*, p. 388.

39. Ibid., p. 371.

40. See for a discussion of other travel writing read by La Roche, Michael Maurer, *Aufklärung und Anglophilie* (Göttingen: Vandenhoeck and Ruprecht, 1987), pp. 154–55.

41. In Wolfgang Griep and Annegret Pelz's *Frauen reisen: Ein bibliographisches Verzeichnis deutschsprachiger Frauenreisen 1700–1810*, Eutiner Kompendien, 1 (Bremen: Temmen, 1995), there is only mention of one (translated) account in German by a woman of travel to England prior to that of La Roche, namely Anne Marie Lepage Fiquet du Boccage's *Reisen der Madame du Bocage durch England, Holland, Frankreich und Italien in Briefen, aus dem Französischen übersetzt* (1776).

42. *Pomona*, 6. Heft (June 1783), p. 544.

43. Ibid., 5. Heft (May 1783), p. 421 (La Roche's emphasis).

44. Ibid, p. 419.

45. Isobel Grundy, 'Books and the Woman: An Eighteenth-Century Owner and her Libraries', *English Studies in Canada*, 20 (1994), 1–22.

46. Petschauer, 'Sophie von LaRoche, Novelist between Reason and Emotion', p. 73; Peter Petschauer, 'Christina Dorothea Leporin (Erxleben), Sophia (Gutermann) von La Roche, and Angelika Kauffmann: Background and Dilemmas of Independence', *Studies in Eighteenth-Century Culture*, 15 (1986), 127–43 (p. 132).

47. La Roche, *Tagebuch*, p. 237.

48. Helmut Kaiser, *Maria Sybilla Merian: Eine Biographie* (Düsseldorf: Artemis and Winkler, 1997), p. 104.

49. Natalie Zemon Davis, *Women on the Margins: Three Seventeenth-Century Lives* (Cambridge, MA: Harvard University Press, 1995), pp. 155–56.

50. La Roche, *Tagebuch*, p. 183.

51. Ibid., p. 240 (La Roche's emphasis).

52. Ibid., p. 236.

53. Ibid., p. 432.

54. Alexander Pope, *Selected Poems* (London: Bloomsbury Poetry Classics, 1994), p. 65.

55. Ibid.

56. La Roche, *Tagebuch*, p. 433.

57. Ibid., p. 242.

58. Ibid., p. 243.

59. Ibid., p. 243.

60. Ibid., p. 243–44 (La Roche's emphasis).

61. Ibid., p. 244.

62. Ibid., p. 8.

63. Ibid.

64. Ibid., p. 9.

65. Ibid., p. 139.

66. Ibid., p. 202.

67. Ibid., pp. 202–03.

68. *Johann Heinrich Mercks Schriften und Briefwechsel*, ed. by Kurt Wolff, 2 vols (Leipzig: Insel, 1909), II, 141 (2 August 1779) (Anna Amalia's emphasis).

69. *ADB*, 95.1 (1790), 265–71 (p. 265).

70. Ibid.

71. *ALZ*, 74, (15 March 1790), 586–87 (p. 586).

72. La Roche, *Tagebuch*, p. 6.

73. Ibid., p. 305.

74. Ibid., p. 257.

75. Moritz, *Werke*, II, 49–51. Joseph Addison had taken a similar approach to his description of St. Peter's in Rome some eighty years earlier. Like Moritz, he attempted to evoke the sense of space and height by standing directly under the cupola, and compared the proportions of the building rather than providing exact dimensions of its parts. See Addison, p. 109.

76. La Roche, *Tagebuch*, p. 328.

77. Ibid., p. 199.

78. Ibid., pp. 425–26.

79. Ibid., p. 557.

80. Ibid., pp. 557–62.

81. Ibid., p. 562.

82. Ibid., pp. 421–22.

83. Madame du Boccage, *Letters concerning England, Holland and Italy. By the celebrated Madam du Boccage, Member of the Academies of Padua, Bologna, Rome and Lyons. Written during her Travels in those Countries*, 2 vols (London: E. and C. Dilly, 1770), I, v.

84. Ibid., pp. v–vi.

85. See the description of St Paul's:

    This church is built of Portland stone, which is not liable to injury by the destructive fumes of sea-coal. It is five hundred feet long, a hundred in breadth at the entrance, and two hundred and twenty-three at the cross.

    In a footnote she adds the dimensions of St Peter's in Rome for comparison: La Roche, *Tagebuch*, pp. 22–23.

86. Ibid., p. 78.

87. Mary Wortley Montagu, *Lady Wortley Montagu: Essays and Poems and 'Simplicity, A Comedy'*, ed. by Robert Halsband and Isobel Grundy (Oxford: Clarendon Press, 1977), pp. 289–90.

88. Helene M. Kastinger Riley, *Die weibliche Muse: Sechs Essays über künstlerisch schaffende Frauen der Goethezeit*, Studies in German Literature, Linguistics and Culture, 8 (Columbia: Camden House, 1986), p. 27.

89. *FGA*, 13 (14 February 1772), 100–02 (p. 101).

90. Ibid., p. 102.

91. *DKV*, I: 17, *Tag und Jahreshefte* (1994), p. 66.

92. *DKV*, II: 4, *Briefe, Tagebücher und Gespräche, 1794–1799* (1998), p. 699.

93. *Goethe und Lavater: Briefe und Tagebücher*, ed. by Heinrich Funck (Weimar: Goethe-Gesellschaft, 1901), p. 219.

94. *Johann Heinrich Mercks Schriften*, II, 18.

95. See her letter to Herder of 27 April or 1 May 1772 (date unsure; Flachsland's italics): 'Endlich ist *Madame de la Roche* bey uns erschienen, aber welch eine andere Erscheinung als die simple erhabene Sternheim! [. . .] sie hat uns mit ihrer allzuvielen *Coquetterie* und *Representation* nicht gefallen' [At last *Madame de la Roche* has appeared at ours, but how different she appears from the simple, sublime Sternheim! She displeased us with her excessive coquettishness and showiness. Meanwhile I have also read the story of the lady von Sternheim. My complete ideal of a woman! Gentle, tender, charitable, proud and virtuous. And deceived.] (*Herders Briefwechsel mit Caroline Flachsland. Nach den Handschriften des Goethe- und Schiller-Archivs herausgegeben*, ed. by Hans Schauer, 2 vols (Weimar: Goethe-Gesellschaft, 1926–28), II, 99). Compare this with her euphoria at having read *Sternheim*, expressed in her letter to her husband of 14 June 1771: 'Ich habe indeßen auch [die] Geschichte der Fräulein von Sternheim gelesen. mein ganzes Ideal von einem Frauenzimmer! sanft, zärtlich, wohlthätig, stolz und tugendhaft. und betrogen' (ibid., I, 238–39).

96. *Diary and Letters of Madame D'Arblay (1778–1840)*, ed. by Austin Dobson, 6 vols (London: Macmillan, 1904–05), III, 29.

97. See Silvia Bovenschen, *Die imaginierte Weiblichkeit: Exemplarische Untersuchungen zu kulturgeschichtlichen und literarischen Präsentationsformen des Weiblichen* (Frankfurt a.M.: Suhrkamp, 1979).

98. See Silke Schlichtmann, *Geschlechterdifferenz in der Literaturrezeption um 1800?*, Untersuchungen zur deutschen Literaturgeschichte, 107 (Tübingen: Niemeyer, 2001).

99. Kraus Worley, p. 96.

100. La Roche, *Tagebuch*, p. 247.

101. Ibid., p. 248.

102. Langner, p. 168.

103. Ibid., p. 171.

104. See Erich Schön, 'Weibliches Lesen: Romanleserinnen im späten 18. Jahrhundert', in *Untersuchungen zum Roman von Frauen um 1800*, ed. by Helga Gallas and Magdalene Heuser (Tübingen: Niemeyer, 1990), pp. 20–40, 23.

105. Peter Seibert, *Der literarische Salon: Literatur und Geselligkeit zwischen Aufklärung und Vormärz* (Stuttgart: Metzler, 1993), pp. 265–80.

106. Ibid., p. 269.

107. Ibid.

108. Forster, I, xii–xiii.

109. *DKV*, I: 18, *Ästhetische Schriften 1771–1805* (1998), p. 13 and *FGA*, 18 (3 March 1772), 141–44 (p. 141).

110. *DKV*, I: 18, p. 14; *FGA*, 18, p. 142.

111. See Gerhard Sauder, 'Empfindsame Reisen' in *Reisekultur: Von der Pilgerfahrt zum modernen Tourismus*, ed. by Hermann Bausinger, Klaus Beyrer, and Gottfried Korff (Munich: Beck, 1991), p. 277.

112. Robert Hassencamp, 'Briefe von Joh. Heinr. Jung-Stilling an Sophie v. La Roche', *Euphorion*, 2 (1895), 577–87 (581).

113. Ibid., 582–83 (Letter of 15 June 1788).

CHAPTER 3

'Die Feder soll unser Sprachrohr seyn': Esther Gad's *Briefe während meines Aufenthalts in England und Portugal*

In 1802 and 1803, the first and second volumes of the *Briefe während meines Aufenthalts in England und Portugal* [*Letters Composed during My Stay in England and Portugal*] written by Esther Bernard (née Gad) were published by Campe in Hamburg. While this work did not receive great acclaim, its appearance did not go wholly unnoticed by literary critics either. The reviewer of the *Allgemeine Literatur-Zeitung* of 20 December 1803 was impressed by the originality of the material on Portugal and intrigued by the account's imaginative use of detail:

> Kleine Begebenheiten weiß eine solche Reisende zu nutzen [. . .] und macht sie den Lesern interessant. Ein Reisender hingegen, der bloß um sich und andere zu unterrichten reiset, muß in einem Lande, wo sehr vieles nicht untersucht ist, erst von der Gewalt der Tatsachen zu lebhaften Aeußerungen gezwungen werden.[1]

> [A lady traveller such as herself knows how to draw on minor occurrences [. . .] and make them interesting for the readers. A gentleman traveller, by contrast, who only travels to instruct himself and others, must, in a country where much has not been studied, first be compelled by the force of events to produce lively utterances.]

Rather slower to appear, the review in the *Neue Allgemeine Deutsche Bibliothek* of 1805 praised the achievements of this 'geistreiches Frauenzimmer' [ingenious lady] and admired the work's expression of fine feeling which was conveyed not only in its subject matter but also its mood.[2] These were, the reviewer implied, what shaped this account more than its factual accuracy or novelty. Moreover:

> Man muß hierauf etwas Rücksicht nehmen, und nicht die unparteyische Kälte eines vielleicht gefühllosern und auf Kleinigkeiten weniger achtenden Mannes erwarten. Auch sind kleine Erzählungen und Verse in die Nachrichten verwebt: man muß also auf den dichterischen, verschönernden Geist etwas abrechnen.[3]

> [We must take this into consideration and not expect the impartial coldness of a perhaps less sensitive man who pays less attention to detail. Moreover short stories and poems are woven into the information: it is therefore important to take into account this work's poetic, embellishing spirit.]

Thus travel writing by women continued into the nineteenth century to be seen as characterized by a subjective reporting style which was influenced by the sensibilities of the viewer and had a greater focus on detail. In the case of Gad's account, the factual prose of the 'Nachrichten' was even interspersed with the unconventional combination of poetry and anecdotal description.

Gad's *Briefe während meines Aufenthalts in England und Portugal* did not represent her literary debut in travel writing. Indeed, it was just one of a series of works which this prodigious figure, often overlooked by scholars of this period, produced in her lifetime. She was born around 1770 in Breslau as the daughter of the Generalpriviligerter Raphael ben Gad and her grandfather was the Hamburg chief rabbi Jonathan Eibenschütz. During her childhood, she enjoyed a thorough education and learned several foreign languages, which later stood her in good stead in her work as a translator. In 1791 she married the merchant Samuel Bernard and had two children by him. This marriage was dissolved in 1796 and she moved to Berlin. As her correspondence demonstrates, she subsequently cultivated friendships with the notable salonnières Henriette Herz and Rahel Varnhagen (who described Esther Gad as 'the clever lady from Breslau'),[4] as well as Elisa von der Recke and Jean Paul. In Berlin she met Wilhelm Friedrich Domeier, personal physician to Prince August Friedrich of England, and an affectionate relationship between them developed. When the Prince moved to Lisbon on account of his asthma in 1801, Dr Domeier accompanied him and Esther followed, via London, with the children. She converted to Christianity, was baptized 'Lucie', married Domeier in London in 1802, and was subsequently known as Esther Lucie Gad Bernard Domeier. She later went to live with Domeier in Malta and her death is thought to have occurred at some point after 1833.

Gad produced a number of smaller works in her earlier years, including the *Beschreibung einer Wasserreise von Aussig nach Dresden* [*Description of a Journey by Water from Aussig to Dresden*], published in the *Deutsche Monatsschrift* in 1799, and several other journal articles on Lisbon and on Portuguese women. Her first book, *Die Geschwister* [*The Siblings*], on which she was working in autumn 1800, never went to press. However, her two-volume *Briefe während meines Aufenthalts in England und Portugal* brought her moderate success and was later republished with a slightly different title (but no obvious differences of content) as the *Briefe über England und Portugal an einen Freund* in 1808. The peripatetic nature of her life in this period, which she recorded in this travel account, was certainly no hindrance to her publishing career. While waiting for the ship to carry her to Malta, she managed, for example, to draw up a collection of four essays which were published under the title *Gesammelte Blätter* [*Collected Papers*]. This work was originally intended to be a two-volume edition, but only the first volume appeared in Leipzig with the Reclam publishing house in 1806. As a translator, Gad was almost as prolific as in her career as a writer. Her translation work included *Die beyden Mütter, oder die Folgen der Verläumdung* [*The Rival Mothers, or Calumny*] (1800–02) from the French of Stéphanie de Genlis, Leucadio Doblado's *Briefe aus Spanien* [*Letters from Spain*] (1824) from the Spanish, and *Der Zwerg. Ein irisches Sittengemälde* [originally entitled *Crohoore of the Billhook*] from the English of John Banim (1828). Gad was not afraid to engage in argument with some of the more enlightened minds of the time, and her *Kritische Auseinandersetzung mehrerer Stellen in dem Buche der Frau von Staël über Deutschland. Mit einer Zueignungsschrift von Herrn Jean Paul Richter* [*Critical Disputation of Several Points in Madame de Staël's book on Germany. With a Dedication to Mr Jean Paul Richter*] was published in German in 1814.

Within the context of the by now extensive and well-established tradition of German writing on England, the *Briefe während meines Aufenthalts in England und Portugal* (1802) did not, arguably, contribute much to contemporary factual knowledge about life in Albion. In terms of factual content, the sections on Portugal, a country hitherto largely off the beaten track of the northern European traveller, were what gave it its novelty value. Comprising two volumes of over 460 pages in total, twenty-eight of the letters written were about England. The first of these, dated Hanover, April 1801, set the journey in motion: subsequent letters carried only place-names, not dates. The third letter, written in Yarmouth, described the boredom of the sea crossing from Cuxhaven and the relief at arriving in England. Following an itinerary that took her and her family through Ipswich and up to London, Gad then spent some time describing life in the capital, its fashions and gossip, the delights of shopping, the works of Aphra Behn and Jonathan Swift, the pleasures of Covent Garden, as well as the cold politeness of the English. The architecture of Westminster Abbey was given a rather cursory examination ('[d]a ich voraussetzen kann, daß dies Gebäude meinen mehrsten Lesern aus genauen Beschreibungen bekannt ist' [since I can presume that this building is known to most of my readers from detailed descriptions][5]) while those buried there, in particular Maria Stuart, were the subject of greater scrutiny. The eleventh letter, which opened with a quotation from Goethe's *Hermann und Dorothea* [*Hermann and Dorothea*], queried the traveller's concern for the new and the useful, when he should have been looking for the good.[6] Good works Gad indeed found performed in the Westminster Lying In Hospital, a nearby orphanage, and the Magdalen Hospital. The thirteenth and fourteenth letters detailed her journey through Bath to the English coast and on to Portugal.

Gad's account of England resumed in the twelfth letter of the second volume as she landed at Falmouth in summer 1802 on her return from Portugal after an unpleasantly stormy sea voyage of eleven days. Salisbury and in particular neighbouring Stonehenge fascinated Gad, who included in her account a lengthy excerpt from Hume's *History of England* (1778) on druids and their violent and barbaric sacrificial practices. By the end of July, Gad was back in London, and discussing what constituted 'beauty' in the capital, how theatrical the rhetorics of the auctioneers at the house of '[e]in Herrn Christie' [a Mr. Christie] were, and with what astonishing ease purchases could be made on credit. 'Meat-pyes', 'Rosinenpudding (plumpudding)', and other such culinary delights were the subjects of later letters, as well as the improvements introduced by the men of the Royal Society, the pleasures of Ranelagh and Vauxhall, and the annual St Bartholomew's Fair. The final letters described excursions to Brighton (in particular the expensive sea bathing facilities to be enjoyed there), Portsmouth, and the Isle of Wight. It closed with a description of the paintings in Shakespeare's Gallery, the artistry of which would also fascinate Horstig.

The foreword and first letter of Gad's account contained more than the standard apology for the possible repetition of material described in other travelogues and the assurance that the account was authentic. Rather, hers was a justification of both form and content which was strategically placed to pre-empt criticism about her divergence from standard practices. This justification of the standpoint from which she was writing was just as important for the reader, she argued, as 'die Zurechtweisung des Mahlers für denjenigen ist, der nicht weiß, wo er stehen muß, um ein Gemälde aus dem gehörigen Gesichtspunkt zu betrachten' [the rebuke of the artist is for those people who do not know where to stand in order to look at a painting from the appropriate viewpoint].[7] The title, which took the form of 'Briefe' [letters] rather than a 'Bericht' [account], immediately suggested to the reader that its author made less of a claim to originality through authoritative description than through informal correspondence. As Gad hastened to observe, her work did indeed find its genesis in a letter to a friend — which Barbara Hahn has suggested could indeed have been Jean Paul, to whom Gad gushed in a letter of September 1800, 'Ich kenne keinen Schriftsteller ältrer oder neurer Zeiten, der so allgemein von den Weibern geliebt wurde, als Sie' [I know of no writer from ancient or modern times who is generally so loved by women as you].[8] Whether or not this initial letter was indeed meant for him, by the closure of her account the letter format she had adopted was really meant to address an audience wider than just one correspondent:

> Den ersten Brief richtete ich wirklich an einen Freund, beym zweiten dachte ich schon an mehrere Freunde und bey den folgenden — dachte ich an ein Publikum. Und betrachten wir dies nicht einigermaßen als unsern Freund, wenn es unsere Werke liest?[9]

> [I did indeed address the first letter to a friend, while writing the second I already thought of several friends and with the next — I thought of an audience. And do we not consider them, to some extent, our friends, when they read our works?]

Such modest claims sought to give the impression that she was not a woman with literary ambitions: quite the contrary, her account evolved from a correspondence conducted, initially at least, in the private sphere. But her open admission of the decision to use an epistolary structure, even if private correspondence no longer underpinned her motivations to record the foreign, revealed a deliberate deployment of this literary device to maintain a sense of privacy and suggest a certain affective proximity between reader and author. The apparent immediacy of the account was also re-emphasized in the first letter: 'Die Feder soll unser Sprachrohr seyn, und jeden Posttag werden Sie erfahren, was ich gesehen und bemerkt habe' [The quill will be our mouthpiece and each day that post is delivered you will learn what I have seen and commented upon].[10] Thus she emphasized the apparent closeness of the relationship between the reader and the narrator. It was as if Gad were almost 'speaking' directly to her correspondent, with such swift dispatch of her letters that the ink had scarcely dried upon them before they were opened and read by their recipient. The structure of these instalments, she was at pains to stress, was not a 'pragmatische Geschichte' [pragmatic story] but rather a collection of facts brought together for readers to interpret as they wished. Nor indeed was it arranged thematically, as had been the case in Archenholtz's *England und Italien* and parts of Moritz's account of England.[11]

Gad's foreword also set a clear agenda in terms of the nature of its content:

> Daß ich manches in meine Bemerkungen über England und Portugal einmischte, was nicht dahin zu gehören scheint, bedarf nur dann einer Entschuldigung, wenn das, was ich einmischte ohne Werth ist; denn alles, was wirklichen Werth hat, steht in jedem Buche an seiner rechten Stelle, und man sollte überall keine starke Scheidewand zwischen Wahrheiten und Wahrheiten ziehen.[12]

> [That I incorporated into my observations on England and Portugal some elements which do not appear to belong there only requires an apology when what I built in has no value, since everything that has true value has its correct place in any book, and one should not make such a strict distinction everywhere between truths and truths.]

Gone, then, was the concern that travellers of late seventeenth-century and early eighteenth-century accounts had shown for the accurate representation of facts and a seemingly 'objective' record of what they had encountered on their journeys. The 'truths' on which Gad focused were of a different order than verifiable facts — they were 'inner truths' which were concerned with issues of human interaction. Indeed, she added, the portrayal of a nation as a whole would not suffer if one sought to weave into it the description of certain people and their fates.[13] Thus, like Moritz to a degree, she developed a mode of representation that depended on the reader's acceptance that the descriptions of individual figures could be extrapolated to stand for a larger entity. Such description on a microtextual level did not only allow for more detailed portrayals. It also gave the author greater scope to focus on her chief preoccupations in this work, namely the fates of individual figures. As she elaborated in her foreword:

> Die Geschichte ganzer Völker hat nur insofern Werth für uns, als sie *belehrt*; die Geschichte einzelner Menschen hingegen, *zieht uns an*. Der Geist vermag es, über das Schicksal ganzer Nationen nachzudenken, aber das Herz kann nur das Schicksal einiger wenigen Menschen mit empfinden.[14]

> [The history of whole peoples is only of any value to us in so far as it *instructs* us; the history of individual people, by contrast, *arrests* us. The mind is capable of contemplating the fate of whole nations, but the heart can only sympathize with the fate of just a few people.]

In between this dichotomy between mind and heart, Gad called for a medial position to be adopted which served a dual end of uniting the emotions and the imagination with reason. Herodotus's historical writing, she enthused, demonstrated how well the ancients knew how to combine the two:

> Sie ist so *unterhaltend* geschrieben und mit so vielen kleinen Anekdoten ver-flochten, daß einige neuere Geschichtschreiber darum dachten, sie sey nicht wahr, weil sie von dem Wahn ausgingen, daß das Schwerfällige die Bedingung des Wahren sey.[15]

[It is written in so *entertaining* a fashion and interwoven with so many small anecdotes that several more recent historians thought as a consequence that it could not be true, because they were under the delusion that ponderousness is the condition for truth.]

Not all late eighteenth- and early nineteenth-century historians would have agreed with Gad's enthusiastic response to the narrative structure of the works of Herodotus, as indeed she realised herself. The aesthetician Johann Georg Sulzer, was highly sceptical of the contribution of Herodotus to accurate historiography, as Daniel Fulda notes.[16] In his *Kurzer Begriff aller Wissenschaften und anderen Theilen der Gelehrsamkeit* [*Brief Guide to all the Sciences and Other Areas of Learning*) (1745), Sulzer argued that it was an absolute must for contemporary scholars to scrutinize again the historical writing of Herodotus's time, 'daß man bey der Geschichte dieser fabelhaften Zeiten, das fabelhafte und allegorische von dem wahrhaften mit mehrerm Fleis absonderte' [so that in the history of these fabulous times, the fabulous and allegorical can be separated with greater diligence from the true].[17] Even if 'serious' intellectuals scorned the use of allegory in non-fictional writing, it was clear that Gad was interested in drawing on narrative practices beyond the realm of literature — and indeed her reference to Herodotus was in itself an important indication of the range of her own scholarship and reading.

Gad's use of the anecdote in her travel account of England in many ways reflected developments both in the literature of the Enlightenment and Romantic periods and in non-fictional forms of writing such as history and biography. The Abbé Reynal's *Anecdotes littéraires* [*Literary Anecdotes*] (1750) and *Anecdotes historiques, militaires et politiques de l'Europe* [*Historical, Military, and Political Anecdotes on Europe*] (1754) belonged to the forerunners of a genre which established itself in Germany with Johann Adam Hiller's *Anecdoten zur Lebensgeschichte großer Regenten und beruehmter Staatsmaenner* [*Anecdotes on the Biography of Great Rulers and Famous Statesmen*] (1762). Among a German-speaking public, anecdotes concerning the private biographies of enlightened absolute rulers such as Frederick II, Peter the Great, and Catherine II made popular reading.[18] The lives of artists, too, were also often recounted in a largely anecdotal fashion, as Karen Junod has demonstrated in her study of Hogarth.[19] While the majority of anecdotes published in the eighteenth century were historiographical in theme, by the start of the nineteenth century, the anecdote had found a firm footing in literary works such as Christoph Martin Wieland's *Hexameron vom Rosenhain* (1805), Achim von Arnim's *Novellensammlung von 1812* [*Novella Collection of 1812*], Johann Peter Hebel's *Schatzkästlein des rheinischen Hausfreunds* [*The Rhenish Family Friend's Small Treasure Chest*] (1811), and Heinrich von Kleist's *Anekdote aus dem letzten preußischen Kriege* [*Anecdote from the Last Prussian War*], which was published in the *Berliner Abendblätter* [*Berlin Evening Papers*] between 1810 and 1811. Indeed, journals eagerly tapped into this growing market and magazines such as the *Deutsche Chronik* [*German Chronical*], *Teutscher Merkur*, *Berlinische Monatsschrift*, and *Flora, Teutschlands Töchter* [*Flora, Germany's Daughters*] became the prime site for the publication of literary and historical anecdotes.[20]

While the anecdote has today become synonymous with unreliability and untrustworthiness, it originally came from the Greek 'an-ekdota' meaning 'unpublished', secret information hitherto not known in the public sphere. Johnson's *Dictionary* of 1755 had defined the word anecdote as 'something yet unpublished; secret history', but by 1773 as he came to prepare the fourth edition, he decided that the word had acquired a second meaning, namely 'a minute passage of private life'.[21] Johann Georg Büsch, writer and economist and Professor of Mathematics in Hamburg, was still stressing the secret and private connotations of the word in his article 'Ueber Anecdoten' [On Anecdotes] published in 1787. The value of the anecdote lay, he emphasized, in capturing a form of oral history: 'Die Geschichte unsrer Zeiten ist gewiß eine der wichtigsten, welche in dem ganzen Laufe menschlicher Begebenheiten vorkommt. Wenn wir dies nicht genugsam erkennen, so wird es die Nachwelt erkennen' [The history of our times is certainly one of the most important which has occurred in the whole course of human activities. Even if we do not recognize this sufficiently, our successors will].[22] Important subjects for anecdotes were figures of political relevance, certainly not the common man. The librarian, writer, and translator Albrecht Christoph Kayser placed less emphasis, however, on the historical importance of the figures in question in his article on anecdotes printed in the *Teutscher Merkur* of 1784:

> Ich definire mir Anekdote so, daß sie eine charakterisirende Herzens- oder Geistesäusserung einer Person enthalte. Es giebt also zweyerley Arten von Anekdoten: eine sucht den sittlichen Charakter, die andere den Geist und Verstand einer Person zu schildern.[23]

> [I define an anecdote thus, that it contains the characteristic expression of a person's heart or mind. There are therefore two forms of anecdote: one which seeks to portray a person's moral character, the other a person's mind and reason.]

The different facets of a person's character were therefore what he deemed of interest to the reading public. But he stressed that the didactic aim of anecdotes was not simply to present us with exemplary role models since they did not show us subjects in an ideal world but in the real one.[24] As a result, anecdotal narrative allowed us to glimpse the unreliability and inconstancy of the human character through focusing on a figure's turns of mood. The common man is often taken by surprise at his own reactions which mere minutes later he regrets:

> Beschämt und gerührt sagt er alsdann zu sich selbst: was hab ich gethan? Wie war mir? Und — diese That oder Rede der Ueberraschung ergriffen und als Anekdote ausposaunt, wie kann sie ein Leben voll thätiger Tugend brandmarken und kränkende Thränen dem Verschrieenen erpressen![25]

> [Shamefaced and moved, he then said to himself: what have I done? What happened to me? And — this act or speech of surprise taken up and broadcast as an anecdote, how much can it stigmatize a life full of active virtue and wrest tears of mortification from the denounced figure!]

Thus the formulation, narration, and reading of anecdotes potentially has a didactic and prosocial effect on the audience, to the extent that they reconsider their own behaviour and attempt to moderate excessive outbursts of feeling for the benefit of their fellow men.

Given that Gad's account was dominated by the anecdotal reporting of conversations with a range of characters (most of them female) whom she met on her travels, how did she deploy the anecdote, in between those sections which were concerned more with factual comment, to encourage empathetic engagement? Who were the subjects of her anecdotes, what was important about their stories and how successful were they in enabling us to gain a more intimate understanding of life in England at the turn of the nineteenth century? The value of the anecdote is not only in what is told but in the very telling and so it will also be important to explore here which rhetorical devices Gad deployed within the anecdotes to convey a greater sense of immediacy or authenticity and thus seek to heighten the reader's empathetic concern. Finally, given that Gad placed such emphasis on this narrative form in her travel writing, what does it tell us about her as a writer, (female) traveller, and observer?

'Die unmittelbare Stimme eines gepeinigten Herzens'

'In England kann jedes Frauenzimmer ohne Begleiter reisen; sie hat nirgend eine unanständige Begegnung, oder auch nur ein unanständiges Wort zu befürchten' [In England every woman can travel unaccompanied, she need never fear an indelicate encounter or an indecent word], Gad noted of travel as an unaccompanied woman through England at the start of the nineteenth century.[26] The anxieties shared by the generation of female travellers before her, like Sophie von La Roche, who had hastened to demonstrate to her readers that she did not travel unchaperoned and, indeed, was journeying principally to visit family members who had settled abroad, had largely disappeared. Just as Moritz had been at pains to concentrate not simply on destinations but also the travel between them, Gad also eagerly used these 'spaces' between her descriptions of places to record encounters with fellow journeyers and the human interest stories they had to tell. Even before they had reached England, she had embarked on the first of her anecdotes, which covered some ten pages. As the rays of the sun illuminated the deck of the ship sailing between Cuxhaven and Yarmouth at around five in the morning, a gentle female voice was to be heard singing on deck a ballad from John Gay's popular tragi-comedy *The What D'ye Call It* (1715). The song is about a damsel lamenting the loss of her lover to the 'cruel ocean' who subsequently expired on seeing the corpse of her drowned beloved float by: Gad fails to sense the burlesque in this and clearly treats it as a piece of tragic writing. Indeed, she includes in her account the full English text and her own German translation — which the reviewer of the *Neue Allgemeine Deutsche Bibliothek* considered amateurish, noting that the childlike simplicity and deep pathos of the original had completely disappeared from the otherwise correct translation.[27] The reason why the women sang this piece, Gad surmised, was because this fellow traveller was in a state of emotional torment:

> Ich glaubte nicht blos gewöhnliche Töne eines Sprachorgans, sondern, wenn ich so sagen darf, die unmittelbare Stimme eines gepeinigten Herzens zu hören. Man hätte ihren Tönen keine angemessenere Worte unterlegen können als: Schmerz! Leiden![28]

[I believed that I was hearing not simply the usual sounds of an organ of speech but, if I may say this, the unmediated voice of a tormented heart. No more appropriate words could have been attributed to her sounds than: Pain! Suffering!]

A leitmotiv throughout the anecdotes contained in the *Briefe während meines Aufenthalts in England und Portugal* was the recounting of precisely this kind of situation: a suffering individual who invites Gad's sympathy and curiosity, and who leads her to reflect on humanity and its injustices. The storm which the passengers had endured the night before, this female figure tells us partly in direct speech, partly in indirect speech reported through Gad, mirrored the mental torment she was suffering herself. But unlike swift changes to the weather, this figure lamented, in certain storms of life no ray of sunshine followed.[29] Having recorded the fellow traveller's words, Gad then broke off the narrative of her conversation with this figure to remark:

> Keine Darstellung eines Leidens macht mehr Eindruck auf den Zuhörer, als die welche dem Erzähler gleichsam entschlüpft ist. Als wenn der Mensch überall das, was ihm nicht bekannt ist, am liebsten auffing! Oder vielleicht auch, weil man dann am sichersten auf Wahrheit rechnen kann.[30]

> [No representation of suffering makes a greater impression on the listener than what has just slipped out of the narrator's mouth. As if people everywhere would prefer to gather information that was unfamiliar to them! Or perhaps also because one can then, with the greatest certainty, expect truth.]

Gad therefore not only allied immediacy of description with the power of the impression that it made on the audience, but also with issues of truth and authenticity. But to whom was Gad referring, when she talked of the 'Zuhörer'? Was she simply referring to herself as the listener to the tale or was she also thinking of her own audience, namely her readers? If she was indeed concerned to evoke in her readers the same emotions of pity and sympathy which she claimed to have felt herself on encountering this figure, then she was presuming that the reader also entered into the suspension of disbelief in such a way that they too 'heard' the subject 'speak'.

In the following paragraph, however, she abruptly distances herself from any mediatory role to reassert her own status in the narrative:

> Jedes Wort, daß diese einnehmende Frau aussprach, vermehrte mein Verlangen ihre Geschichte zu wissen; aber ich ehrte ihr Unglück und ihr Stillschweigen darüber, und da ich mich jeder unbescheidenen Frage enthielt, und sie wohl einsah, daß ich nicht blos Neugierde, sondern ein edles Interesse aus Schonung unterdrückte, so belohnte sie mich dadurch, daß sie mir sagte, daß ihre Leiden von einer Art wären, die keine menschliche Hülfe, ja keine göttliche Hülfe vermindern könnte.[31]

> [Every word which this likeable woman uttered increased my desire to know her story; but I respected her unhappiness and her silence on it, and since I abstained from posing any immodest question and she comprehended well that I suppressed not mere curiosity but a noble interest to protect her feelings, she rewarded me by saying that her suffering was of a kind that no human aid, indeed no divine help, could allay.]

Thus Gad constructs a position for herself as an empathetic individual which also emphasizes the authenticity of her own feelings towards the suffering subject. Wishing to present herself as a woman of integrity rather than merely some *Schaulustige*, she seeks to demonstrate that her curiosity was not of an improper kind. That Gad's aid was in vain — as this figure lamented, since neither human nor divine help could alleviate her anguish — lay in the nature of the figure's situation. 'Sie litt durch die Verrätherei, durch die Ungerechtigkeit eines geliebten Menschen', Gad reports, 'und dies ist vielleicht das einzige moralische Uebel, gegen welches es kein Heilmittel giebt' [She suffered as a result of betrayal, due to the injustice of a beloved person and this is perhaps the only moral evil for which there is no cure].[32] The specific suffering of one individual is therefore extrapolated to become part of a wider moral issue. To the blows of fate, Gad remarks, we are more or less immune since time passes and the wound heals, but the injustice of a beloved friend cuts a wound which bleeds forever, while revenge, man's natural weapon against such injustices, only serves in such cases to damage the injured party more.[33] Thus Gad uses this encounter as a platform for airing moral concerns which far outweigh national issues. Even before she has arrived in England, she therefore seems bent less on uncovering national differences and specific characteristics of 'Englishness' than on demonstrating that there is a common denominator to human suffering.

As she draws this scene to a close, Gad informs the reader that this female figure had promised her that she would write down her story for her as soon as she reached London, 'und hat mir im voraus erlaubt, sie Ihnen dann mitzutheilen' [and has allowed me to communicate it to you in advance].[34] The reader, she tries to suggest, has been offered privileged access to this information, an intimate insight into a particular individual's life, and in so doing Gad creates the potential for a sense of enhanced emotional proximity. The footnote which Gad appended to this statement showed a certain nervous self-reflexiveness, however: 'Ich werde diese Geschichte mit einigen Abänderungen, bey einer andern Gelegenheit mittheilen, wenn ich erst wissen werde, wie man meine häufigen Einschaltungen dieser Art aufgenommen hat' [I will, with a few changes, make this story public on another occasion, once I know how my frequent interjections of this kind have been received].[35] The fact that she was concerned about audience reception even (or particularly) at this very early stage in her account suggests a highly crafted narrative that belies an apparent artlessness. What it also suggests is that she was crucially aware of the experimental nature of her travelogue, its unconventional form, and potential transgression of a number of unwritten rules about non-fictional travel writing at the turn of the nineteenth century.

'Lassen Sie den Muth nicht sinken; es ist mit den Zeiten wie mit den Menschen'

Scarcely ten pages later, having described the cumbersome process of transferring from the larger vessel which brought them from Germany to smaller boats which took them to the shore, as well as the tipping of coach drivers in England, Gad shifted into her second anecdotal sequence. Some thirty miles from the coast, a young woman stepped into the carriage and the occupants, who included Gad, a cleric, and an older woman, soon entered into conversation. The younger woman declared that she had not been out during the Easter weekend just passed, since people had now become so dreadful that it was impossible to keep polite company.[36] The older woman retorted that people were no worse than they were forty years previously, although they were perhaps more pretentious and concerned with outer appearance. These were, however, not failings which many people were taken in by and did not gnaw at social values. The cleric, by contrast, considered envious talk and defamation to be on the increase in a society growing ever more materialistic. Envy, he commented, was the driving force behind the constant search for the new and had even affected the book market.[37] As he elaborated, while books in previous years might have met with a critical reception from envious competitors, new publications did not used to appear on the market so quickly and therefore readers had time to consider and form their own opinion of the work in question. Now, the cleric growled, books appeared so quickly that there was no time to defend a newly published work against its critics before the public gaze had shifted uncompromisingly to the next. His was the age-old cry that everything had been better in the past. Gad switched out of recording his opinion in direct speech and shifted the spotlight onto herself. Here, she adopts the role of adviser that she could not fully assume in the previous anecdote:

> Ich sagte zu dem hübschen jungen Mädchen, lassen Sie den Muth nicht sinken; es ist mit den Zeiten wie mit den Menschen: man lobt beyde, wenn sie nicht mehr da sind. [. . .] Der sechszigjährige Mensch sieht auf das neue Zeitalter mit zu alten Augen, so wie er vielleicht auf das alte Zeitalter mit zu jungen Augen sah.[38]

> [I said to the pretty young girl, do not be disheartened; it is with the times as with people: both are praised when they are no longer there. [. . .] The sixty-year-old looks on the new era with eyes that are too old, just as he perhaps looked on the old era with eyes too young.]

Thus she encourages the younger traveller to look more positively on the current state of society and appears to be making a general comment on the inability of the older generation to adapt to the changes wrought by the younger. Whether her comments — and those of her fellow travellers — are focused in particular on English society and English culture is hard to tell. Implicitly, of course, the cleric's criticisms reflect the profound changes in material culture which characterized eighteenth-century Britain and the spreading affluence of the privileged classes that could be witnessed in new leisure pursuits, forms of interior decoration, and ever richer apparel. Explicitly, though, Gad's use of the anecdote was here more a tacit endorsement of the potential universality of the (darker) human emotions.

The Destructive Power of Empathetic Reading: 'Der Schluß wird Ihr Herz verwunden'

The longest anecdote in the first volume of the *Briefe während meines Aufenthalts in England und Portugal* covered well over twenty pages and drew on an encounter between Gad and the friend of a dragoon regiment captain whom she met at a staging inn on the way to Bath. As her fellow travellers were eating, Gad's eye was caught by the captain sitting by the fireplace with his son on his lap whose soul seemed veiled in mourning, like his body too, lost in thought or perhaps with even no thoughts at all.[39] Moving away from the description of this cameo scene for a moment, she notes:

> Die Natur, oder was es sonst seyn mag, mahlt alle Leidenschaften mit stärkern Tinten auf die Gesichter der Engländer, als auf die Gesichter anderer Nationen. Wenn in ihrem Herzen Zorn ist, zeigt sich in ihrem Gesichte Wuth; Liebe sieht wie Enthusiasmus, und Gram wie Schwermuth bey ihnen aus.[40]

> [Nature, or whatever else it might be, paints all these passions with stronger colours on the faces of the English than on the countenances of other nations. When there is anger in their hearts, there is ire on their faces; love looks like enthusiasm and affliction like melancholy with them.]

This ability to 'read' the emotions on the face of the English suggested that they were not a staid and unemotional people, and it was precisely this susceptibility to emotional display which Gad appeared to consider a national characteristic. Indeed, perhaps it was this very perception of the English as the embodiment of *Empfindsamkeit* which encouraged her to view them through an emotionally highly charged lens. Gad's response to the sight of the unhappy figure is highly empathetic, 'denn sein sichtbarer Schmerz war in meine Brust übergegangen' [for his visible pain had entered my breast].[41] This 'emotional contagion', as Keen has termed it (akin to Hume's 'rays of passions, sentiments, and opinions [that] may often be reverberated'),[42] was initiated through the sight of the suffering figure.[43] It not only evoked a sense of melancholy in Gad. It prevented her from sleeping altogether in the coach in which she travelled on from the inn:

> Wenn sich aber die Seele mit regem Mitgefühl, und mit allem was die Einbildungskraft hinzuthut, einen fremden Schmerz lebhaft vorstellt, und wenn sie, wie es jetzt mein Fall war, von Vermuthung zu Vermuthung irrt, dann kann man nicht einschlafen.[44]

> [When, however, the soul vividly imagines a stranger's pain with active sympathy and with all that the powers of the imagination add, and when, as in my case, wanders from assumption to assumption, then one cannot fall asleep.]

This extreme sense of pity and concern for a stranger with whom Gad had not even exchanged a word seems rather excessive to modern sensibility. Indeed, her construction of herself as the pitying observer begins to feel rather contrived for its constant re-emphasis.

The story gathers pace, however, as morning breaks. Gad enters into conversation with a young man who is clearly a companion of the fireside figure and who is travelling in the coach party with Gad. She examines him with open interest, she notes, like a messenger who brings favourable news or like a miser looks upon a cash box.[45] Her analogy is not an entirely productive one since it suggests a form of inappropriate curiosity which fulfils desires that are not wholly humanitarian and prosocial. So great is Gad's unhappiness — 'meine unüberwindliche Traurigkeit' [my insurmountable unhappiness] as she, somewhat exaggeratedly, terms it — that the conversation starts, ironically, by the young man asking her what makes her so unhappy. Gad implies, therefore, that she has become the very mirror of the captain's suffering. She explains that it is the apparent sadness of his companion that has so upset her and entreats him to tell her the circumstances of his melancholy. His story is, again, one of broken promises and apparent betrayal. The captain fell in love with a young woman, Elisa, of great virtue and sound education, lodging nearby. He promised to make her his wife on the death of his uncle, without whose permission he could not marry. They lived together in his country residence outside London for three years and she bore him a son. He then received news that his uncle was dying and returned home one month later in a state of great sadness. Six months went by, Elisa was pregnant again, but the captain still did not fulfil his promise. Just after he had left for London to legalize the marriage, without telling Elisa of his intentions, she drowned herself in the river.

This anecdote is interesting less for its content and its overt appeal to the emotions than for the structure which Gad uses to weave her own responses into the narrative as it is being told by the young man. Near the start of the anecdote, the captain comes home and exclaims to his companion:

> Ach mein Freund, rief er aus, als er in mein Zimmer trat, ich liebe nicht blos, ich werde auch mit der größten Wärme wieder geliebt, und ich muß den Engel fliehen.★)
> (Entsetzlich, sagte ich seufzend; erst bemühet er sich um ihre Liebe, und da er das Geständniß derselben erhalten hat, will er fliehen.)[46]

> [Ah, my friend, he cried, as he entered my room, it is not just that I love, for my love is returned with the greatest warmth and I must flee from this angel.★)
> (Dreadful, I said sighing. First he tries to gain her love and when he has received the avowal of it, he wants to flee.)]

In this multi-layered narration both the teller of the anecdote and its commentator are presented to the reader. That Gad's remarks are in parentheses suggests that they should be considered marginal, yet the empathetic force of these comments ('Entsetzlich, sagte ich seufzend') is such that they cannot go disregarded by the reader. Indeed, the asterisked footnote to the captain's assertion that he must flee from Elisa is directed still more assertively at the reader:

> Ich wünsche, daß viele meiner Leserinnen diese Inconsequenz unglaublich finden mögen, aber ich *fürchte*, daß einige sie nicht nur glaublich, sondern alltäglich finden werden.[47]

[I would wish to think that many of my female readers might find this inconsistency incredible, but I *fear* that several of them will find it not only credible but a common occurrence.]

Whether Gad had automatically assumed that the only readers of her account would be women, or whether she simply felt the need to address those of her readers who were female, is unclear. But the concern which Gad expresses at such a situation, in which men frequently desert women who had hoped to become their partners, is again presented as a warning coming from an experienced, older, female figure and in many ways it draws the reader's attention more to the sympathetic figure of Gad than her subject.

At the end of the following paragraph, Gad inserts her opinion into the text in a similar manner. In the captain's defence, his friend argues:

> Wenn er also als ein ehrlicher Mann gegen Miß Gibber handeln wollte, was blieb ihm nun anders übrig, als sie zu fliehen, oder seinem braven Onkel das gegebene Ehrenwort zu brechen?
>
> (Elende Ausflucht, sagte ich schmerzhaft; nachdem er Feuerstoffe in das Herz des armen Mädchens geworfen hatte, welche Härte war es, sie dann fliehen zu wollen!)[48]

> [If he therefore wanted to act like an honest man towards Miss Gibber, what else was now left for him to do but to flee or break his promise to his good uncle?
>
> (Miserable excuse, I said sorely, after he had poured fuel on the flames of the poor girl's heart, how cruel it was then to want to flee from her!)]

Deploying a vocabulary of misery, cruelty, and pain, Gad therefore seeks to heighten the reader's empathetic response to the situation by again using the technique of putting her own suffering on display. The phrase 'Entsetzlich, sagte ich seufzend' is echoed here in the similar construction 'Elende Ausflucht, sagte ich schmerzhaft' — and indeed has become rather formulaic by the time it has been remodelled on a third occasion a couple of pages later as 'Unglückliches Geschöpf, sagte ich theilnehmend; welche Irrthümer hast du!' [Unhappy creature, I said sympathetically, how mistaken you are!].[49]

At intervals, Gad interrupted the narrator of the anecdote not only to offer her advice or opinion on the story as it developed. She also included those passages where the narrator conversed directly with her and thus focused more closely on herself as a sentient being:

> Wenn ich vorausgesehen hätte, sagte mein freundlicher Reisegefährte, daß Sie so vielen Antheil an dieser Geschichte nehmen würden, so hätte ich Ihnen die Mittheilung derselben gewiß abgeschlagen. Ich fürchte, der Schluß wird Ihr Herz verwunden, und ich vermuthe, Sie sind ohnehin selbst nicht glücklich, sonst könnte wohl schwerlich fremder Kummer so vielen Eindruck auf Sie machen.[50]

> [If I had known, said my friendly companion, that you would sympathize so greatly with this story, I would certainly have refused to tell it you. I fear that the ending will wound your heart and I suspect that you are in any case not happy yourself, otherwise a stranger's worries would hardly make such an impression on you.]

Here Gad gestures at the very dangers to listeners (or readers) of being too strongly affected by the suffering to which narrative, and their own imaginative engagement with it, exposes them. She also forces the reader to consider in what frame of mind Gad herself travels and whether her more or less permanent departure from Germany does not induce a melancholy which she shares with the figures whom she describes. Her forthright response to this is quite the opposite, for as she observes, if she were unhappy herself then she could not be responsive to the suffering of others:

> Wir halten unsere eigenen Leiden immer für viel größer als die Leiden anderer, nicht blos aus Egoismus, sondern weil wir unsern Schmerz *empfinden*, und anderer ihren uns nur *vorstellen.*[51]

> [We consider our own suffering to be far greater than that of others, not out of pure selfishness, but because we *feel* our pain and can only *imagine* that of others.]

This statement seems to run counter to what Gad has been suggesting all along in her construction of herself as an empathetic figure. For if she is suggesting that we cannot feel the pain of a suffering individual but can only represent it in our mind, then this rather gainsays her own assertions that she directly felt the pain of the unhappy figures she describes.

'Ein Anathema gegen weibliche Gelehrsamkeit'

The first volume of Gad's *Briefe während meines Aufenthalts in England und Portugal* was therefore heavily characterized by an emphasis on the importance of affairs of the heart. This sustained deployment of the 'empfindsamer Blick' [sentient gaze] and of the description of Gad's own emotional state is not to modern taste: indeed, as Editha Ulrich has caustically remarked, these outpourings of sentimentality appear just as superficial as in the works of Sophie von La Roche.[52] The second volume was noticeably less anecdotal in structure. Indeed, it only comprised one rather long anecdote, the subject of which was once again male–female relations: the inconstancy of men and the subordinate position of women in marriage. But this anecdote was much more controlled in its inclusion of empathetic language and made a series of points about women's education and emancipation which were both coherently argued and rationally formulated. The anecdote which served as a basis for this argumentation concerned the daughter of the narrator, an older woman whom Gad met in the mail coach from Portsmouth to London. The daughter had been well educated by her father without regard to gender differences and excelled at musical composition.[53] Among her many suitors was a young man who was particularly impressed by her piano-playing skills and seemed to value her musical prowess. After their marriage, however, cracks in their relationship began to show since the husband's assessment of women was that they either tended to hysteria or affectation.[54] As if her husband's reduction of women to these traditionally 'female' traits was not enough, when the daughter sought solace in learned undertakings, he later felt intellectually trumped although he had originally encouraged them:

Sie suchte ihre Muße zu den gewohnten Studien anzuwenden. Dies missfiel dem Manne anfangs gar nicht; ja wenn sie ihre gelehrten Beschäftigungen unterließ, wie man alles zu nennen pflegt, was eine Frau thut, wenn es nicht kochen ist, so war er der Erste welcher ihr darüber Vorwürfe machte.[55]

[She sought to turn her leisure to her customary studies. This initially did not displease her husband; indeed when she neglected her intellectual pursuits, as one calls anything which a woman does that is not cooking, he was the first to reproach her for it.]

Although the words come from the mouth of the older woman, they are very clearly in line with Gad's own fierce criticism of the limitation of women to the domestic sphere and their general exclusion from intellectual activities. As the narrator of the anecdote continues:

Der Ehemann einer ununterrichteten Frau hält, wenn er aufgebracht ist, ihre Dummheit für die Quelle seines Unwillens, und alles Unglücks in der bürgerlichen Gesellschaft. Der Ehemann einer gebildeten Frau hingegen, mißt alle Leiden, die zuweilen aus ungleichen Temperamenten und aus widrigen Verhältnissen entstehen, der weiblichen Geistesbildung bey, und mit jeder Klage stößt er dann ein Anathema gegen weibliche Gelehrsamkeit aus![56]

[When angry, the husband of an uneducated woman considers her stupidity to be the source of his displeasure, and of all unhappiness in society. The husband of an educated woman, by contrast, attributes all the suffering which derives from unequal temperaments and adverse circumstances to female intellectual education and with every complaint he expresses a hatred of female learning!]

Thus women are always in the weaker position, since the supportive or destructive role they play in the marital relationship is determined by their husband. By way of conclusion of the anecdote, the mother remarks that her daughter and son-in-law could indeed have lived happily together but only if he had been wiser, and not if she had been less wise.[57] The speaker is, intriguingly, thus calling for the better education of men rather than women if society is to become more enlightened and marriage remain a stable institution.

Thus the theme of women's intellectual independence — which Gad had claimed in the first volume to be one of her chief concerns for visiting England — came more strongly to the fore in the second volume.[58] While Britain boasted a host of male writers and intellectuals such as the philosopher Francis (Lord) Bacon or the statesman Lord Chesterfield, women too had made important contributions to learning. The 'tasteful' travel account by the Duchess of Devonshire, Elizabeth Cavendish, *Sketch of a Descriptive Journey through Switzerland* (1796), was just such an example, Gad noted (and thereby implicitly valorized her own work as the account of a travelling woman).[59] But she was not only interested in the position of aristocratic women in British society. She dedicated the whole of the seventeenth letter in the second volume, written from London, to the state of education in England and the daily routine that characterized life in both day and boarding schools. There were, of course, a few good schools for women and excellent women teachers too, Gad noted, and no better proof of this fact could be found than in the figure of 'Marie Wolstonekroft [sic], die verdienstvolle Vertheidigerin der weiblichen Rechte'

[Mary Wollstonecraft, the meritorious defender of women's rights], who had been headmistress of a girls' school, and Margaret Bryan, who ran a boarding school and seminary for girls at Blackheath and published *A Compendious System of Astronomy* in 1797.[60] Beyond intellectual pursuits, women were also actively involved in more practical forms of work, not least seamstressing, because it was not considered proper for a woman in England to be clothed by a tailor. This provided women of the lower classes with work and some measure of financial independence:

> So bleibt es doch immer eine von den Vorzügen dieses Landes, daß den Frauenzimmern hier tausendfache Mittel gelassen sind, sich auf eine anständige Art selbst zu ernähren, und sich des größten Erdenglücks, der Unabhängigkeit [. . .] zu versichern.[61]
>
> [It therefore always remains one of the virtues of this country that women have access to thousands of different means of supporting themselves decently and guaranteeing them the greatest happiness on earth, independence.]

The advantages of such a system were many, Gad argued, not least that men were no longer the main breadwinners and under great pressure to provide for wife and children but also that women could gain a sense of their own worth.[62]

Gad therefore exploited what she clearly felt to be the 'modern' working and teaching environments that she had witnessed in England to promote her own agenda about the role that women should play in society. Thus, in contrast to previous sections of her travel account, she used sympathetic interest as a means to demonstrate the progress women had made in establishing a more equal footing with men. Gad voiced similar ideas in the third essay of the *Gesammelte Blätter* entitled 'Briefe eines jungen Frauenzimmers' [Letters of a Young Woman] in which she stressed the importance of education and informative reading for women as educators of future generations. Indeed, she argued provocatively, if women were only meant by nature to be wives, then there would be no reason for them not to remain stupid and uneducated.[63] On an intellectual level, marriage was advantageous to very few women indeed, she asserted. The only profit they could make from their learning in such situations was to draw on it as a form of solace in enabling them to bear their unhappiness with greater calm. But if they were to produce children and ensure that they were offered the best possible upbringing, then women's education was essential:

> Da aber diesem angebeteten und verachteten Geschlecht auch Mutterpflichten übertragen sind, so wäre es doch rathsam, denke ich, man ließe es Kenntnisse erwerben, damit endlich Kinder durch vernünftige Mütter erzogen, und nicht, wie meine armen Cousinen und zahllose andere Kinder, wechselsweise vernachlässigt und gepeinigt würden.[64]
>
> [Since, however, maternal duties are conferred upon this worshipped and despised sex, it would be advisable, I think, if they were allowed to gain knowledge so that children would at last be brought up by sensible mothers and not, like my poor cousins and countless other children, neglected and tormented by turns.]

While stressing the role of women in the domestic sphere, Gad therefore also emphasized their crucial function as transmitters of information to future generations, whether in the nursery, the kitchen, or elsewhere.

If women's rights were very much on Gad's mind as she penned her travel account in 1802 and 1803, her standpoint on this subject had already been articulated most forcefully some five years earlier. In 1798, Christian Daniel Voß, editor of the journal the *Der Kosmpolit*, had allowed her to publish there her 'Einige Aeußerungen über Hrn. Kampe'ns Behauptungen, die weibliche Gelehrsamkeit betreffend'.[65] This was a fierce and feisty rebuttal of Joachim Heinrich Campe's *Väterlicher Rath für meine Tochter. Ein Gegenstück zum Theophron. Der erwachsenen weiblichen Jugend gewidmet* [*Paternal Advice for My Daughter. A Complement to Theophron. Dedicated to Adult Young Ladies*] (1789), which reinforced the traditional woman's role as that of spouse, housewife, and mother.[66] Gad's response, a '*Kampfschrift*' against Kampe, as Karin Rudert has neatly termed it, attacked three main premises of his work.[67] Firstly, Campe had recommended to his daughter that she should on no account become an intellectual or a writer since she would neglect her household tasks. Gad argued that high-ranking intellectual men were at the same time administrative officials, preachers, or lawyers and therefore able to combine several tasks, just as a woman could run a household and also apply herself to studies.[68] Moreover, she declared, domestic affairs were not so very far estranged from the sciences and the arts and to be involved in both would be beneficial for each. Campe's second objection was that women were physically too weak to endure the exhausting practice of intellectual thought, to which Gad responded that male thinkers were often those with the weakest bodies.[69] The third objection which Campe had made, namely that women's desire for learning would only attract the hatred and envy of other women and also some men, was countered by Gad with the ironic remark that women who could tie a nice bow would certainly be favoured above those who could understand Euclid, since men had taken it upon themselves to reduce women to beings '[die] keinen Kern haben' [who have no core].[70]

Gad: 'eine empfindsame Reisende'?

Gad did not deploy such fierce rhetoric in the *Briefe während meines Aufenthalts in England und Portugal* but drew instead on other narrative devices to construct an image of herself as a sentient but intellectual female figure. Her travelogue included references to a vast range of writers and their works, from Herodotus and Gay, previously mentioned, to Kant's *Anthropologie* [*Anthropology*], Leibniz's *Philosophie* [*Philosophy*], Johann Georg Hamann's *Denkwürdigkeiten des Sokrates* [*Socratic Memorabilia*], and Lessing's *Minna von Barnhelm*. In the field of translation too, Gad clearly felt herself able to comment on the quality of Anne Dacier's rendering of Homer ('hie und da ein wenig französirt' [here and there a little frenchified]) in contrast to Pope's, as well as Schlegel's translation of Shakespeare.[71] Gad's display of her own reading was demonstrative of the intellectual demands she made of herself. It also called to mind the second essay in the *Gesammelte Blätter* in which she considered how the process of reading affected us. 'Einige Fingerzeige zu einer zweckmäßigen Wahl beim Lesen' [A Few Pointers to the Expedient Selection of Reading Material] not only ranges across a number of different issues but also makes a series of quite provocative statements. One might have expected of an intellectual woman like Gad that she only prescribed reading of the most learned texts. But as she remarked at the start of her essay,

> Es gibt eine Zeit für alles, selbst für das Lesen unbedeutender Romane. Man muß durch leere Vorhallen gehen, ehe man ins innere Heiligthum der Musen gelangt, wo der Geist für jede ihnen geweihete Stunde den schönsten beglückendsten Lohn erhält.[72]

> [There is a time for everything, even for the reading of unimportant novels. Once must proceed through empty atria, before one reaches the inner sanctum of the Muses, where the mind receives the most pleasant and most pleasant reward for every sanctified hour.]

She therefore stressed that the act of reading was in itself important, if only as a form of mental exercise as a result of which the intellect could be trained to move on to more taxing reading. The novel was a thoroughly useful genre, she argued, in this respect: 'Gute Romane, deren es aber freilich nur sehr wenige giebt, führen den Leser mehrere Schritte näher zu einer wissenschaftlichen Geistesbildung, welche das Ziel alles Lesens seyn sollte' [Good novels, of which there are admittedly only very few, draw the reader several steps closer to an intellectual education of the mind, which should be the goal of all reading].[73] What she understood precisely by 'wissenschaftliche Geistesbildung' is harder to decipher — did it cover reading of the classics, of historical and theological works, the natural sciences even? — but Gad was scathing in her criticism of those English novels now flooding the German book market in which nothing of any great import happened:

> Die Heldin der meisten neuern englischen Romanse, welche in Deutschland, selbst in einer mittelmäßigen Uebersetzung, mit höchstem Eifer gelesen werden, erzählt gewöhnlich mit der größten Weitschweifigkeit, daß sie sich angekleidet hat, und wie sie sich angekleidet hat; daß sie des Morgens einige Briefe geschrieben, und einige empfangen [hat].[74]

> [The heroine of most of the more recent English novels, which are read with great alacrity in Germany even in a mediocre translation, commonly narrates with the greatest prolixity that she got dressed and how she got dressed, that she wrote a few letters in the morning and received a few.]

Her criticism therefore seems levelled against the popular sentimental and moralizing novels of the day in which women's lives were indeed reduced to those few trivial events which they had under their own control. Gad had little time for such 'langweiliges Geschwätz' [boring gossip], as she termed it, the plot of which consisted of nothing more than regaling how Ms Elisa went upstairs, or put on her straw hat or shawl (possibly a reference to Wilhelmine Karoline von Wobeser's *Elisa oder das Weib, wie es seyn sollte*, published in 1795).[75] The flight from reality offered by the reading of such mundane and slow-paced texts was, for Gad, a foolish renunciation of all that their own lives could give them. The everyday conversations between the people and routine events described there, which were themselves often given using everyday language, were 'bloß ein matter Wiederschein, oder vielmehr der verlängerte Schatten des wirklichen Lebens' [simply a dull reflection, or rather the lengthened shadow of real life].[76]

For all that we might now consider parts of Gad's work to represent moments of 'failed empathy' because of their overwrought affective appeal, it is important to view it within the context of its time. Heinrich Ludwig de Marées's two-volume *Anleitung zur Lektüre* [*Guidance on Reading*] of 1806 contained a list of over a hundred pages of recommended reading. For the genre of travel writing, his selection included the works of Emilie von Berlepsch, Friederike Brun, and Esther Domeier (geb. Gad). To place Gad alongside other key women writers of the period would suggest that her work was considered to have valuable merit in giving readers a new angle on the foreign. Her use of the anecdotal was not, in itself, a particularly unusual narrative device deployed at that time to give readers the impression of immediate access to the emotions of the characters in question. What was striking about Gad's work was, however, its sustained adoption of this strategy in travel writing, as the first volume of the *Briefe während meines Aufenthalts in England und Portugal* demonstrated. That her agenda shifted rather sharply in the second volume suggests that she herself had realized that the overwrought sensibility demonstrated in the first volume, its tendency to place increased focus on the author herself as the centre of attention, and its failure to be truly informative about life in Britain, detracted greatly from her account. While her concern in the second part was not to distance herself completely from the figure of the sentient woman, the latter volume sought to offer a more balanced picture of the intellectual role which women could play within the realm of domesticity despite their cruel treatment at the hands of men. England, Gad therefore gave us strongly to believe, was in many ways the epitome not just of technological progress but of advances in the standing, treatment, and educational improvement of women.

Notes to Chapter 3

1. *ALZ*, 4: 344 (1803), cols 545–48 (col. 545).
2. *NADB*, 102 (1805), 213–18 (213).
3. Ibid.
4. Rahel Varnhagen, *Rahel. Ein Buch des Andenkens für ihre Freunde*, 3 vols (Berlin: Duncker and Humblot, 1834), I, 162.
5. Esther Gad, *Briefe während meines Aufenthalts in England und Portugal an einen Freund von E. Bernard geb, Gad*, 2 vols (Hamburg: Campe, 1802–03), I, 122–23.
6. Ibid., p. 134.
7. Ibid., p. ix.
8. Barbara Hahn, '"Geliebtester Schrifsteller". Esther Gads Korrespondenz mit Jean Paul', *Jahrbuch der Jean Paul Gesellschaft*, 25 (1990), 7–42 (p. 31).
9. Gad, *Briefe*, I, p. x.
10. Ibid., p. 5.
11. Ibid., p. 6.
12. Ibid., p. xi.
13. Ibid.
14. Ibid., pp. xi–xii (Gad's emphasis).
15. Ibid., p. xii (Gad's emphasis).
16. Daniel Fulda, *Wissenschaft aus Kunst: Die Entstehung der modernen deutschen Geschichtsschreibung 1760–1860* (Berlin: De Gruyter, 1996), p. 341.
17. Johann Georg Sulzer, *Kurzer Begriff aller Wissenschaften und anderen Theilen der Gelehrsamkeit worin jeder nach seinem Inhalt, Nuzen u. Vollkommenheit kuerzlich beschr. wird*, 2nd edn (Leipzig: Langenheim, 1759), p. 32.

18. Sonja Hilzinger, *Anekdotisches Erzählen im Zeitalter der Aufklärung: Zum Stuktur- und Funktionswandel der Gattung Anekdote in Historiographie, Publizistik und Literatur des 18. Jahrhunderts* (Stuttgart: M und P Verlag für Wissenschaft und Forschung, 1997), p. 55.

19. Karen Junod, 'Drawing Pictures in Words: The Anecdote as Spatial Form in Biographies of Hogarth', in *The Space of English*, ed. by David Spurr and Cornelia Tschichold (Tübingen: Narr, 2005), pp. 119–34.

20. See Hilzinger, pp. 95–138 and Walter E. Schäfer, 'Anekdotische Erzählformen und der Begriff Anekdote im Zeitalter der Aufklärung', *Zeitschrift für deutsche Philologie*, 104 (1985), 185–204.

21. Quoted in *The Oxford Book of Literary Anecdotes*, ed. by James Sutherland (Oxford: Oxford University Press, 1975), p. v.

22. Johann Georg Büsch, 'Ueber Anekdoten, insonderheit über die Anekdoten unserer Zeit', *Historisch-politisches Magazin, nebst litterarischen Nachrichten* (1787), 272–86 (p. 279).

23. Albrecht Christoph Kayser, 'Ueber den Werth der Anekdoten', *TM* (1784), 82–86 (p. 82).

24. Ibid.

25. Ibid., p. 84.

26. Gad, *Briefe*, I, 154.

27. *NADB*, 102 (1805), 213–18 (p. 213)

28. Gad, *Briefe*, I, 36.

29. Ibid., p. 38.

30. Ibid.

31. Ibid., pp. 38–39.

32. Ibid., p. 39.

33. Ibid.

34. Ibid., p. 40.

35. Ibid.

36. Ibid., p. 51.

37. Ibid., p. 53.

38. Ibid., p. 55.

39. Ibid., p. 156.

40. Ibid.

41. Ibid.

42. David Hume, *A Treatise of Human Nature*, 3 vols (London: Noon, 1739–40), II (1739), 157.

43. Keen, p. 42.

44. Gad, *Briefe*, I, 157.

45. Ibid.

46. Ibid., p. 164.

47. Ibid. (Gad's emphasis).

48. Ibid., p. 165.

49. Ibid., p. 170

50. Ibid., p. 171.

51. Ibid., pp. 171–72 (Gad's emphasis).

52. Editha Ulrich, 'Reiseberichte als Medium der Fremderfahrung: Esther Bernards Wandlung in Briefen über England', in *Entdeckung und Selbstentdeckung: Die Begegnung europäischer Reisender mit dem England und Irland der Neuzeit*, ed. by Otfried Dankelmann (Frankfurt a.M.: Lang, 1999), pp. 11–49 (p. 32).

53. Gad, *Briefe*, II, 351.

54. Ibid., p. 352.

55. Ibid., p. 353.

56. Ibid., p. 355.

57. Ibid.

58. Gad, *Briefe*, I, 83

59. Gad, *Briefe*, II, 379.

60. Ibid., p. 254.

61. Ibid., pp. 256–57.

62. Ibid., p. 257.

63. Esther Gad, *Gesammelte Blätter*, 2 vols (Leipzig: Reclam, 1806), I (II unpublished), 154.
64. Ibid.
65. Esther Gad, 'Einige Aeußerungen über Hrn. Kampe'ns Behauptungen, die weibliche Gelehrsamkeit betreffend', *DK*, 3 (1798), 577–90.
66. Campe's *Theophron, oder der erfahrne Rathgeber für die unerfahrne Jugend* had appeared in 1783.
67. Karin Rudert, 'Die Wiederentdeckung einer "deutschen Wollstonecraft": Esther Gad Bernard Domeier für Gleichberechtigung der Frauen und Juden', *Quaderni. Università degli studi die Lecce, Facoltà di magistero, Dipartimento di lingue e letterature straniere*, 10 (1988), 213–61 (p. 227).
68. Gad, 'Einige Aeußerungen', p. 579.
69. Ibid., p. 582.
70. Ibid., p. 584.
71. Gad, *Briefe*, I, 98–99.
72. Esther Gad, 'Einige Fingerzeige zu einer zweckmäßigen Wahl beim Lesen', in *Gesammelte Blätter*, I, pp. 109–32, p. 113.
73. Ibid.
74. Ibid., p. 115.
75. Ibid., p. 116.
76. Ibid.

CHAPTER 4

Light and Landscape in Carl Gottlieb Horstig's
Reise nach Frankreich, England und Holland
zu Anfange des Jahres 1803[*]

A series of articles on London and its environs appeared between 1803 and 1804 in the journal *London und Paris*, one of the most important channels which regularly fed German readers with information on England. Numbering fourteen in total, these articles roamed across an astonishing range of topics. They included a detailed account of those German speakers living in England, such as the chemist Friedrich Accum, the Austrian clergyman Daniel Gruber, the astronomer Wilhelm Herschel, and Rudolph Ackermann, a pioneer in the process of waterproofing materials and paper. They lamented the smokiness of British open fireplaces, debated the exclusion of women from the British Museum and the Royal Society, lauded the quality of German landscape gardens such as Wörlitz (which now rivalled the English originals in planned finesse), and enthused about the beauty of the landscape along the Thames. Their author marvelled at the view from St. Paul's of the matrix of roads disappearing into the horizon, discovered in the poetic works of Robert Bloomfield 'natürliches Gefühl, wahre dichterische Einbildungskraft, [. . .] süße Einfalt und ungekünstelte Zartheit' [natural feeling, true poetic imagination, sweet simplicity, and unaffected tenderness][1] and declared the paintings in Aldermann Boydell's Shakespeare Gallery on Pall Mall to carry an effect that tended to the fantastic.[2] Although these accounts did not cover more than about seventy pages in total, they nevertheless gave an interesting insight into what had fascinated their author, Carl (or Karl) Gottlieb Horstig, one of the lesser known German travellers to England of his time.[3]

What was most striking about these articles was not their factual content: after all, information on developments in English society, culture, and politics were reaching German audiences on a weekly, if not daily, basis. Rather, it was their mode of representation. The majority of these brief reports were not factual but impressionistic and highlighted the extent to which Horstig viewed the foreign in terms of pictorial constructions. In his description of the Thames as it passed through London, he was, for example, less interested in the shipping, its cargo and activities at the port, than in the aesthetic impact of the scene on the observer: 'Mahlerischer werden die Ansichten des schiffreichen Stroms in der Gegend von Westmünster, von wo aus man das Ufer der Themse ungehindert erreichen, und bis in eine weite Entfernung hinaus verfolgen kann' [The views of this river with its busy shipping become more picturesque in the area of Westminster, where the eye can see the banks of the Thames unhindered and follow it well into the distance].[4] Such preoccupations with viewing landscape through the eyes of an artist were what also characterized his travel account on England, the *Reise nach Frankreich, England und Holland zu Anfange des Jahres 1803* [*Journey to France, England and Holland at the Start of the Year 1803*], which appeared in 1806.

This might seem surprising, given that Horstig is principally remembered — if remembered he is at all[5] — for the *Erleichterte Deutsche Stenographie* [*Simplified German Stenography*] (1797), a milestone in the development of shorthand in German. But Horstig's oeuvre was prolific, ranging across music, theology, education, and (landscape) art to travel writing. Born in 1763 the son of a schoolteacher, Horstig appears to have enjoyed a particularly thorough education. He studied Theology in Leipzig and by 1793 was preacher and Konstitorialrat in Bückeburg (Lower Saxony). One year later he was made head preacher in Bückeburg, as well as superintendent of schools and the figure responsible for education in the county of Lippe. These tasks meant that until 1803 his travel was more or less confined to Germany and early accounts record Horstig's journeys undertaken either locally or at least within Germany to Hildesheim (1797) and Rinteln (1799), to Bad Pyrmont where he met Goethe in 1801 (who counted Horstig among the important men he met there),[6] and to the Harz region (1803). After early retirement in 1803 and a move to Heidelberg, his curiosity then drew him to destinations further afield such as France, England and the Netherlands (1806), Vienna (1815), and Switzerland (1822). In his earlier years he produced an impressive array of publications in the field of music and pedagogy: obituaries of Johann Christoph Bach and Franziskus Neubauer (1798), collections of songs including *Kinderlieder und Melodien* [*Children's Songs and Melodies*] (1798), and articles on the teaching of singing in school. His theoretical work on pictorial art attested to a keen awareness of the debates of the time concerning aesthetic manipulation in supposedly 'natural' landscape scenes. The essay 'Ueber das Pittoreske in der Malerey' [On the Picturesque in Painting] (1793) made an important contribution to contemporary debate on how to define the picturesque as a rigorous category, while a series of articles published between 1792 and 1795, including 'Über die Natur und das Wesen schöner Empfindungen' [On the Nature and Character of Pleasant Sensations] (1792), openly engaged with contemporary debate about sentimental association and aesthetic taste, notably in the works of the Scottish aesthetician Archibald Alison (1757–1839). An article entitled 'Ueber den Werth der Symbole' [On the Value of Symbols], published in *Der Genius der Zeit* [*The Genius of the Age*] in September 1794, explored the associative nature of ideas and the emotions conveyed by particular symbols. Horstig's *Briefe über die mahlerische Perspektive* [*Letters on Picturesque Perspective*] (1797), lavishly illustrated with detailed diagrams indicating lines of perspective and vanishing points, showed a concern to bridge the gap between the mathematically precise system of perspective, capable of representing objects with complete geometrical accuracy, and the practice of landscape painting.[7]

In one of his later excursions into aesthetics, Horstig mused in his contribution to

Carl Wilhelm Grote's 1817 anthology *Zeitlosen* [*The Timeless*], 'Woher kam es, daß ich von jeher mehr Vergnügen darüber empfand, etwas durch Zeichnung als durch Worte ausgedrückt zu finden?' [Why was it that I always found greater pleasure in finding something expressed as a drawing than in words?][8] The reason, he suggested, lay in the superiority of visual over textual description. As he elaborated, drawing gave an unadulterated rendering of the subject as it had been visualized in the eye and soul of the observer.[9] Thus visual art appeared to offer an unmediated representation of the scene, creating the illusion that the spectator was at the place being described. Pictorial description could also be equated with the very act of viewing. It allowed the eye to roam and contemplate, as if the viewer could see the scene complete in his mind's eye. More than this, though, visual representation had the capacity to mobilize both the 'Auge' and the 'Seele', not only transporting the beholder in his imagination to the landscape described, but also moving him in mind and spirit. Nevertheless, for all his emphasis on the visual, Horstig was not wholly dismissive of the descriptive powers of the written word. Nothing offers the eye of the thinker as much to consider at one moment as a page of writing, he observed.[10] Each word on a page had the potential to call up in the mind's eye a new picture, while every thought that flowed from these words opened up a new world for him.[11]

In linking visual representation with immediacy, Horstig had touched upon a crucial paradox underlying eighteenth-century aesthetics. Within what Helmut J. Schneider has termed an 'aesthetics of illusionism', painting sought to achieve the coalescence of vision and reality, image and nature.[12] But while painters and poets alike strove to represent nature in a pure, unmediated fashion, they could never escape the fact that visual or textual descriptions remained precisely that: re-presentations, re-constructions of landscape scenes. These were always created by a beholder viewing and describing the world according to a known set of visual practices for an audience who had learnt to interpret the natural world within a particular framework of reference. Thus the art of landscape painting lay in concealing the manipulation inherent in its staged arrangement of so-called 'natural' scenes. As Horstig stressed in the foreword to his account of travel to England, the *Reise nach Frankreich, England und Holland zu Anfange des Jahres 1803*, this was a tension of which he was crucially aware:

> Bey der Mittheilung dessen, was die Seele schönes von außen empfängt, muß noch außer dem Gesichtspunkte, den man sich dabey erwählte, das stille Zusammenfassen in Betrachtung kommen, woraus das neue Bild hervorgeht.[13]

> [In communicating those pleasant impulses the soul receives from outside, one must consider, besides the point of view which was selected, the quiet compilation of features from which the new picture springs.]

The impression which an audience gained of a given scene, whether described verbally or visually, was therefore shaped not only by the viewpoint and angle of perspective adopted by the author or artist. The scene was also refracted once more in the process of description where it was re-composed and structured to produce a 'neues Bild'.

This chapter broadly asks two questions: how did codes of visual ordering and comprehension used by German travellers such as Horstig construct landscape scenes that encouraged readerly engagement? Which rhetorical strategies did they apply to give the impression to their readership of unmediated access to the scenes represented? The first section examines Horstig's own understanding of the picturesque within the broader aesthetic framework laid down by earlier German aestheticians working on landscape, and by *doyens* of the picturesque such as William Gilpin and Uvedale Price. It also focuses on the relationship between the category of the picturesque and sentimental association, examining in particular Horstig's critical engagement with Alison's work. How did this influence the viewing practices adopted by Horstig and his 'reading' of the land-, sea- and townscapes he encountered? A second section offers a detailed reading of Horstig's travel account focusing in particular on light and motion in two key settings, Dover and London. In so doing it seeks to examine how, through his use of light in landscape, Horstig conferred a kinetic quality upon natural description that seemed to make the scene more direct, immediate, and emotionally engaging.

'Die bilderreiche oft sogar metrische, prosaisch-poetische Sprache'

Admittedly, the itinerary of Horstig's account scarcely marked it out as a picturesque tour. He did not venture as far north as the Lake District, as far west as the Welsh border, nor did he explore Hampshire and the Isle of Wight, the landscape of which Gilpin had 'discovered' in 1798. Horstig's journey, which took him little further than London and its environs, was conceivably curtailed by his illness at that time. Depression, or a form of nervous breakdown, the alarming effects of which his doctor witnessed in 1803,[14] suddenly meant that Horstig no longer had the energy to maintain his punishing routine of seventeen-hour working days.[15] Work commitments too might have forced him to keep his stay in England relatively brief — he was still presiding over *Consistorialsitzungen* in January of that year and by mid-April 1805 was back in Bückeburg.[16] Of the 248 pages which his account comprised, the first twenty-five described the Horstigs' journey from Pyrmont through Höxter to Kassel, where they spent several days exploring the museums and in particular delighting at the collection of Old Masters held in this city, before passing on through Frankfurt, Mainz, and Worms to the French border. A good half of the account was devoted to regaling the reader with the Horstigs' journey through France, which included a detailed survey of Paris, its art museums, Institute for the Blind, Botanical Gardens, the Tuileries, and the palace at Versailles.

Following a description of the sea-crossing from Calais to Dover, Horstig then turned to the delights of England, which included a brief mention of Canterbury (a smaller city than Horstig had expected)[17] and an extensive exploration of the capital, with one brief excursion to Windsor. Horstig's account of England, like those before him, ranged across a series of topics, from the sheer number of churches and chapels in London to the figure of Professor Fischer of Mannheim, a specialist on optics and astronomy. Most of the key subjects of British architecture had already been mentioned by previous travellers, Horstig lamented, and passed swiftly through the British Museum before heading on to examine the paintings at the studio of the Flemish landscapist, Hendrik de Cort. The 'magische Wirkung' [magical effect] and 'bezaubernde Tiefe' [enchanting depth] of the pictures in the Shakespeare Gallery which were positioned in a way that favoured their use of perspective enchanted Horstig.[18] The performance of Händel's *Messiah* which they heard in Covent Garden he deemed 'unforgettable' and the landscape they viewed around Windsor, Islington, and Primrose Hill most striking.[19] 'Unsere Reisepässe sind unterzeichnet, unsere Abschiedsbesuche sind gemacht' [Our passports have been signed and our farewell visits paid] remarked Horstig some thirty pages before the end of his account and, following a difficult crossing from Harwich to the Netherlands, dedicated the rest of his account to the Dutch cities of Harlem and Amsterdam (a city view interesting to a painter's eye) and the return home.[20]

In terms of structure, Horstig opted neither for an obviously epistolary approach nor for a journal format. Composed of 104 sections which bore neither date nor location, his account had clearly moved away from the need to demonstrate its authenticity through rhetorical strategies, such as the form of the letter or diary to suggest immediacy or privacy. While each section tended to focus on one specific topic, the layout was not such that the reader felt that the material had been organized with a clear thematic structure in mind. What did, however, remain a leitmotiv throughout his work was his interest in the arts and in pictorial representation, as his woodcut of Montmartre and engraving of Dover, which illustrated this work, demonstrated. Indeed the *Reise nach England, Frankreich und Holland* in its practices of viewing and description owed much to conventions of scenic description that drew on the picturesque, on perspective, and on the handling of light.

The 'bilderreiche oft sogar metrische, prosaisch-poetische Sprache' [visually rich, often even metrical, prosaic-poetic language],[21] which the *Allgemeine Literatur-Zeitung* saw as characterizing Horstig's account of a journey from Germany to London undertaken in the first three months of 1803, offered an important site of overlap between the visual and the textual through the 'painterly' style of poetic language and picturesque viewing practices. To see the British countryside in picturesque terms was certainly in keeping with perception of landscape in England at that time. Gilpin had published descriptions of picturesque tours to the River Wye, Cumberland, Wales, and the Southern Counties in the 1780s and 1790s.[22] However Gilpin's fame as popularizer of the picturesque lay not simply in the textual descriptions found in his travel accounts. His principal theoretical work on the picturesque, the *Three Essays* (1792), also included a section on 'Sketching landscape' which encouraged amateur drawing of the kind which Horstig must have undertaken to produce the illustrations for his account. Although picturesque travel in England reached its apogee in the last decade of the eighteenth century, the picturesque would continue to fascinate German travellers until well into the 1820s.[23] While the lure of Italy's *campagna* meant that at the end of the eighteenth century artists such as Jakob Philipp Hackert and Johann Christian Reichart were filling their sketchbooks with classical landscapes, other German artists such as Johann Christian Klengel (1751–1824), appointed Professor of Landscape Painting in Dresden in 1800, and Adrian Zingg (1734–1816) were increasingly drawn to the landscape of home.[24]

Horstig published a brief, somewhat curious, article entitled 'Einfluß der

Umgebung' [The Influence of the Surroundings] in the 1808 edition of the *Morgenblatt für gebildete Stände*. It affirmed his preoccupation with the evocative and kinetic possibilities of the description of light in landscape. His essay, presented as a discussion between mother and daughter, focused on the importance of light in influencing the spectator's emotional response to his surroundings.[25] There was no-one on earth, asserted the mother, who was wholly insensitive to the influence of light. Indeed, she continued:

> Das Licht erweckt jedesmal den Menschen, sey es die aufgehende Sonne am Morgen oder die angezündete Kerze bey der Nacht. [. . .] Je mannigfaltiger nun das Licht von allen Seiten dich berührt, desto lebendiger wirkt es auf dich zurück, und du kannst dem Einfluße, auch wenn du wolltest, nicht widerstehen, so lange du dein Auge offen hältst.[26]

> [Light inspires people again and again, whether as the rising sun in the morning or the candle lit at night. [. . .] The more that light affects us in a variety of different ways from all sides, the more vivid is its impression upon us and you cannot resist this influence, even if you wished to, as long as you hold your eye open.]

Thus different sources of light — the soft glow of a candle, or the bright rays of dawn — could have markedly different effects on the mood of the observer. The more varied the light sources, the more intense was the effect on the observer. As the paintings which William Turner, Thomas Girtin, and Philippe Jacques de Loutherbourg had begun to produce by the end of the eighteenth century powerfully demonstrated, light did more than merely illuminate a scene. It could evoke powerful emotions in the observer that broke with the serene, verdant luminosity of classical landscape art. The boldness of atmospheric effect, the juxtaposition of brightness and shadow, and the energy and movement that light could encapsulate, fundamentally changed the way in which landscape was 'read' and represented.

'Die Kunst das Würkliche zum Dramatischen umzubilden'

Passing through Kassel on his way to England in the spring of 1803, Horstig paid a brief visit to the city's art gallery. He noted in his travelogue that he had viewed with delight Claude Lorrain's collection of two pairs of canvases known as 'The Four Times of The Day'.[27] Each of these four pictures conveyed an atmosphere of its own, showing a glowing sunset and a cool afternoon in the first pair, a serene morning and the light just before sunrise in the second.[28] That Horstig should show himself an ardent admirer of Lorrain's work was very much in keeping with the spirit of the time. But what was striking about these scenes which Horstig brought to the reader's attention was precisely the way in which each handled light in landscape differently. Indeed the angle, tone, and intensity of the sun's rays, the explicit inclusion of the orb of the sun in the first, and its implicit presence through its rays in the remaining three canvases, produced dramatically different effects. While these works by Lorrain played quite deliberately with light in landscape, this subject had remained largely unexplored by German aestheticians working on landscape art until the late eighteenth century.

In his *Brief über die Landschaftmahlerey* [*Letters on Landscape Painting*] (1770), Salomon Gessner had noted that the eye could learn to discover picturesque qualities in even the most mundane of objects. Even a stone, held in the sunlight, could create a series of interesting effects. These were dependent on the play of light, shadow, and reflection upon it.[29] It was only later in the decade that Merck addressed the importance of light in landscape painting in a more sophisticated way.[30] His essay 'Ueber die Landschaft-Mahlerey' [On Landscape Painting] printed in the *Teutscher Merkur* of 1777 sought to imbue landscape scenes with greater poetic feeling. It argued for a new aesthetics of landscape which better accommodated those components of 'Gefühl' [feeling] and 'Geschmack' [taste] that characterized appreciation of this genre.[31] However, he adopted a mildly ironic stance towards the desperation with which budding artists sought to blind the spectator with 'Effekt', while failing to grasp what constituted the essential qualities of a pleasing work of art. Light and shadow were essential components of a landscape painting, not simply for their ability to demarcate what lay in the sun and in the shade. They were also vital elements determining the mood into which the painter and later the viewer of the canvas would be transported. Merck also observed, though, that if light was a unifying force in painting, it was not one that should render the scene homogeneous. Monotony was to be strenuously avoided, since it was the varying patterns made by light and shadow as they played on the landscape that interested the eye: the 'Kunst das Würkliche zum Dramatischen umzubilden' [the art of transforming the real into the dramatic] lay precisely in catching the lighting of a scene accurately but creatively, losing nothing of the landscape's structure or mood.[32]

Merck's reflections on the importance of variety and 'interest' in landscape echoed — even if they did not explicitly acknowledge — the much more detailed theoretical precepts set out by Gilpin some nine years earlier in his *Essay upon Prints*. Georg Friedrich Kunth's translation of the *Observations, Relative Chiefly to Picturesque Beauty* (1786) was published in 1792, while Gilpin's journey through the west of England and the Isle of Wight (1798) appeared in translation in 1805. Thus by the time Horstig came to work on the picturesque and to write his account of the journey he made to England in 1803, Gilpin was not an unknown name in Germany. Indeed, the lemma on landscape in Sulzer's *Allgemeine Theorie* referred to the *Observations on the River Wye* (1782), Gilpin's first tour book, as 'voll feiner Bemerkungen für den Landschaftsmahler' [full of fine observations for the landscape painter].[33]

Gilpin defined the picturesque as 'that peculiar kind of beauty, which is agreeable in a picture',[34] and, later, as those objects 'which please from some quality, capable of being *illustrated by painting*'.[35] But while the first of these comments seemed to ally the picturesque with the beautiful, Gilpin sought to clarify the distinction between these two categories in the theoretical discussion 'On Picturesque Beauty' in the first of his *Three Essays* (1792). Beauty, 'in real objects' was distinguished by smoothness and neatness, as Gilpin felt Burke had rightly observed.[36] 'The higher the marble is polished, the brighter the silver is rubbed, and the more the mahogany shines, the more each is considered as an object of beauty'.[37] Rough objects were intrinsically more interesting, Gilpin argued, because they offered a variety of tints and forms, rather than a uniformity of colour or shape. The picturesque eye took its subject matter from nature, but also sought the interest of irregularity in it: 'It is the various surfaces of objects, sometimes turning to the light in one way, and sometimes in another, that give the painter his choice of opportunities in massing, and graduating both his lights, and shades'.[38] The picturesque artist should seek to represent not just the play of light off a rough surface, but the richness of the hues and 'the beauty also of *catching lights*'.[39] Thus 'visual irritation' was a key aspect of the spectator's enjoyment gained from the picturesque.

Uvedale Price's *Essay on the Picturesque* (1794), and his later work *A Dialogue on the Distinct Characters of the Picturesque and the Beautiful* (1801), gave a new impetus to the discussion of the picturesque. He disagreed with Gilpin's assumption that the beautiful and the picturesque could be allied to each other. The landscape feature in the natural world which most clearly exemplified the difference between the two was, he argued, water:

> A calm, clear lake, with the reflections of all that surrounds it, viewed under the influence of a setting sun, at the close of an evening clear and serene as its own surface, is perhaps, of all scenes, the most congenial to our ideas of beauty [. . .]. On the other hand, all water of which the surface is broken, and the motion abrupt and irregular, [. . .] universally accords with our ideas of the picturesque.[40]

The picturesque was characterized for Price by variety, intricacy, and abruptness, the beautiful by smooth undulation. These different surfaces also determined how light played variously upon them: the smooth surface acted as a mirror sending back a clean reflection, while a broken surface sent out gleams of light in all directions. Sublimity was to be found in uniform conditions, such as the 'equal gloom' of a heavy sky before a storm, or a blaze of light unmixed with shade.[41] A complex relationship between light and movement was therefore forged within the category of the picturesque which embodied a series of tensions. While Gilpin's attempt to visualize the landscape in terms of rules governing painting implicitly reduced the picturesque scene to stasis and arrest, Price's notion of the picturesque was one in which motion in light and water picked out essential notes of interest in the scene. Even if there was no great swell of movement in the natural forces that the scene described, the sharp points of light that glinted out sent the observer's eye darting across this seascape as his attention was caught briefly by each, absorbing him in the view.

While Gilpin and Price had focused primarily on those features of landscape which gave visual satisfaction, the theologian and aesthetician Archibald Alison offered a different appraisal of the application of natural scenery. His *Essays on the Nature and Principles of Taste* (1790) argued that the satisfaction gained from viewing a landscape was not due solely to the visual stimulation which it afforded, but rather to its involvement of the imagination in the scene. Horstig engaged directly with Alison's work in the series of articles 'Ueber die Natur und das Wesen schöner Empfindungen. Veranlaßt durch Alisons Versuch über den Geschmack' published in the *Neue Bibliothek der schönen Wissenschaften und der freyen Künste* and more indirectly in his article on the picturesque, 'Ueber das Pittoreske in der Malerey', which appeared in Sulzer's *Nachträge* (1793). Alison suggested that the pleasure derived from viewing a landscape was essentially one of association. In the *Essays on the Nature and Principles of Taste* he argued that beauty was not a quality of objects but rather a feeling in the perceiver's mind. Beauty could not therefore be reduced to a simple perceptual form, and no single term or principle was sufficient to describe the emotion involved. Rather, beauty consisted of an emotion that elicited an association of ideas, a 'train of thought', performed by the imagination.[42] Perception alone was not sufficient to explain our aesthetic response to it:

> The gay lustre of a morning in spring, or the mild radiance of a summer evening, [. . .] we are conscious of a variety of images in our minds, our hearts swell with emotions, of which the objects before us seem to afford no adequate cause.[43]

It was impossible to describe objects of taste without referring to the feelings they inspired. The faculty of the imagination had a key role to play for Alison in the transformation of beautiful objects into emotionally productive ones. 'The landscapes of Claude Lorrain', he argued, '[. . .] excite feeble emotions in our minds when our attention is confined to the qualities they present to our senses'.[44] But the force of our imagination allowed us to 'lose ourselves amid the number of images that pass before our minds' and then subsequently to 'waken at last from this play of fancy, as from the charm of a romantic dream'.[45] Thus the process of visual perception gave way to the recall of associated images which transported the observer into a mood of dream-like contemplation, intensified by the activity of the imagination.

Horstig refuted Alison's ideas by reasoning that the initial sensation evinced in the observer on viewing a beautiful object had an immediate effect upon him.[46] In other words, he did not feel that it was founded upon the application of association. The fact that a sense of beauty was evinced in us without the involvement of the imagination or a 'train of ideas' was, Horstig argued, clear from physiological evidence. Our appreciation of beauty depended on how tense our nerves were, and accordingly how pleasing or painful an impression a particular image had upon us:

> Rührt es nicht von der jedesmaligen Beschaffenheit unsrer Nerven her, ob eine helle Farbe, ein heller Ton, einen süßen oder schmerzhaften Eindruck auf uns machen soll? [. . .] Wird der Mangel an Lichtstrahlen bei dem, dessen angegriffne Organe Schonung verlangen, nicht ein angenehmeres Gefühl hervorbringen, als die heftigere Berührung lebendiger Farben, die wegen ihrer vielen Lichtstrahlen weit mehr Erschütterung bewürken?[47]

> [Does it not depend individually on the condition of our nerves whether a light colour, a bright tone, makes a sweet or painful impression on us? [. . .] Will the lack of light rays not evince a more pleasant feeling in one whose worn-out organs demand protection from the fiercer contact with vivid colours which, because of their many rays of light, create far more disquiet?]

Our response to the world around us was therefore dependent less upon the forces of our imagination than on the impression it made physically on our sense faculties. But as Horstig also added, our nerves were not capable of withstanding for a long time exposure to the beautiful, which wore down the sensations through its very uniformity.[48] Rather, variety and change were necessary to keep the senses alive to the beautiful. Karl Heinrich Heydenreich, Alison's German translator, was less categorical in his dismissal of the importance of the imagination in raising particular ideas of aesthetic sensation. He suggested that Alison had not defined clearly enough which type of imagination he was referring to: whether he meant the power to bring disparate ideas together in one's mind, the power to recall past events, or the power to construct from previous ideas new concepts. In any case, though, he argued, it was essentially wrong to attribute aesthetic sensations wholly and exclusively to it.[49]

Horstig's essay 'Ueber das Pittoreske in der Malerey' (1793)[50] expanded on the ideas that he had introduced in his critical commentary on Alison's work. Beauty, he argued, was an inherent characteristic of a scene, rather than an element borrowed from neighbouring features or associated ideas.[51] For him what was of paramount importance in picturesque painting was the accurate representation of the object in question. While a picture of a house in which we have grown up carries with it a thousand happy memories, it is not the beauty of the house that draws us to make these associations, but the artist's ability to give a true and accurate representation of the scene that allows us to be transported to it.[52] Horstig's discussion of the mobilization of emotion was one that seemed to pare visual perception down to the very rules of optics:

> Das Auge kann nur von Lichstrahlen afficirt werden. Auf die Beschaffenheit dieser Lichtstrahlen also kommt es beym Maler an, ob er die Empfindung, deren er sich jetzt bey Betrachtung eines Gegenstandes bewußt wird, schön nennen soll oder nicht.[53]

> [The eye can only be affected by rays of light. For the painter it depends on the qualities of these rays of light as to whether the sensation of which he becomes conscious on viewing an object should be termed beautiful or not.]

The more that an object could return the light rays that were directed upon it in such a way as to catch the observer's attention, the more this would evince an emotional response. It was therefore only really the surface of an object, its colour and form, that came under the artist's consideration. The reason why picturesque scenes seemed to appeal to our emotions more when we encountered them in art than in nature was that the purpose of art was to sensitize us to the beautiful. In the real world there were few beautiful objects which were not overshadowed by less beautiful objects in their immediate surroundings. Aesthetic beauty in the natural world was bought at a high price, Horstig observed: see how difficult it is to scale a sublimely high, craggy cliff or to cross a ruined bridge.[54] In art we could engage effortlessly with the picturesque, and since nothing detracted from our pleasure, the need was awakened in us to see beautiful things and to learn to appreciate the beautiful. The picturesque taught us to develop taste, not through recourse to what pleased, but through an immediate appreciation of beauty, through the immediate effect of the beautiful.[55]

Dover: 'Das ungewohnte Schauspiel der vorbeysegelnden Schiffe'

At sunset on a late January afternoon in 1803, the Horstigs' ship bringing them from the French coast sailed into Dover harbour. As they waited to dock, Horstig described the scene encountered:

> Das ungewohnte Schauspiel der vorbeysegelnden Schiffe, und vor allen der untergehenden Sonne, die vor meinem Blicke zum ersten Male den reinen Horizont berührte, hielt mich lange auf dem Verdeck zurück, wo ich mit meinen Gefährten so lange verweilte, bis wir uns allein nur von Himmel und Wasser umgeben sahen. [. . .] Der Anblick des neuen schiffreichen Hafens von Dover, dessen weiße Felsenbänke wir im Mondenschimmer durch die Segel blinken sahen, hatte für uns etwas bezauberndes.[56]

> [The unfamiliar spectacle of the ships sailing by and above all the setting sun, which before my eyes touched the unadulterated horizon for the first time, kept me on the deck for a long time, where I stayed with my fellow travellers until we only saw ourselves surrounded by sky and water. [. . .] The view of the new harbour at Dover with its many ships, whose white cliffs we saw gleaming in the moonlight through the sails, had something magical for us.]

The scene which Horstig constructs of Dover is one that is obviously alive with movement, the ships passing to and fro in the harbour. But acting as a backdrop against this, motion of a different order is described, which emphasizes the temporality of the narrative as the sun sets and moonlight picks out the sails in different hues. Horstig and his fellow spectators appear to be static subjects while these other components in the scene move about them. The shift from evening to night in one scene merges two different qualities of light in a manner that is reminiscent of the images comprising Lorrain's *Four Times of the Day*. The light which Horstig describes at Dover harbour is 'magical', not the glaring rays of the midday sun but rather the soft light of dusk giving way to moonlight which picks out the cliffs. The cliffs themselves are rough and therefore reflect the light in a way that offers picturesque interest, while the view of them and the light reflected back from them is broken by the sails passing, thus providing that mild visual 'irritation' with which artists of the picturesque sought to catch the observer's eye.

The 'Schauspiel' continues the next day as Horstig climbs the chalk cliffs overlooking the harbour:

> Kaum waren wir den weißen, mit Feuersteinen überall durchwachsenen Kreidenberg, der sich mit den hohen senkrecht abgeschnittenen Felsenbänken in die See hineinwirft, zur Hälfte hinaufgestiegen; kaum sahen wir über die Straßen und Thürme von Dover hinweg, als sich das prachtvollste Schauspiel vor unsern Blicken öffnete.[57]

> [We had scarcely climbed halfway up the white chalk hill, covered with flintstones, which, with high vertically cut banks of cliffs, throws itself into the sea; we were scarcely able to look beyond the streets and towers of Dover, when the most splendid theatrical scene opened up before our eyes.]

Here the scenic description is of quite a different order. The picturesque detail of the harbour enclosed by the white cliffs and the horizontal movement of the boats gives way to the sublime of sharp, vertical structures which 'cast themselves' into the sea. The scene now seems to be constructed in terms of the horizontal and vertical axes shaping the landscape. Ascending the side of the cliffs below Dover Castle, they look across the bay from this higher vantage point:

> Die weite endlose See, die gegen Mittag an Frankreichs nachbarliche Küste

schlägt, und gegen Abend bis nach Amerika sich ausdehnt, lag tief unter uns in ihrer unbeschränkten horizontalen Fläche vor den Augen ausgebreitet.[58]

[The wide endless sea, which around midday breaks on France's neighbouring shore and around evening extends to America, lay far below us, its boundless horizontal surface spread out before our eyes.]

The physical sublimity inherent in the scale of the cliff-face above them shifts to sublime descriptions of the boundlessness of the sea, 'endlos' and 'unbeschränkt'. Admittedly, this is tempered by Horstig's efforts to delimit it geographically, through his reference to the coasts of France and America. This uncertainty about how to convey the far and the near in text — an illustration would convey it through different colour tones and set the horizon as the point of visual limitation — pointed up the disparity between visual intention and verbal description. It was this lack of clear, concrete pointers to mark distance that obliged Horstig to set them himself by these rhetorical means. The difficulty which this seemed to present for him was perhaps indicative of the problems encountered when responding to and attempting to verbalize a primarily non-verbal image such as landscape. It suggested that while by the time Horstig was travelling, certain formal properties of landscape painting had been established, the same could not really be said of the verbal 'painting' of landscape in German travel writing.

As Horstig looked across the bay from their viewpoint halfway up the cliffs, the sunlight that had seemed so mild the evening before now took on quite a different character:

Heiß, wie ein brennender Spiegel, strahlte die Sonne aus den Wellen zurück, und vervielfachte ihre Flamme in tausend funkelnden Wellen. Nah und fern schwammen vereinzelte Schiffe umher, deren fernste Spur wir mit dem bewaffneten Auge kaum verfolgen konnten.[59]

[Hot, like a burning mirror, the sun shone back at us from the waves and multiplied its flames into a thousand sparkling waves. Near and far, single ships sailed about, the furthest trails of which we could scarcely follow with the weaponed eye.]

The sun as the sole source of power and energy becomes an almost violent force, its rays mirrored in the water's surface, burning back up towards the viewers. But as the wind catches the still water and its evenness is broken by the rippling effect of the waves, the sunlight dissolves into a series of glints and sparks and the edge is taken off the sublime rendering by a more picturesque description. Light remains the one unifying force in the picture, the 'flame' which is refracted into myriad different waves and glimmers. The exhilaration of changing light and atmosphere, especially across large stretches of water, and the movement reflected in the water invite readerly involvement. By looking through binoculars, Horstig brings background action to the fore, playing with depth in a way that reinforces that dimension of the scene and enhances the extent of the sun's power. His reference to binoculars or a telescope (the 'bewaffnet[es] Auge') which enabled him to see further than the naked eye recalled the fact that much landscape viewing and painting in that period was not solely the product of 'natural' visual processes. Many travellers and painters

FIG. 4.1. Carl Gottlieb Horstig, *Der Ilsenstein, from Tageblätter unserer Reise in und um den Harz* (Dresden: Gerlach, 1803), plate V

carried with them a 'Claude glass', which was a small mirror, slightly convex in shape, with its surface tinted a dark colour which abstracted the subject reflected in it from its surroundings. It reduced and simplified the colour and tonal range of scenes and scenery to give them a painterly quality. Horstig's use of the term 'bewaffnet' might be ironic, but it also pointed to a certain violence with which the spectator who sought to see more than he could without such optical aids distorted the scene before him, interfering with the natural process of viewing.

Horstig's *Tageblätter unsrer Reise in und um den Harz* of 1803 were richly and powerfully illustrated, with accomplished pieces showing his mastery of the sublime (Fig. 4.1). Yet there was only one, rather naïve, engraving to accompany the account of his journey to England, that of Dover harbour (Fig. 4.2), a scene not unusual at that time. Dover and the Kent area had become one of the key sections of coastline that

Der Hafen von Dover.

Der Oderteich vom Oderdamme gesehn.

FIG 4.2 (above). Carl Gottlieb Horstig, *Der Hafen von Dover*, frontispiece to the *Reise nach Frankreich, England und Holland zu Anfange des Jahres 1803* (Berlin: Maurer, 1806)
© British Library Board. All Rights Reserved (10105.b.6.).

FIG 4.3 (below). Carl Gottlieb Horstig, *Der Oderteich vom Oderdamme gesehn*, from *Tageblätter unserer Reise in und um den Harz* (Dresden: Gerlach, 1803), plate XV
© British Library Board. All Rights Reserved (10260.e.14.).

inspired picturesque painters.[60] The principal marine genre through the Classical and into the picturesque period was the harbour, with plenty of activity and details of the shoreline vying with the ships for importance. By the second quarter of the nineteenth century, the coast had continued to increase its attraction to landscape painters, but previous 'long-shore' views, usually from a hill on one side of the resort, were giving way to the depiction of shorter parts of coastal scenery.[61] While the earlier focus on Kent had been marine and coastal, by the Romantic period there was less interest in the great antiquarian buildings such as Dover Castle. Indeed, Horstig only briefly paused to mention it as 'die viereckige Burg, die Wilhelm der Eroberer baute, von alten Thürmen umgeben, deren Ursprung man vom Julius Caesar herleitet' [the square castle, which William the Conqueror built, surrounded by old towers whose origins are to be found in Julius Caesar's time].[62]

Horstig's illustration of the shore is an altogether 'safe' piece which keeps the reader at arm's length. The sweep of the coast and the curve of the harbour form the central line of the picture, linking foreground with middle distance, as was traditionally the case in the long-shore view.[63] It is a picture organized in terms of enclosure, rather like the textual description of their arrival the evening before. The passage of the ships heading out to sea or returning from abroad only hints at the boundless breadth of the sea beyond. Like Horstig's drawing of the *Oderteich* (Fig. 4.3), an illustration accompanying his travels to the Harz, light remained the single dominating idea. Horstig was keen to emphasize the cloud formations and the light reflected off the rippling water. The sun itself only made its presence felt by casting oblique rays through the cloud onto the sea. Nevertheless, this illustration is intriguing not only for its use of light and the angle of perspective selected: the viewpoint itself is interesting precisely for what it did *not* show. For Horstig did not focus on the white cliffs which had formed one of the points in his textual description. By the time that he was journeying, these had acquired weighty cultural value not only as the symbolic gateway to Britain but as the site of one of the most dramatic scenes in Shakespeare's *King Lear*.[64] Nor indeed did he include the castle, whose history he had briefly summed up in the text. Castles and abbeys, and in particular their dilapidated remains, had acquired an almost theatrical status within the picturesque cult of ruins. Tradition, the passage of time, nostalgia: all were embodied in such buildings. If the major shift that painting had undergone at the end of the eighteenth century was from the historical to landscape, landscape itself now disguised a variety of forms of history. Yet Horstig chose to ignore this, standing with his back to the castle and surveying the scene out to sea. The town itself was included in Horstig's work in a rather simplistic fashion. In the middle ground on the far right it picked out the church spire, a traditional symbol of refuge, but otherwise was not concerned to focus on any scenes of human interest. The scene was therefore dominated by its use of light and an almost exclusive concentration on the topography of the landscape, rather than through an attempt to engage the spectator's interest in human activity in the scene. If anything, the human element is arbitrary and the scene is about the prospect, the reflection of light off the waves, and the free fluidity of the elements of light and water, if treated in a rather stiff, unpoetic manner.

The disparity between the visual and the literary landscapes which Horstig creates invites further examination. The illustration seems guided by the desire to imitate rather than to represent. It fails to engage with the reader's imagination as the literary portrayal did. The powerful personal associations that the verbal description conjured up are absent from the illustration despite the fact that the combination of sunlight, clouded sky, and water could produce highly powerful emotive effects. Certainly practical limitations (such as the time he could allow himself to make a sketch, or weather conditions) might explain why it was that the visual and the textual descriptions vary so much. Horstig's sketch of the bay seemed to owe more to the stasis that underlay Gilpin's understanding of the picturesque than the more dynamic conception of it characterizing the work of Price.

'Eine Abend-Scene, ein bewegtes Gemälde'

Horstig's description of the harbour as like a 'Schauspiel' seems at first sight to do no more than reinforce the notion that the scene before his eyes was like a 'performance'. However, this term carried greater weight in this period. Goethe's *Werther* abounded with words like 'Szene', 'Schauspiel', or 'Schauplatz' which attested to the theatrical character that underpinned the representation of the natural scene.[65] Such a 'staging of nature', to borrow Helmut J. Schneider's phrase, was highly paradoxical in its apparent pursuit of descriptive immediacy while being obviously illusionistic in its very undertaking.[66] By the time Horstig came to describe his travel to England, a couple of decades after the appearance of *Werther*, the overlap between landscape and the theatrical had begun to take on a still more concrete shape. Towards the end of the eighteenth century, painters were becoming deeply involved with topographical illustration in the theatre, de Loutherbourg's stage scenery being a case in point. His *Eidophusikon*, the forerunner to the peep-show, first performed at Lisle Street in February 1781, used three-dimensional sets, lighting, and sound effects to represent shipwrecks and natural wonders such as Niagara Falls. It attempted to present motion through the presentation of successive pictures. The *Panorama*, an enormous canvas attached to the inside of a rotunda that revolved slowly around the spectators seated in the centre, and later the diorama, gigantic paintings exhibited under changing light while the auditorium slowly revolved, were both the early nineteenth century's equivalent of virtual reality. Together with the *Phantasmagoria*, these concentrated on the projection of images onto a screen, creating an at times crude, but effective, combination of light and movement. These breathtaking visual displays radically rethought the imaginative possibilities of landscape painting. Size became an important factor in commanding the reader's attention, creating an effect that sought at the very least to impress if not to overpower.[67]

Horstig was clearly aware of these developments in the world of optics and the theatre. Passing through Paris on their way to London, the Horstigs were left with a lasting impression of the function of light and movement in the new theatre of effect. Two 'mechanisch[e] Kunstwerk[e] von seltner Schönheit und Pracht' [mechanical works of art of rare beauty and splendour] shown at the Palais

Royal fired his imagination. One was a scene particularly rich in movement, representing an Indian town complete with exotic blooms opening and closing, a bronze elephant whose silver trunk and ears moved to and fro as the creature bent down, and liveried servants who marched around the creature in circles.[68] What the mechanical arts were capable of when they were combined with artifice to blind the unexpecting eye of the tasteful observer, Horstig commented, was demonstrated here.[69] The Panorama in Paris, 'A View of Paris from the Tuilieries', also came under close scrutiny, in terms of both the mechanics behind its creation of optical illusion and the artistry with which scenes were drawn and presented. The effects of light and shadow in the canvases painted for it by Pierre Prévost were in Horstig's estimation successful, the foreground less so, but the use of perspective 'unvergleichlich gut' [incomparably good]. In sum, he noted:

> Ich möchte sagen, der erste Anblick dünkt uns märchenhaft zu seyn, so unsicher und schwankend sind die ersten Effekte des Anschauns, wenn man aus der Dunkelheit auf einmal in das blendende Licht hervortritt. Je länger man aber von dem erhöhten Mittelpunkte in die runde Welt hineinschaut, desto lebendiger fühlt man sich nach und nach, bey immer zunehmender Täuschung, in die Wirklichkeit versetzt.[70]

> [I would say that the first view seems to us like a fairy-tale, so unsteady and wavering are the first effects of one's observation, when one suddenly steps out of the darkness into the blinding light. The longer one looks from the raised centre into the round world, the more vividly one feels oneself gradually transported into reality through an increasing process of deception.]

In this theatre of effect, moving and changing scenery, which was controlled by mechanical means, entirely supplanted actor and play. If anything, the spectator had now become the actor, centrally positioned in a landscape that turned about him. It was this centrality of the spectator in the landscape that emphasized the key difference between the experience of nature and the viewing of a landscape. It was precisely this sense that Horstig (and his reader) had as he surveyed the scene coming into Dover harbour; less so as Horstig surveyed the bay from the prospect further up the cliffs.

A short piece entitled 'Die Kirche am See' (The Church by the Sea), written either by Horstig or by his wife for the July 1805 edition of Halem's monthly journal *Irene*, points up more clearly the influence that mechanical and optical devices had on the way in which landscape might be visualized and described.[71] The maritime scene which it depicts bears a striking resemblance to Horstig's description of Dover harbour. The reflection of the light in the shimmering water, the movement of the sails to and fro, and the animation by the wind and the waves endow the natural world with a kinetic energy. Taking a step back to view the scene, the author then draws an interesting parallel with the mechanical performances of the type that the Palais Royal offered its spectators:

> Die zurückeilenden Fischer-Kähne, die ihre Beute in großen Körben nah an dem Ufer einsenkten, die Torfschiffe, die mit der letzten Last, die sie heut führen sollten, von den Moorufern wiederkamen, die dreisten Fischerknaben, die, der See ganz gewohnt, zum Vergnügen sich singend auf den Wellen

schaukelten, alles dieses bildete eine Abend-Scene, ein bewegtes Gemälde, das die bewunderten *tableaux mechaniques* [sic] in Paris weit hinter sich ließ.[72]

[The fishing boats, hastening to return to the harbour, which lowered their spoils in great baskets into the water near the shore, the turf ships, which returned from the banks of the moor with the last load that they would carry today, the cheeky fisherboys who, entirely used to the sea, rocked to and fro, singing on the waves for pleasure, all this painted an evening scene, a moving painting, which left the admired mechanical paintings in Paris in the shade.]

That it was a scene more powerful than the *tableaux mécaniques* was indeed a striking remark, given the fascination and wonder with which Susette's husband had looked upon them. But perhaps in stressing that even those forms of representation, which at that time were at the very forefront of advances in visual technology, fell short of conveying the scene, this was a reminder of just how difficult it was to convey all that affected the human senses — be it light, movement, or mood — when describing the natural world.

London: 'ein prachtvolles Gemälde'

Even when travelling towards and through London, Horstig was sensitive to the picturesque possibilities of the landscape around him. 'Aber eine so liebliche Country zu sehen, von solchen anmuthsvollen Hügeln und Thälern eingeschlossen, [. . .] das hatte ich nicht erwartet' [But to see such pleasant countryside, enclosed by such graceful hills and valleys, [. . .] that was something I had not expected], wrote Horstig a few miles into his journey on the road from Dover to London.[73] The great views, he added, were still also characterized by grace and pleasantness, which the imposing size of some landscape paintings preferred to deny.[74] The English countryside had therefore satisfied Horstig's taste for the picturesque not simply in the classic charm of rolling hills and valleys, but also in panoramic views. Indeed Horstig's own taste in landscape painting was sufficiently broad to accommodate a variety of different styles and forms. Hendrik de Cort, whose work Horstig judged on a brief visit to his London studio to be so excellently accomplished, indeed on a par with the great masters, produced not only valley scenes but also canvases depicting a broader sweep of landscape.[75]

London, Horstig was keen to stress from the outset, was less crowded, less grey, and, with the unforeseeable bends in the Thames, in many ways a more picturesque city than the Paris that they had just left. This description of London as 'picturesque' demonstrated that he was not intent on offering a representation of the country and the city in terms that constructed them as opposing and separate entities. Landscape did indeed signify for him a mix of peace, solitude, and visual pleasure, but he did not set it as some rural idyll against the ugliness of the conventional cityscape. Nor indeed did the sprawl of the city encroach voraciously upon the landscape in Horstig's reading of the natural environment. Traditionally, the picturesque was implicitly shaped by notions of anti-industrialism, grounded in an ideology which celebrated with nostalgic enthusiasm a oneness with nature that represented a mode of living long past.[76] Horstig's aesthetic reading of both landscape and cityscape remained primarily topographical rather than political.

Approaching London, he was not concerned to point up differences between an agrarian and an industrial way of life. Indeed, no such sharp distinction seemed to manifest itself between the urban and the rural, and a near seamless overlap from the picturesque viewing of the landscape to that of the cityscape seemed to take place. At Chatham he marvelled at the level of the roads below the horizon:

> Von hier aus bis London sieht man die Themse mit Schiffen bedeckt, wie man sie zu Calais und Dover nicht größer und mannigfaltiger finden kann. Es macht eine besondere Wirkung, die hohen Dreymaster auf flacher Erde hinfahren zu sehen, wenn der Standpunkt so niedrig ist, daß man kein Wasser mehr erblickt. Sie scheinen mitten in der anmuthigen Landschaft auf dem festen Boden hinzugleiten.[77]

> [Looking from this point towards London, one sees the Thames covered with ships, as large and as many as one could not even find at Calais or Dover. It makes a particular impression upon one, to see the high threemasters sailing on flat earth, when the viewing point is so low that one can no longer see water. They seem to glide across firm soil in the middle of the graceful landscape.]

From this low standpoint, the spectator has a far greater sense of being enveloped in, even overwhelmed by, the beauty of the landscape, a sense of moving through and being in it. While the neo-classical painter and poet took a prospect view, surveying the landscape from a high viewpoint, the picturesque observer selected a vantage point that was far lower. From this perspective, Horstig could visually enhance the power that the landscape held over him and his fellow spectators. By focusing specifically on the flow of the river into London it was as if he used the medium of water to connect the rural and the urban, to introduce the city into his description in a way that was smooth and unhindered, emphasizing continuity rather than difference.

If water, and the movement it created, fascinated Horstig, the seeming fluidity of fog that hung over the capital was another aspect to which he repeatedly returned:

> Ueberall weiter großer Raum, freye Aussichten durch die Nebenstraßen [. . .] ehe wir noch die große Themsebrücke erreichten, von der wir die Westminsterabtey aus dem grauen Nebel der Nacht hervorragen und mit ihren alten Thürmen uns entgegenwinken sahen.[78]

> [Everywhere wide, open space, unhindered views through the sidestreets [. . .] even before we got to the great Thames bridge, from which we saw Westminster Abbey towering up out of the grey mist and beckoning to us with its old towers.]

While the size of the towers of Westminster Abbey rising up out of the fog could lend itself to sublime rather than picturesque description, Horstig blunts the edge of sublime awe by suggesting that the towers greet the onlooking travellers. His later description of the spire of St Paul's and of the Tower uses fog as a means to reinforce a sense of distance and depth:

> Da sieht man die eigentliche Stadt London gerade vor sich liegen, die Pauls-kirche in der Mitte und zu beyden Seiten von der Westminsterabtey bis zum Towr [sic], Gebäude und Thürme in fortlaufender Abstufung — ein prachtvolles Gemälde.[79]

[There one sees the actual city of London lying before one, the Church of St
Paul's in the middle and, on both sides of Westminster Abbey to the Tower,
buildings and towers in consecutive tiers — a splendid picture.]

Precisely because fog dampened illumination and reflection, it was also a means
of creating atmosphere that the debate around light and its importance in painting
had left largely untouched. The layer of fog spread across the city in its background
allowed him to pick out more easily points of interest such as spires and domes of
key buildings. As such it appeared to extend picturesque viewing practices to the
city. It allowed the observing eye to operate in the same way as it had done when
viewing landscape, darting to and fro, linking points of interest in that same state
of 'visual irritation'.

But for all that it seemed that Horstig was intent on viewing England through a
picturesque lens, he was not prepared to offer the standard picturesque account that
reiterated previous exclamations of wonder at particular scenes. Moritz's account
memorably acknowledged the beauty of the scenery around Richmond. Recording
his meeting with the by now aging Sophie von La Roche at Offenbach before his
departure for England, Horstig had also praised her descriptions of Richmond,
Windsor, and Kew for being so memorable since she knew how to choose well
the most pleasant spots from which to give her descriptions of landscape and to
make Pope's residence at Twickenham on the Thames or the wide views from the
terrace at Windsor and the gardens of Kew highly memorable.[80] But given that her
account was published in the late 1780s, by the time that Horstig was travelling
some twenty years later, it had become something of a commonplace to find these
spots charming. Horstig could not wholly oppose the visual 'canonization' of these
points:

> Zwar bietet Richmondhill, dieser hochbelobte Hügel, den man von fern schon
> erblickt, noch mehr die Terrasse von Windsor, dem Auge ein überraschend
> schönes Schauspiel dar. Doch sind beyde nur ein paar unbedeutende Anhöhen,
> wenn man sie mit den erhabenen Standpunkten einer Gebirgsgegend
> vergleichen will.[81]

> [Richmond Hill, this highly praised hill, which one can see from far away,
> and still more the terrace at Windsor, does certainly offer a surprisingly
> pleasant theatrical scene. However, both are only a few unimportant points of
> high ground, if you wish to compare them with the sublime viewpoints in a
> mountainous landscape.]

Horstig was therefore also quick to compare the London scenes with the sublime
power of the mountains that he knew from Germany and find the picturesque
wanting, perhaps because the former gave him greater opportunity for emotional
investment. Thus for all that Horstig was well versed in the evocative possibilities
that the picturesque carried with it, as he neared the end of his journey to England,
he reinforced the fact that the sublime had greater power to move the spectator
or reader by dint not merely of the standpoints that it assumed, but through the
emotional investment in the landscape that it elicited.

The movement which Horstig incorporated into his textual descriptions of land-scape in England was therefore one primarily determined by light. Rather than peopling his landscapes with figures who themselves would bring motion into the scene, he used sunlight, particularly in combination with water, to imbue an otherwise largely static landscape with energy. This provoked kinetic sensations based on the explorative glance of the spectator whose eye he could catch with moving, flickering lights. The aesthetic category of the picturesque was particularly suited to this form of representation, given its preoccupation with irregularity and roughness of surface, as well as sudden changes from light to dark. But Horstig's recognition of the wildness and 'natural' appearance of landscape as an aesthetic source of pleasure was not such that he saw fit to imbue features of the landscape, sun, or water with any particular form of symbolism, as artists such as Philipp Otto Runge or Caspar David Friedrich more overtly did. Moreover, Horstig sought to skirt around the political implications of the picturesque — that its focus on ruins or traditional buildings might have some relation to national identity — by largely effacing the political and the social from the scenes described and seeing them through a resolutely ahistorical lens.

Thus, for Horstig, the affective power of the landscape lay principally in its aesthetic qualities. That his own engraving of the harbour at Dover did not really carry the same force as his linguistic description of it suggests that, on his return, he was able to hone and revise the language of his narrative, whereas his sketch could not benefit from such revisions since he no longer had this scene before him. The sensations evoked by the scenery also seemed to be immeasurably more durable than any picture he still had in his mind's eye of the countryside that had so fascinated him on the south coast of England. As a result, the engraving of Dover harbour remained really rather primitive in comparison with the illustrations published in his other travelogues. The verbal description, by contrast, was woven into a well-crafted account that gave the reader glimpses of a sophisticated, strikingly visual, and highly original writing style. Admittedly, Horstig's use of description in many ways remained closely allied to the technique of picturesque painting, but in his *Reise nach Frankreich, England und Holland* he also succeeded in demonstrating that this could be a most productive category not only for conveying impressions of the English landscape but also for exploring the complexities of representation itself.

Notes to Chapter 4

* Horst-Eberhard von Horstig holds an incomplete copy of the 483-page manuscript of Richard Graewe's biography of Horstig, which was later considerably shortened for publication: see Richard Graewe, *Carl Gottlieb Horstig, 1763–1835: Das Lebensbild eines vielseitigen Genies aus Goethes Freundeskreis* (Hildesheim: August Lax, 1974). Horst-Eberhard von Horstig confirmed that it did not appear from this manuscript that Graewe had conducted any research into Horstig's use of landscape aesthetics that would have otherwise remained unpublished (correspondence of 25.06.04).

1. *London und Paris*, 12 (1803), 33.

2. Ibid., p. 101.

3. The Horstig family were raised to the aristocracy in 1840, five years after Carl Gottlieb's death, by Ludwig I of Bavaria. For this reason he is not referred to as 'von Horstig', in contrast to his successors.

4. *London und Paris*, 12 (1803), 193.

5. There is no mention of Horstig in either the *Allgemeine Deutsche Biographie* or the *Neue Deutsche Biographie*.

6. *DKV*, I:17, p. 80.

7. In this respect, Horstig's work was a continuation of research into perspective published in Germany by J. G. Lambert (1759) and Johann Michael Röder (1796), and in England by Brook Taylor (1715) and J. M. W. Turner's own teacher Thomas Malton (1776). See 'Perspective', in Johann Samuel Ersch and Johann Gottfried Gruber, *Allgemeine Encyclopädie der Wissenschaften und Künste in alphabetischer Folge* (Leipzig: Brockhaus, 1818–89), Section 3, 17 (1842), pp. 70–85. Turner himself was appointed Professor of Perspective at the Royal Academy in 1807 and lectured on perspective from January 1811. See Maurice Davies, *Turner as Professor: The Artist and Linear Perspective* (London: Tate Gallery, 1992).

8. 'Reflexe von Horstig', in Carl Wilhelm Grote [pseudonym of Carl Treuthold], *Zeitlosen: Eine Blüthenlese aus den Gaben der Freunde und eignen Dichtungen*, Erstes Gewinde (Wesel: Becker, 1817), pp. 177–95 (p. 177).

9. Ibid.

10. Ibid., p. 179.

11. Ibid., p. 180.

12. See Helmut J. Schneider, 'The Staging of the Gaze: Aesthetic Illusion and the Scene of Nature in the Eighteenth Century', in *Reflecting Senses: Perception and Appearance in Literature, Culture, and the Arts*, ed. by Walter Pape and Frederick Burwick (Berlin: de Gruyter, 1995), pp. 77–95.

13. Carl Gottlieb Horstig, *Reise nach Frankreich, England und Holland zu Anfange des Jahres 1803* (Berlin: Maurer, 1806), p. iii.

14. Graewe, pp. 73–74.

15. Ibid., p. 30.

16. Ibid., p. 73.

17. Horstig, *Reise*, p. 150.

18. Ibid., p. 197.

19. Ibid., pp. 200, 204–12.

20. Ibid., p. 234.

21. Anonymous review, *ALZ*, 53 (1807), 424.

22. William Gilpin, *Observations on the River Wye, and Several Parts of South Wales, Relative chiefly to Picturesque Beauty; Made in the Summer of 1770* (London: Blamire, 1782); *Observations, Relative Chiefly to Picturesque Beauty, Made in the Year 1772, on Several Parts of England; Particularly the Mountains, and Lakes of Cumberland, and Westmoreland* (London: Blamire, 1786); *Observations on the Western Parts of England: Relative Chiefly to Picturesque Beauty; to which are Added, a Few Remarks on the Picturesque Beauties of the Isle of Wight* (London: Cadell and Davies, 1798).

23. See for example P. Rosenwall [pseudonym of Gottfried Friedrich Peter Rauschnick], *Mahlerische Ansichten und Bemerkungen auf einer Reise durch Holland, die Rheinlande, Baden, die Schweiz und Württemberg*, 2 vols (Mainz: Kupferberg, 1824).

24. See the preface to *Die Entdeckung der Wirklichkeit: Deutsche Malerei und Zeichnung, 1765–1815*, exhibition catalogue, Museum Georg Schäfer, Schweinfurt, 15 June–2 November 2003, ed. by Bruno Bushart (Leipzig: Seemann Henschel, 2003) for a helpful commentary on new currents in German painting of the period.

25. *MgS*, 261 (1808), 1041–42.

26. Ibid., p. 1042.

27. Horstig, *Reise*, p. 7.

28. Marcel Röthlisberger, in his work *Claude Lorrain: The Paintings*, 2 vols (New York: Hacker Art Books, 1979), argues that these four paintings were not originally intended by Claude as a series, although they were all painted for the same client Henri van Halmale. They have continued to be known as 'The Four Times of the Day' ever since they were described thus in the *Verzeichnis der . . . Gemählde-Sammlung in Cassel* (1783). They were removed from Kassel under Napoleon in

1806 and placed in Malmaison, the residence of Empress Joséphine. In 1812 copies were made and bequeathed in 1814 to the Mittelrheinisches Landesmuseum in Mainz where they now hang (Röthlisberger, I, 362–64).

29. Salomon Gessner, *Brief über die Landschaftmahlerey an Herrn Fuesslin, den Verfasser der Geschichte der besten Künstler in der Schweitz* (Zurich: Orell, Geßner, Füeßli und Compagnie, 1770), p. 246.

30. For a valuable examination of light in German theoretical work, see August Langen, 'Zur Lichtsymbolik der deutschen Romantik', in *Märchen, Mythos, Dichtung: Festschrift zum 90. Geburtstag Friedrich von Leyens am 19. August 1963*, ed. by Hugo Kuhn and Kurt Schier (Munich: Beck, 1963), pp. 447–85.

31. *TM* (1777), III, 275.

32. Ibid., pp. 276–78 (p. 278).

33. Johann Georg Sulzer, *Allgemeine Theorie der schönen Künste in einzeln, nach alphabetischer Ordnung der Kunstwörter auf einander folgenden, Artikeln abgehandelt*, 2nd edn, 4 vols (Leipzig: Weidmann, 1792–94), III (1793), 153.

34. William Gilpin, *An Essay upon Prints: Containing Remarks upon the Principles of Picturesque Beauty* (London: Robson, 1768), p. x.

35. William Gilpin, *Three Essays: On Picturesque Beauty; on Picturesque Travel, and on Sketching Landscape* (London: Blamire, 1792), p. 3.

36. Ibid., p. 4. See Edmund Burke, *A Philosophical Enquiry into the Origin of our Ideas of the Sublime and Beautiful*, ed. by Adam Philips (Oxford: Oxford University Press, 1990), part III: section XXVII, , p. 113: 'beauty should be smooth and polished, [. . .] shun the right line, yet deviate from it insensibly; [. . .] be light and delicate'.

37. Gilpin, *Three Essays*, p. 3.

38. Ibid., p. 20.

39. Ibid. (Gilpin's emphasis).

40. Uvedale Price, *An Essay on the Picturesque, as Compared with the Sublime and the Beautiful* (London: Robson, 1794), pp. 53–54.

41. Ibid. p. 54.

42. Archibald Alison, *Essays on the Nature and Principles of Taste* (London: Robinson, 1790), p. 2.

43. Ibid., pp. 2–3.

44. Ibid., p. 11.

45. Ibid.

46. Carl Gottlieb Horstig, 'Ueber die Natur und das Wesen schöner Empfindungen. Veranlaßt durch Alisons Versuch über den Geschmack', *NBsWfK*, 46 (1792), 3–20 (p. 5).

47. Ibid., p. 6.

48. Carl Gottlieb Horstig, 'Fortsetzung über die Natur und das Wesen schöner Empfindungen', *NBsWfK*, 49 (1793), 195–228 (p. 201).

49. Archibald Alison, *Ueber den Geschmack, dessen Natur und Grundsätze*, verdeutscht und mit Anmerkungen und Abhandlungen begleitet von K. H. Heydenreich, 2 vols (Leipzig: Weygand, 1792), I, 199–200.

50. Carl Gottlieb Horstig, 'Ueber das Pittoreske in der Malerey', *Nachträge zu Sulzers allgemeiner Theorie der schönen Künste* (Leipzig: Dyk, 1792–1808), II: 1 (1793), 31–40.

51. Ibid., p. 31.

52. Ibid., p. 32.

53. Ibid., p. 33.

54. Ibid., p. 38.

55. Ibid., p. 40.

56. Horstig, *Reise*, pp. 144–45.

57. Ibid., p. 146.

58. Ibid., pp. 146–47.

59. Ibid., p. 147.

60. Peter Howard, *Landscapes: The Artists' Vision* (London: Routledge, 1991), p. 46.

61. Ibid., p. 90.

62. Horstig, *Reise*, p. 147.

63. Howard, *Landscapes*, p. 71.

64. See also though Johann Friedrich Karl Grimm's *Bemerkungen eines Reisenden durch Deutschland, Frankreich, England und Holland in Briefen an seine Freunde*, 3 vols (Altenburg: Richter, 1775), II, 278–79, in which he reacts against the romanticization of the white cliffs of Dover by describing them as 'Felsen [. . .] ganz weiß, aus Kreide, ungefähr hundert und dreysig Fuß hoch, aber bey weiten nicht so steil und so fürchterlich, wie sie Shakespeare macht'.

65. Schneider, 'The Staging of the Gaze', p. 78.

66. Ibid. Walter Pape reminds us that Goethe would have objected to the term 'Täuschung' himself, since the eye was incapable of illusion, as it simply functioned according to scientific laws. See Pape's essay '"Die Sinne triegen nicht": Perception and Landscapes in Classical Goethe', in *Reflecting Senses: Perception and Appearance in Literature, Culture, and the Arts*, ed. by Walter Pape and Frederick Burwick (Berlin: de Gruyter, 1995), pp. 96–121 (pp. 96–97).

67. See in particular Ann Bermingham's excellent article 'Landscape-O-Rama: The Exhibition Landscape at Somerset House and the Rise of Popular Landscape Entertainments', in *Art on the Line: The Royal Academy Exhibitions at Somerset House, 1780–1836*, ed. by David Solkin (London: Paul Mellon Centre for Studies in British Art, 2001), pp. 127–44.

68. Horstig, *Reise*, p. 110.

69. Ibid.

70. Ibid, pp. 126–27.

71. *Irene* (July 1805), 235–36. Authorship of this article is unclear. The contents page of the journal gives it as 'Horstig', while at the end of the article is printed 'S. Horstig'. Susette Horstig contributed numerous articles to this journal, including 'Die Wanderungen der jungen Künstlerin', describing the Horstigs' journey with Ursula Magdalena Prestel in 1801 (*Irene* (June 1802), 179–90). A brief introductory note by Horstig to his wife's article is fulsome in its praise of her work and suggests that he was a close reader of her writing and a fervent supporter of her literary aspirations. Nina d'Aubigny von Engelbronner, Susette's sister, a writer, teacher, composer, and singer, was also an intrepid traveller. She moved to London in 1803 (where the Horstigs visited her), and published a series of articles between 1804 and 1806 in the magazine *London und Paris* on her travels to London and on life in the capital. She later journeyed through Asia and Africa, returning to Germany in 1819 and settling in Dresden in 1820.

72. *Irene*, p. 236.

73. Horstig, *Reise*, p. 148.

74. Ibid., p. 149.

75. Ibid., p. 190.

76. See Ann Bermingham, *Landscape and Ideology: The English Rustic Tradition, 1740–1860* (London: Thames and Hudson, 1987), pp. 73–83; also *The Politics of the Picturesque: Literature, Landscape and Aesthetics since 1770*, ed. by Stephen Copley and Peter Garside (Cambridge: Cambridge University Press, 1994).

77. Horstig, *Reise*, p. 150.

78. Ibid., p. 152.

79. Ibid., pp. 195–96.

80. Ibid., p. 17.

81. Ibid., p. 207.

CHAPTER 5

Sympathy and Spectacle:
Visual Representation in Johanna Schopenhauer's
Reise durch England und Schottland

In the preface to her novel *Gabriele*, completed in 1819, Johanna Schopenhauer cast a critical glance over her publications thus far. These largely comprised accounts of her travels to England and Scotland, to the Netherlands, Paris and southern France, and along the Rhine. The scenes depicted in them were, she summarized:

> Abbildungen nach der Natur, mit möglichster Wahrheit wiedergegeben, wie ich sie auffaßte. Ich möchte sie Landschaftsgemälde nennen, auf denen ich mich bemühte, jeden treu kopierten Gegenstand genau an den Platz hinzustellen, wo er in der Wirklichkeit sich befindet, indem ich mich wohl hüthete, den Regeln der Gruppirung oder dem Zauber des Effekts das kleinste Opfer zu bringen.[1]

> [depictions from nature, reproduced with the greatest possible veracity, as I interpreted it. I would like to call them landscape paintings, in which I endeavoured to place every faithfully copied object in exactly the spot where it can be found in reality, while I also guarded against making sacrifices with regard to the rules about the grouping of objects or the magic of effect.]

At first sight, these comments serve to reinforce that claim to authentic, accurate observation and description which travel writers had conventionally been making for the past hundred years or more. But as this chapter will seek to show, these were the considered words of a woman whose travel accounts are clearly constructed through the eyes of an artist and art critic. Johanna Schopenhauer's account of travel through Britain between 1803 and 1805 could not be the *Kunstreise* that the journey she made through Belgium some twenty years later admiring paintings by old masters and Flemish Primitives clearly was. Nevertheless her presentation of certain scenes, notably landscapes, and of particular figures whom she encountered both in rural and urban settings owes much to the modes of presentation used in painting and in the performing arts at that time. This chapter explores how her viewing practices inform the textual descriptions she used and how, by evoking sympathy on the part of the reader with the figures portrayed, these representational strategies sought to offer an affectively engaging account of Britain.

While she is best remembered as the author of *Gabriele*, Johanna Schopenhauer made her debut not as a writer of literature but as an art critic. Her avid interest in art appreciation, which was already apparent in early articles on contemporaries such as Gerhard von Kügelgen and Caspar David Friedrich, would later develop into the artistic sensitivities displayed in her detailed study of Dutch and Flemish painting, *Johann van Eyck und seine Nachfolger* (1822). Famous habitués of her Weimar salon established in 1806 included Goethe, the director of the Weimar drawing academy Heinrich Meyer, the highly successful portrait and history painter Caroline Bardua, and the aesthetician Carl Ludwig Fernow. Fernow was one of the closest of Johanna Schopenhauer's friends; following his death in 1808, she compiled his biography not only to discharge her duties as a friend, but also to cancel his debts with his publisher Cotta. In his collection of essays known as the *Römische Studien* (1806–08), inspired by his prolonged stay in Rome in the 1790s, Fernow included an essay which was one of the most detailed treatises on landscape aesthetics to that date. Thus the *Teegesellschaften*, held on Thursday and Sunday nights at Johanna Schopenhauer's house in Weimar, brought together some of the greatest artistic minds of that time to be found in any of the German states.[2]

Goethe, Fernow, and many like them had been magnetized by the form and the light of the Italian countryside in the classical arcadian visions embodied by Nicolas Poussin or Claude Lorrain. However, as the eighteenth century drew to a close, it was increasingly the landscape of Britain that caught the imagination of German travellers. It lured those in search of views that recalled Salvator Rosa's violent depictions of rugged, wild scenery which positively revelled in nature's imperfections.[3] Gilpin's travel accounts, in their stimulation of a vogue for picturesque travel, encouraged the appreciation not just of the wild beauty of Wales and the Lake District, but also of the sublime splendour of Derbyshire. By the third quarter of the century, the Peak District in particular, with its lofty crags and gloomy caves, had become one of the finest painting grounds for British landscape artists, while the works of writers such as Arthur Young and Thomas Gray also expressed a new interest in the barren, mountainous landscape of Derbyshire.

But German interest in Britain was not stimulated solely by its topographical delights: rapid scientific and technological advances in England had motivated Germans to travel since the 1750s. Heinrich Floris Schopenhauer, Johanna's merchant husband, set an itinerary which included a tour of the Midlands precisely because it allowed them to visit the mines, furnaces, and rolling mills of Britain's industrial heartland. Her account, originally published in 1813, was followed by a revised and extended version in 1818 which covered more than 800 pages in total. It was not constructed as diary entries or letters, but as separate numbered sections, which generally focused on a particular place or theme. Her account of England began by describing how they travelled from Dover up to London, took in the spring art exhibition in Somerset House, stopped off to admire Woburn Abbey, Stowe with its impressive gardens, and Blenheim Palace (where Schopenhauer took an immediate dislike to the tour guide's verbosity), before reaching Birmingham. From there they journeyed on to Derby, Matlock, and Castleton, stopping briefly at Chatsworth on the way. Manchester's spinning factories ('ein Wunder der Industrie' [an industrial marvel]) constituted the next port of call, followed by Leeds, its air thick and black with coal dust. Returning from Scotland — where the Schopenhauers had visited the Edinburgh races, admired the Ossianic scenery of Dalmally, and had been terrified by the sharp inclines around Lanark — they passed through the Lake District to reach Liverpool. Bristol and Bath broke the journey on the way back down to London. Here she covered the well-beaten tracks to Drury Lane, Covent Garden, Vauxhall, the British Museum and Westminster Abbey. She did, however, also find time to visit less famous sights including Boydell's collection of Shakespeare illustrations, Merlin's Museum of mechanical toys and the Weeks Museum, where she marvelled at a lifesize silver swan swimming in a crystal pool. Thus her account represented an interesting combination of landscape and art appreciation interspersed with both impressive and highly disturbing scenes of industrial labour.

Johanna Schopenhauer's concern to represent natural scenery 'mit möglichster Wahrheit', as she had noted retrospectively in *Gabriele*, meant that she chose to engage directly with one highly problematic aspect in the representation of late eighteenth- and early nineteenth-century landscape: the encroachment of industry and industrial labour upon it. English artists had already appropriated this theme in a way that produced thought-provoking, if not highly dramatic, results. *Arkwright's Cotton Mills by Night* (1782–83) and *View in Matlock Dale* (c. 1780–85) by Joseph Wright of Derby showed that the influence of industry on landscape could be benign and unthreatening, if industrial features such as the mills, or the chimney of a local lead-mine on the horizon, were introduced into the picture using a sense of scale which kept in check their influence on the landscape. However, not all depictions of the British industrial scene were quite so untroubled. Philippe Jacques de Loutherbourg's *Coalbrook Dale by Night* (1801) reproduced the blast furnace as an infernal, apocalyptic scene. The incorporation of factories and industrial labour into the landscape was therefore potentially problematic, but the entry of mine, mill, and factory workers into the aesthetic domain raised still more difficult issues about the relationship between the artist and the labouring poor, which addressed complex notions of sympathy and of social criticism.

While Schopenhauer's cameos of industrialists such as Matthew Boulton were vivacious and colourful, emphasizing their valuable contribution to progress, she was also quick to highlight the plight of industrial labour in the countryside. Recent research has explored Johanna Schopenhauer's position within the aesthetic programme of the Weimarer Kunstfreunde [Weimar Lovers of Art], whose prize competitions and periodical, the *Propyläen*, were devoted to the propagation of an overtly neo-classical doctrine.[4] However, her treatment of accessory figures ('staffage') in the landscape, in particular the labouring poor, marks a clear shift away from classical aesthetic ideals. A detailed reading of her travel account of Britain, the *Reise durch England und Schottland* (1813), aims to demonstrate firstly why, according to the aesthetic theories current at the time, the inclusion of industrial labour in landscape scenes was so problematic. Then it explores why she deliberately chose to invest such interest in these figures and asks how both moral and social constraints on the depiction of the labouring poor affected her aesthetic representation of them.[5] The second section considers how two other aspects of early nineteenth-century performing art — the *Attitüde* and the *lebendes Bild* ('tableau vivant') — influenced the modes of representation Johanna Schopenhauer used to portray figures sympathetically in her account of her journey through Britain.

'Die ärmlichsten Gestalten, welche die Phantasie nur erdenken kann'

If William Gilpin had enthused about the 'sublime and wonderful scenes' in the vales around Matlock in Derbyshire, the 'wild scenes of the Peak' were a landscape, he noted bluntly, that he 'left without regret'.[6] But the wild desolation, the giant rocky outcrops, the eerie caverns, mines, and caves of the area around Castleton in North Derbyshire were a major attraction to tourists travelling there with a variety of motivations. Above all, those of a more Romantic persuasion willingly fell victim to the tourist trap that the showcaves at Castleton had already become by the late 1780s. The Peak Cavern, with its vast entrance set in a gorge beneath the ruins of Peveril Castle, was a particular favourite. Its chambers led down into a series of galleries and an underground canal tunnel which had been excavated by lead miners in the 1770s.[7] The Blue John Cavern had passages leading into inlets where Blue John fluorspar continued to be mined to the end of the eighteenth century, while the Tree Cliff Cavern, within the same cave system, led to an inner series of caves profusely decorated with stalactites and stalagmites. It was also the geological singularity of the location — the limestone was rich in fossil specimens of aquatic animals — which drew more cool-headed scientists such as Joseph Banks ('discoverer' of Fingal's Cave) and Alexander von Humboldt to explore the richness of its depths.

In her description of Derbyshire scenery in the *Reise durch England und Schottland*, Johanna Schopenhauer placed the initial emphasis on the power of the natural setting:[8]

> Ein enges, schauerliches Thal empfieng uns: kein Baum, keine Spur von Vegetation, nur nackte und steile Felsen, zwischen denen wir uns ängstlich hindurchwinden mußten, die jeden Augenblick den Weg zu versperren schienen.[9]
>
> [A narrow, eerie valley received us: no tree, no trace of vegetation, only bare and steep cliffs, which seemed to block our path at every moment and between which we had to wend our way fearfully.]

The scene was constructed in such a way that the readers were not mere spectators. It was also invested with a dynamism which drew readers into the landscape as it gradually unfolded around them, rather than formally presenting a scene in beautiful stasis. The rhetoric of the sublime, which implicitly evinced the negative pleasure of terror, invited the reader to empathize with the danger felt by the travellers. It mobilized a series of emotions which reinforced the inferiority of the aesthetic subject in the face of nature: the fear instilled in the travellers as they traced a route between the steep-sided cliff faces which threatened to halt their progress, the solitude, the austerity of the sheer drops of rock with no trace of vegetation to soften their harshness.

As they travelled on, leaving imposing factory buildings behind them, they entered a landscape bereft of human habitation which lacked the harmony of natural beauty:

> Zu Anfange sahen wir noch zwischen durch ansehnliche Fabrikgebäude von großem Umfange; auch diese verschwanden. Wir durchreisten jetzt die traurigste, ödeste, schauerlichste Gegend in England, die Bleiminen von Derbyshire.[10]

[Initially we still saw from time to time impressive factory buildings of considerable size; but these also disappeared. We were now travelling through the most miserable, empty, and wretched landscape in England, the Derbyshire lead mines.]

Wild, desolate, and terrible, this landscape seemed to embody those features which characterized paintings by Salvator Rosa. But Johanna Schopenhauer was not content to focus solely on scenery. Impressive though the natural phenomena of this area were, on her 'canvas' she would not allow the human figures inhabiting it to be rendered insignificant. Instead, she allows Castleton's impressive scenery to fade into the backround, making it a backdrop for groups of workers who are sketched in as occupying the foreground:

> Es waren deren unzählige von allen Seiten zu sehen, zwischen durch die ärmlichsten, aus Feldsteinen aufgethürmten Hütten, vor ihnen langsam wandelnde bleiche Gestalten, Bewohner dieser Oede, von der schrecklichen Arbeit in den Bleiminen entkräftet.[11]

> [Countless numbers of them could be seen from all sides, in between the poorest huts, constructed out of piles of stones, before them slowly moving pale figures, inhabitants of this wasteland, exhausted by the dreadful work in the lead mines.]

Her landscape description is not composed as one free of human interest. Wraith-like human figures occupy the scene, turning the centre of attention upon themselves. The pale spectres which drift back and forth before her gaze are more than mere staffage figures suitably located to emphasize the awesome grandeur of the scene: they imbue it with a sense of narrative. Their exploitation by the mining industry is inscribed upon their bodies, rendering them 'bleiche Gestalten'.

As the travellers progress into the mouth of the Peak Cavern, her concern switches back to the natural singularity of the location:

> Vor der Wölbung hängen ungeheure, bizarr geformte Tropfsteine; wildes Gesträuch rankt dazwischen, Epheu umwindet sie und flattert in leichten Kränzen darum her. Felsenstücke hängen herab, Untergang drohend dem Haupte dessen, der vorwitzig in die Geheimnisse der Unterwelt dringen will.[12]

> [Huge, bizarrely shaped stalactites hang from the cave's entrance, which is surrounded by a maze of bushes and wreathed in fine tendrils of ivy. Lumps of rock were perched so precariously from the roof that they seemed to threaten disaster for the over-inquisitive, who might be too anxious to penetrate the secrets of the underworld below.]

Using description which seems to draw heavily on the visual vocabulary of the Gothic novel, she already forewarns the reader that they are entering an underworld which seems governed by different laws.[13] As they walk into the first cavern itself, once again it is less the sublime natural surroundings which catch Johanna Schopenhauer's eye than the figures of women and children, members of a group of twine-spinners who live underground:

> Wir traten in die Höhle; die dunkle Nacht ward dem allmählich sich daran gewöhnenden Auge zur Dämmerung. Bald unterschieden wir darin eine Menge Weiber und Kinder, ämsig spinnend, die ärmlichsten Gestalten, welche

die Phantasie nur erdenken kann. Gnomen gleich hocken sie in dieser kalten feuchten Dunkelheit und fristen kümmerlich ihr armes Leben; [. . .] Dies ist die unterirdische Stadt, von der mancher Reisende gefabelt hat.[14]

[We entered the cave and the black night changed to dusk as our eyes grew gradually accustomed to the gloom. We could soon distinguish the many figures of women and children, busily spinning, creatures, as miserable as the imagination can conceive. Cowering like gnomes, they live out their wretched existence in this cold damp darkness. [. . .] This is the subterranean city, about which many a traveller has written fantastic tales.]

The scene is not constructed as a static landscape. The reader must wait for the traveller's eyes to grow accustomed to the gloom in the interior of the caves, in order to make out the figures as they loom up out of the darkness. These gnome-like, deformed creatures could not be further from the classical beauties of Claude Lorrain or the pastoral fresh-faced labourers in a landscape by Aelbert Cuyp. Like the wraith-like figures who work in the lead-mines, there is something eerie, if not grotesque, about them. Their presence deliberately jars, disturbing any sense of harmony between man and nature. But here, the darker side to the industrial revolution is punctuated by moments of extraordinary empathy with individuals working in what Johanna Schopenhauer clearly implies are inhumane conditions. The inhabitants of the 'underworld' survive in the cold, damp darkness that is so obviously the converse of the sunlit warmth of the environment in which they should naturally be living. These 'ärmlichste Gestalten' are described in a way that evinces an urgent concern with the material conditions of the poor in England. In locating these figures within the landscape, she refuses to uncouple aesthetic value from practical use by inserting them into some sterile, bucolic tableau. Her barbed criticism of previous travellers who exploited the drama of the scene ('die unterirdische Stadt, von der mancher Reisende gefabelt hat'), while turning a blind eye to the realities of social inequality, likewise challenges conventional scenic tourism.

Johanna Schopenhauer's description of them is more than just earnest criticism of the plight of industrial labour. It is a calculated attempt to evoke in readers a sense of sympathy with these figures, drawing them into the scene by calling on her powers of imagination to project herself into the figures of the workers. This construction of an affective bond between observer and observed explicitly queried the social and moral justification for the spinners to be working under such conditions. But her critique is, paradoxically, tempered in the same breath by the rhetoric of her gaze. The figures being watched do not look back at her and respond. They are not singled out for individual treatment; they are not given names or family histories. The identity assigned to them remains that determined by their profession. They are kept collectively anonymous, at a certain emotional distance.

Once the spinners apprehend that the travellers are there, they surround them, begging vociferously. At this point, the social dynamics of the scene change drastically:

Ungestüm bettelnd umgaben sie uns, sowie sie uns gewahrten; wir waren froh, nach dem Rate der Wirtin in *Castleton*, eine Menge Kupfergeld eingesteckt zu

haben, um uns loszukaufen. [. . .] Die Wärme der Höhle im Winter, die ein
eigentliches Haus entbehrlich macht, der kleine Gewinn, den die neugierigen
Fremden ihnen gewähren, besonders aber die Freiheit von Angaben, welche
nur auf der Oberwelt, im Sonnenlichte gefordert werden, bewegt diese Armen,
eine so unfreundliche Wohnung zu wählen.[15]

[As soon as they became aware of us, they surrounded us, begging noisily,
so that we were glad we had followed the advice of our landlady in *Castleton*
and taken a fair number of coppers with which to pay our ransom. [. . .] The
warmth provided by the cavern in winter, making a proper house unnecessary,
the small profit they can make from curious visitors, and above all the freedom
from having to pay taxes which are only demanded in the world above ground,
in the sunlight, these are the factors that make the poor souls choose this
unfriendly place as their abode.]

The nature of the affective involvement changes with it. Before, the travellers
were presented as active spectators looking upon passive individuals; now, the
subject of their gaze rounds upon them clamouring for money. Here, as it becomes
clear that the travellers have the wherewithal to offer charity, notions of affective
identification break down and observer and observed withdraw to socially defined
roles. At this point Johanna Schopenhauer appears to make an affective volte-face
as these positions crystallize. The cave which the spinners inhabit, previously dark
and dank, is now warm enough to serve adequately as a home; the few pennies they
gain by begging or by showing visitors round the caves are now income on which
they avoid paying the necessary dues.

    This seemingly abrupt withdrawal of emotional investment by the author in the
scene is related to the highly complex series of codes according to which sympathy
operates. Sympathy is essentially a form of affective transport that momentarily
transcends social distance. It works on the assumption that social distinctions are
momentarily suspended and that spectators consider themselves to be on the same
level as the suffering subject they observe. The moment of close, or actual, bodily
contact as the labourers surround the travellers to beg seems to catalyse a shift in
perception and representation on Johanna Schopenhauer's part. It is as if she is
jolted out of her role as painter of this 'cameo', stepping back from the scene to
assume once again her position as a travel writer and as a woman making the (albeit
rather unwilling) gesture of charity. A play of proximity and distance is at work
in these descriptions which culminates in her acceptance of that polarity between
the 'Fremder' and the 'Autochtonen' which Friedrich Wilhelm von Schelling had
alluded to in his *Philosophie der Kunst* (1802):

In dem angenommenen Fall, wo die Landschaftsmalerei ihre Schildereien
mit Menschen belebt, muß doch eine Nothwendigkeit in ihr Verhältniß zu
denselben gebracht werden. [. . .] Die Menschen müssen daher entweder als
gleichsam auf der Stelle gewachsen, als Autochtonen geschildert werden,
oder sie müssen auch durch die im Verhältniß zu der Landschaft fremde Art
ihres Wesens, Aussehens, ja selbst der Bekleidung, als Fremde, als Wanderer
dargestellt werden.[16]

[In the case in question, in which landscape painting enlivens its pictures with
people, the necessity of these figures must be seen in relation to these paintings.

[. . .] The human figures must therefore either be portrayed as if they were native to that place, as indigenous, or they must be portrayed as foreign, as wayfarers, through their foreign manner in relationship to the landscape and even indeed through their clothing.]

This he had seen as a key difference to be underlined in establishing the relationship of figures in scenic description to the landscape itself. Its application to Johanna Schopenhauer's landscape composition raises the question: just who is 'fremd' and who 'autochton' in this scene? The miners are portrayed as carrying out work that seems so unnatural that it is almost they who are the 'strange' forces fighting nature, while it is Johanna Schopenhauer, the scenic traveller, who is — elsewhere at least — seeking unity with the natural world. Then again, it is the practicalities of financial 'Nothwendigkeit' which force these 'ärmlichste Gestalten' into this distorted relationship with their environment. Material necessity locates them, unwilling subjects, within the landscape. Their spectator, by contrast, is the free spirit, the 'Wanderer', who is not shackled by demeaning labour at the service of money. This distinction between 'fremd' and 'autochton' here demarcates boundaries of authority, rather than simply of belonging, which demonstrate the partiality (an implicit negation of disinterest) of the spectator and her account.

The Individual and the Landscape

To what extent did Johanna Schopenhauer's description of industrial labour in the landscape depart from what was being propounded by theorists of landscape art in the period? In his essay 'Wahrheit und Wahrscheinlichkeit der Kunstwerke' [Truth and Probability in Works of Art] (1798), Goethe argued that the truth of nature ('das Naturwahre') and the truth of art ('das Kunstwahre') were two discrete entities. The artist should in no way attempt to give his work the appearance of nature: indeed this would debase his very artistry.[17] The truth of art was to be found in an 'eine innere Wahrheit, die aus der Konsequenz eines Kunstwerks entspringt'.[18] It relied on the appreciation of the work of art as a microcosm, in which everything within it was subject to its own laws and judged according to its own terms. A perfect and complete picture was what the artist should seek to give, in accordance with a mind harmoniously developed and formed. These processes of selection and composition which Goethe described evidently did not propound a realism of the kind glimpsed in Johanna Schopenhauer's textual description of labouring figures in the landscape. In a short essay, 'Etwas über Staffage landschaftlicher Darstellung' [On Staffage in Landscape Description], published in the *Propyläen* (1800), Goethe argued that the inclusion of historical or mythological characters into landscape was altogether difficult since they drew our attention away from everything else: in so doing, they disturbed the balance of the painting.[19] They pointed to issues which lay outside it and were therefore not inherent in the landscape before the viewer's eye. While less illustrious individuals could people a landscape, it was vital that figures which peopled a landscape did not dominate it, but rather blended in to it.[20]

Goethe's short essay, 'Ruysdael als Dichter' (1816), gives his clearest signal regarding the significance that should be ascribed to staffage in a landscape setting.[21] What particularly intrigued observers in Ruisdael's *Ruined Monastery by a River,* Goethe suggested, was the draughtsman in the foreground sitting with his back towards them. This figure was not the frequently misused staffage element but rather someone whom they beheld with emotion because he was both meaningful and effective. He could even be, Goethe suggested, Ruisdael himself:

> Er sitzt hier als Betrachter, als Repräsentant von Allen, welche das Bild künftig beschauen werden, welche sich mit ihm in die Betrachtung der Vergangenheit und Gegenwart, die sich so lieblich durch einander webt, gern vertiefen mögen.[22]

> [He sits here as an observer, a representative of all future viewers of the painting, who through him would like to delve with him into that contemplation of past and present, which so charmingly interweave themselves.]

Unlike the fisherman and the herders who were going about their business, this small, but key, foreground figure was, like the spectator, taking stock of the scene. He thus occupied a liminal position between being in the scene and observing it. By considering this draughtsman representative of all future spectators, Goethe implied that as we beheld the painting, we implicitly projected ourselves into this figure, who acted as our entry point into the scene. He served as a surrogate beholder in the picture for the observer outside the painting.

Carl Ludwig Fernow, in his work on landscape painting, particularly the essay 'Über die Landschaftmalerei' [On Landscape Painting] in the *Römische Studien,* also paid close attention to the notion of staffage.[23] In landscape painting *stricto sensu,* human figures should never rise in status from being merely accessory details in the landscape to form the focal point of the action:

> Es giebt aber ein Verhältnis der Figuren zur Landschaft, wo jene aufhören, Staffirung zu seyn, und wo diese *Scene* und *Fond* ihrer Handlung wird. Zu diesem Verhältnisse darf es *in der Landschaftmalerei* nie kommen, weil Gemälde der Art aufhören würden, Landschaften zu seyn. Menschliche Figuren interessiren schon durch sich selbst mehr, als landschaftliche Gegenstände, besonders wenn sie durch ihre Bedeutsamkeit oder durch ihr Handeln noch ein besonderes Interesse erhalten.[24]

> [There is, however, a relationship between figures and the landscape in which they cease to be staffage and where this becomes the *scene* and *background* to their actions. This should never occur in *landscape painting* since pictures of this kind would cease to be landscapes. Human figures are in themselves more interesting as objects in landscape, particularly when they acquire a specific relevance through their significance or their actions.]

However, a landscape which showed a delightful but unpopulated scene without any trace of human habitation would also be dissatisfying:

> so wird eine Landschaft bedeutender, ihr Karakter wird bestimmter, ihr Inhalt reicher und poetischer, ihr Eindruck klarer und befriedigender, mit einem Worte: die Darstellung einer idealischen Naturscene wird ästhetisch-interessanter, wenn sie, wie die wirkliche Natur, als ein Aufenthalt lebender Wesen erscheint; wenn sie durch Menschen und Thiere, durch Kunstprodukte der Kultur, durch interessante Ereignisse und Auftritte belebt wird.[25]

[thus a landscape becomes more significant, its character more sharply defined, its content richer and more poetic, its expression clearer and more satisfying, in a word: the representation of an idealistic natural scene becomes more aesthetically interesting when, like nature in reality, it appears as the habitation of living beings; when it is enlivened by people and animals, by artistic cultural products, by interesting events and scenes.]

Natural landscape still remained a place of (limited) human activity which gave the scene added aesthetic value. Goethe always maintained that a landscape should be peopled with figures, however insignificant. However, Fernow went further than Goethe in stressing the importance of narrative within landscape painting. He more readily acknowledged the value of human figures in constructing meaning in scenic description.

The Cave as Theatrical Space

How had other travellers viewed the same scene and in what way was Johanna Schopenhauer's approach so very different? In his *Tour through Different Parts of England, Scotland and Wales*, made in 1778, Richard Joseph Sulivan described the Peak's Hole thus:

> Being arrived at the entrance, which is forty-two feet high, and one hundred and twenty feet wide, the attention is caught by cottages scattered up and down in this dark abode, and a multitude of women and children spinning at wheels.[26]

While he did not choose to ignore the spinners, he offered a dispassionate account of these workers at the mouth of the cave. Karl Philipp Moritz's narrative of his journey through England some twenty years earlier referred only in passing to the community of spinners living underground, describing them as 'vergnügt und fröhlich', since the day on which he visited was a Sunday and they could play with their children in front of their huts.[27]

The Reverend Richard Warner's account, *A Tour through the Northern Counties of England, and the Borders of Scotland* (1802), showed greater sensitivity to the peculiarity of the combination of manufacturing and nature that was being carried out in the cave.

> At the foot of that [a dark and gloomy precipice] to the right is seen a gulf forty-two feet high, a hundred and twenty wide, and about ninety deep, formed by a depressed arch of great regularity. Here a singular combination is produced — human habitations and manufacturing machines (the appendages of some twine-makers, who have fixed their residence within this cavern) blending with the sublime features of the natural scenery.[28]

He still referred to the mathematical dimensions of the cave to convey scientifically a sense of its size. But he also concentrated specifically on the twine-spinners for just one moment, acknowledging the strangeness of the combination of industry and nature. Warner's final remark that the twine-spinners blend well into the sublimity of the surrounding cave does not seem entirely consonant with his initial assessment of the scene as 'singular'. Underneath his controlled description lies an awkwardness, a sense that these spinners are out of place, but no real attempt is made to identify with their condition.

William Westall, Associate of the Royal Academy, and the landscape artist on board HMS *Investigator* during its circumnavigation of Australia by Matthew Flinders, later produced both a verbal and visual description of the Peak Cavern. In his *Great Britain Illustrated: A Series of Original Views* (1830), he acknowledged that there were

> persons employed in the manufacture of twine [. . .] carrying on their work in the Cave without experiencing the heats of summer or the colds of winter season; occasionally acting as guides to the visitors of this romantic spot.[29]

However, passing over the hardships which these labourers suffered, his interest focused more on the impressive scenery of the 'romantic spot' than on those who dwelt in it, as the accompanying illustration confirms (Fig. 5.1).

The figures in the engraving are tiny, barely visible against the dark of the cave's interior and the heavy rock walls curving over the scene. A line of poles receding into the cave accentuates the sense of depth. Man's loss of significance in the face of such impressive and imposing surroundings convincingly evoked a sense of scale and space which sought to convey the emotional power of the scenery. Westall's rendering of the scene therefore made few real concessions to affection and in so doing reversed the set of priorities which characterized Johanna Schopenhauer's account.

Perhaps the visual and dramatic rendering of the Peak Cavern which shows the most interesting parallels with Schopenhauer's account was by de Loutherbourg. In 1778 he made a series of sketching trips to Derbyshire and Kent which were to become the basis for forthcoming Drury Lane productions and other artistic endeavours. His representation of Castleton and in particular the Peak Cavern figured in one of the scenes in his play *The Wonders of Derbyshire* (1779), while an aquatint of Peak's Hole was reproduced in *The Romantic and Picturesque Scenery of England and Wales* (1805). Johanna Schopenhauer certainly did not witness the theatrical performances (she first set foot on British soil in 1787). Nor is there any evidence to show that Goethe, for all his interest in stage design and scenery, knew of de Loutherbourg's groundbreaking work. Nevertheless, comparisons between de Loutherbourg's forms of representation and hers are valuable in enabling us to understand more about the way in which Johanna Schopenhauer conceived of the mine scene and the figures occupying it.

When, on 8 January 1779, David Garrick's Drury Lane Theatre held the opening night of the pantomime *The Wonders of Derbyshire* or *Harlequin in the Peak*, it met with a tumultuous reception. Nothing quite like it had been seen in British theatre. It was, the *Morning Chronicle* enthused, 'in the truest sense of the words, a wonderful work, and superior to any thing the stage has presented to the publick eye'.[30] The play, which included scenes from Chatsworth, Dove-Dale, the lead mines, and the Peak Cavern, became a staple of the Drury Lane repertoire and was performed forty-nine times. A curious London audience had certainly been kept on tenterhooks, awaiting the opening night of this play which was delayed on several occasions because the costly scenery took seven months to complete.[31]

Drawn by W.Westall,A.R.A.

E.Finden sculp.

ENTRANCE TO THE PEAK CAVERN.
DERBYSHIRE.

FIG. 5.1. William Westall, Entrance to the Peak Cavern from
Great Britain Illustrated: A Series of Original Views (London: Tilt, 1830)
Reproduced by permission of Cambridge University Library.

Two things were technically groundbreaking about the stage sets: firstly, the use of a whole series of 'flats', or pieces supported by braces placed on the stage, which broke up the scene into a series of small elements, thus enhancing the scene's depth and distance and adding a greater sense of perspective; and secondly the reform in lighting, which enabled more subtle transitions to take place which could broaden the range of effects. The arrangement of the flats also meant the construction of theatrical space in a way which demanded a new relationship between the actor and the scenery. Where opera had called for the close interaction between the performer and the setting because of its emphasis on spectacle, in pre-Romantic drama, scenery was very much kept 'in its place' by performer and stage architect.[32] The performers on stage and the scenery were now more closely integrated into the scenery, creating a symbiotic relationship between the two.

If de Loutherbourg could ally painting and scenery in his radically different scenic vision of the Peak Cavern, Schopenhauer allied painting and textual description in her travel account to aim likewise at attaining the three-dimensional representation of this scene in the mind of the reader. Once she had placed the labourers in front of the backdrop she had previously sketched in, her description also took on the character of a painting being performed, a *lebendes Bild*. Seeing the workers in these terms goes some way to understanding why it was that she found it so startling that they should beg. These figures, held by the spectator's gaze as if they were within a painting, stepped out of the 'frame' as they came to demand money, becoming alarmingly mobile against the wishes of the beholder. But the sense of movement in this scene comes not only from the figures which people it. It also arises from the play with light and lack of light which echoes the moment in modern theatre where the house lights dim and the figures on stage are illuminated. Thus Johanna Schopenhauer's textual description of the twine-spinners in the Peak Cavern not only draws its inspiration, as did de Loutherbourg's stage set, from landscape painting, but also borrows effects from the theatre in its attempt to construct for the reader a vital, dynamic, and also sympathetic picture of the labouring poor in England.

The Performance of Sympathy

If, in her *Reise durch England und Schottland*, Schopenhauer presented within the framework of landscape painting figures to whom she was drawn sympathetically, others were described in ways which drew on quite different forms of representation. Some specific individuals were described as if they were the living counterparts of pitied, distressed figures in well-known paintings or sculptures, and were made to move and perform as if their canvas or marble counterparts had come to life. In portraying them in this way, Schopenhauer keyed into two types of performance very popular at the time, namely the *Attitüde* and the *tableau*, both of which were plastomimic art forms that reflected the essential shift which the body underwent from the mid-eighteenth century onwards as the site of the visual expression of feeling.

One of the earliest eye-witness accounts of the 'attitudes' held by Emma Hamilton, wife of Sir William Hamilton, British ambassador to Naples, was given by Goethe in his *Italienische Reise* (1816–17). She performed a series of dramatic poses based chiefly on famous antique sculptures but also on figures in murals, often dressed in a classical white tunic with a shawl which she would drape over herself or let fall halfway. Her performances embodied both the physical representation of classical art and the expression of emotion. But it was not simply the dramatic presentation of feeling which underpinned Emma Hamilton's popularity. The affective investment by spectators in the scene in such a way that they were left 'bald erschüttert, bald gerührt, bald zum Mitleid, zur Mitfreude, zum Abscheu, zur Liebe hingerissen' [now shocked, now moved, now compelled to feel sympathy, shared joy, abhorrence, love], was a key element of the performance.[33] Emma Hamilton's German counterparts included most notably Henriette Hendel-Schütz, who extended the repertoire of the *Attitüde* to include not only classical poses but also scenes from the works of Dürer, Cranach, and Raphael.[34] Goethe's praise of her performance at the Rathaus in Weimar in 1810 was primarily for the 'neue Kunstansichten' which it offered.[35] What fascinated him about the *Attitüde*, as his detailed essay on the purpose of the theatrical devices in his own monodrama *Proserpina* made clear, was its hybridity: a '[s]chöne, anständige körperliche Bewegung, an die Würde der Plastik, an die Lebendigkeit der Malerei erinnernd' [a beautiful, decorous bodily movement, recalling the dignity of sculpture, the vividness of painting].[36] It drew on sculpture and painting in a way which embodied both stasis and movement and therefore fused plastic and pictorial art with performance in new and exciting ways.

The *tableau*, by contrast, was characterized by stasis. It involved the simulation of a well-known painting by a group of people imitating the positions held by the figures on the canvas. By the start of the nineteenth century, it had become a flourishing parlour game. This fashion for assuming the poses of characters in Anthony Van Dyck's *Belisarius* or Gerard Terborch's *Paternal Admonition* reflected the renewed preoccupation on the part of an educated public with emotional investment in the spectacle of compassion, commiseration, and pity in the realms both of life and of art. Goethe's *Die Wahlverwandtschaften* (1809) is traditionally seen as having made the performance of *lebende Bilder* a fashionable activity in its own right in Germany. This work is also considered to have influenced its use in subsequent literary works such as E. T. A. Hoffmann's *Nachricht von den neuesten Schicksalen des Hundes Berganza* (1813) and Johanna Schopenhauer's *Gabriele*.

Birgit Jooss's recent study has focused not only on the historical development of the *Attitüde* and the *lebende Bilder*, the figures who performed them, and the images they sought to imitate.[37] It has also examined their use within the realm of literature, concentrating on their symbolic function in fictional works, most notably Goethe's *Die Wahlverwandtschaften*. However, the function of these forms of representation in non-fictional writing, in particular travel narratives, has been overlooked by scholars both of the performing arts and of Johanna Schopenhauer's oeuvre. Despite discussions of the relevance of *tableaux vivants* in *Gabriele*, scant attention has been paid to her inclusion of them in her non-fictional travelogue on Britain.[38] By examining how Johanna Schopenhauer represents in her travel writing tragic figures who perform *lebende Bilder* and *Attitüden*, the following sections seek to explore the complex mapping of theatricality, affective expression, and sympathetic spectatorship in her travelogue on England and Scotland.

Sarah Siddons, Ann of Swansea, and the 'weiblicher Belisar'

The image of the blind beggar Belisarius receiving alms was one of the most popular subjects in painting in the last quarter of the eighteenth century. Goethe had, of course, also brought it to an educated German public's attention by making it one of the *lebende Bilder* performed in *Die Wahlverwandtschaften*. This novel, which Johanna Schopenhauer had declared to be one of her favourite texts, is also considered to have been a key source of inspiration for the *tableaux* which the characters in her own later work *Gabriele* perform. Little can be established about when and how Johanna Schopenhauer started to write up for publication purposes the notes she had compiled while on her travels through Britain between 1803 and 1805. Her account was not published in its entirety until 1813. Part of it also appeared earlier in the 1811 edition of *London und Paris*, although the section on begging in London, in which this reference to Belisarius occurs, was not included in this

FIG. 5.2. Jacques Louis David, *Bélisaire, reconnu par un soldat qui avait servi sous lui au moment qu'une femme lui fait l'aumône*, 1781, Lille, Musée des Beaux-Arts

article.[39] Given that her account was not published in full until four years after *Die Wahlverwandtschaften*, it therefore seems fair to assume that Goethe's inclusion of the Belisarius picture in his novel of 1809 inspired Johanna Schopenhauer to refer to it in her own later work.

What was it about the figure of Belisarius that caught not just Goethe's imagination in the late eighteenth and early nineteenth centuries? According to the Roman historian Procopius, Belisarius was a highly successful general under the Roman emperor Justinian, and won important victories over the Vandals and the Goths. Nevertheless, on several occasions his actions incurred suspicions of disloyalty on the part of the emperor, who accused him of plotting against his life and eventually stripped him of his office. By the seventeenth century, Belisarius had come to be portrayed as the legendary figure of an aged, blind man, wrongfully accused, who was forced to end his days dependent on charity.[40] Jean-François Marmontel's philosophical novel *Bélisaire* (1767), which used the legend of Belisarius to criticize the government, society, and religious doctrine of the time, helped to strengthen this image of the persecuted innocent man which was highly appealing to the excessively sentimental audience of the time.[41] This work encouraged renewed interest in the figure of Belisarius in French painting in the last quarter of the eighteenth century. He was the subject of paintings by Louis Jean-Jacques Durameau (1775), Jean-François Pierre Peyron (1779), and, most notably, Jacques Louis David (1781) (Fig. 5.2).

How did Johanna Schopenhauer incorporate the Belisarius motif into her work and to which rhetorical ends? The most obvious transformation which she made was that of gender. In her section on mendicants in London, she projected the figure of the downtrodden, yet courageous, Roman general onto the sister of the renowned actress Sarah Siddons to create what she would later call her 'weiblicher Belisar'. Siddons was an iconic figure of the British stage with a career spanning more than five decades. She was not only painted by the likes of Gainsborough and Reynolds in various character parts, particularly as the tragic figure of Lady Macbeth, but also held a series of attitudes captured by Gilbert Austin in his *Chironomia* (1806) (Fig. 5.3).

Tragedy too had its place in the life of the sister of Sarah Siddons, Ann Hatton, also known as 'Ann of Swansea':

> Man hielt sie allgemein für eine, durch verschuldete und unverschuldete Unglücksfälle, so tief gesunkene Schwester der berühmten Schauspielerin *Siddons*, wenigstens trug sie eine unverkennbare Aehnlichkeit mit dieser in ihren Zügen. Dieselbe hohe, edle Gestalt, derselbe Adel in Blick und Miene, nur älter, blaß und wie versteinert durch lange Gewohnheit des Unglücks.[42]

> [She was generally reputed to be a sister of the famous actress, Mrs Siddons, and it was said that a series of tragedies, some self-inflicted, some accidental, had caused her to sink so low. She certainly bore an unmistakable likeness to the actress, and had the same tall noble figure and distinguished expression, though she was somewhat older, pale, her features hardened by her long run of misfortune.]

Hatton's life was indeed characterized by 'verschuldete und unverschuldete Unglücksfälle' which she made no attempt to hide — indeed every attempt to publicize. Afflicted with lameness and a squint from infancy, she had married a provincial actor, only to find that he was already married to someone else.[43] On being discovered, he abandoned her to an impoverished existence. In October 1783 advertisements in the London papers appeared, identifying her as the younger sister of Messrs Kemble and Siddons, to whom she had applied in vain for money. Six years later she was accidentally shot in the eye at a brothel in Covent Garden. She again used press coverage to embarrass her prominent family further by allowing details of this incident, and her attempted suicide in Westminster Abbey, to be made public. In 1793 Ann Hatton left for America, accompanied by her second husband, returning to Britain and settling in Wales around 1800. Her autobiographical poetry[44] and her string of lurid but popular Gothic novels made her a popular novelist and poet in Swansea until her death in 1838.[45]

While the *Reise durch England und Schottland* claims to record the Schopenhauers' second journey to England between 1803 and 1805, the description of Ann Hatton appears to relate more closely to images of her circulating in England on the Schopenhauers' first tour in 1787. If Ann Hatton was indeed 'handsome and finely

FIG. 5.3. Gilbert Austin, 'Seven Attitudes by Mrs. Siddons', from
Chironomia; or, a Treatise on Rhetorical Delivery (London: Cadell and Davies, 1806)
Reproduced by permission of Cambridge University Library.

proportioned[46] in early life — which corresponds to the grace and majesty accorded
to her by Johanna Schopenhauer — by the time John Barber encountered her in
Swansea around the turn of the century, this 'sister of the English Melpomene [. . .]
laboured under the misfortune of lameness, and the encumbrance of more human
flesh than I ever saw crowded in one female figure'.[47] The composite picture
which Johanna Schopenhauer created therefore did not merely draw on the two-
dimensional image from David's canvas. To add movement, she also projected upon
this begging figure the grace, regal poise, and striking features of Sarah Siddons,
whose Covent Garden performances in Thomas Southerne's *Isabella* and August
von Kotzebue's *Pizarro* the Schopenhauers had attended in late September and mid-
October 1803.[48]

The description of Ann Hatton continued thus:

> Oft begegnete uns diese wunderbare Erscheinung. Sie trug immer einen
> schwarz seidnen Hut, der nicht so tief in's Gesicht ging, daß man nicht dessen

Züge hätte bemerken können; ein grün wollnes Kleid, eine schneeweiße große Schürze und ein eben solches Halstuch. Schweigend, mit stolzem Ernst wandelt sie, gestützt auf zwei Krücken, langsam und ungehindert durch die Menge.[49]

[We often saw this curious apparition. She always wore a dark silk hat, which did not cover so much of her face that one could not note her features; a green woollen dress, a large snow-white apron, and a similar kerchief. As she slowly walked along, silently and with pride, supported on two crutches, the crowd made way for her.]

The silence, which accompanies this 'performance', serves to heighten the beholder's awareness of bodily attitude, gesture, and features. If Johanna Schopenhauer called attention to Hatton's 'Blick und Miene' — Sarah Siddons's dark eyes had also made her an electrifying, passionate performer — she refers to the power of facial expression to engage the reader's sympathies with the actress, although she does not directly comment on Hatton's features. As the figure starts to move, a whole series of inversions and revisions of the original Belisarius painting begin to take place. These affect not only the spatial configurations between actors but the original conferral of implied stasis and movement.

The tragedy of Belisarius's fate is articulated by his body itself, deformed as it is by blindness and lameness into immobility. The tension in the scene lies precisely in his physical inferiority both through deformity and through his sedentary position in relation to the standing soldier, while, wrongly condemned, he occupies the morally superior position. Johanna Schopenhauer's re-vision of the scene reverses these relationships. It makes the tall noble female figure dominate by standing, looking down upon her subjects 'mit dem Anstande einer Königin'. She is the mobile, if crippled, body seen to pass through and beyond the crowd of onlookers. The description continues:

Sie forderte nicht, sie bat nicht, aber reichliche Gaben wurden ihr dennoch von allen Seiten geboten, Jeder fühlte sich gezwungen, getrieben, ihr zu geben. Es war, als müsse man ihr danken, daß sie die gebotne Gabe nur nahm. Sie dankte nicht; mit dem Anstande einer Königin nahm sie das Dargebotene und wandelte stumm weiter wie ein Geist.[50]

[She never asked for anything, did not beg, but the public seemed to feel obliged, even driven, to give her something and gifts were showered upon her. It was as if they wished to thank her for accepting their gifts, and she, with the gracious manners of a queen, received their offerings as her due, without thanks, and then moved on like some apparition.]

However, the act of giving returns the scene to those same power relationships inherent in pictorial representations of Belisarius. Ann Hatton is presented as the heroic, suffering figure who is able to transcend physical constraint, assured of her moral superiority. The confrontation between the figures in the crowd giving alms and the suffering woman raises important issues about the moral aspects of the relationship between sympathy and spectacle in this period. Her spectators are 'gezwungen', 'getrieben', by guilt to give money. But this is the eager public display of compassion by a group of onlookers who remain faceless and anonymous. The pity which Ann Hatton evokes in them is one of charitable sympathy, the need to salve one's social conscience, rather than emotional investment in her situation. Her refusal to thank them breaks with the normal course of give-and-take in the articulation of sympathy. Her rejection of the terms on which this sympathy is offered constitutes a reaction against the recipient's implicit subjugation in such a situation and an affirmation that forcing one's sympathy upon an individual is implicitly demeaning for that person.

The visual contact between the 'weiblicher Belisar' and her audience is, as a result of her (partial) blindness, kept to a minimum. Since eighteenth-century theories of meaning and identity depended on the belief that sight was the principal bodily sense, its converse, blindness, remained a subject of intense fascination.[51] Indeed, interpretations of the Belisarius-tableau in *Die Wahlverwandtschaften* have traditionally focused on the leitmotiv of metaphorical sight and blindness with regard to the figure of Ottilie.[52] However, Michael Fried has shown, in an analysis of Diderot's discussion of Van Dyck's *Belisarius*, that the 'blindness' in the picture could be of an altogether different order. For what Diderot found compelling in the painting was not so much the figure of Belisarius, but rather the soldier facing him. The soldier was so completely absorbed in the act of beholding the begging figure that he was 'blind' to all else.[53] The dominance of the gazing soldier established the moral value of the painting, because it confirmed Belisarius's heroic status and thereby secured the moral meaning of the composition as a whole.[54] Just as Belisarius drew the pensive gaze of the soldier, so Johanna Schopenhauer's female counterpart 'absorbed' the attention of the onlooking crowd, similarly reinforcing Ann Hatton's status as the heroic figure in this *tableau*.

More importantly, Diderot believed that paintings and plays should advance the fiction that their beholders were absent, non-existent. The actors should be oblivious, 'blind', to the audience. The spectators should feel as if they had been forgotten, ignored, unaddressed. This notion of 'absorption' embodied by the soldier, Fried argues, determines not only the moral significance of the Belisarius figure but more generally the picture's status as a painting.[55] While the soldier functioned as a kind of surrogate beholder who mediated between the actual viewer and the painting, allowing intimate access into the picture, this also neutralized the beholder's presence in front of the Belisarius spectacle. The 'actors' in the scene were 'performing' as if no spectators were present. Johanna Schopenhauer's 'weiblicher Belisar' drew the attention of the onlookers in such a way that their viewing was focused on Ann Hatton and on no-one or nothing else in the scene. They are, therefore, the surrogate beholders in this scene through whose eyes we can also choose to observe the 'weiblicher Belisarius'. The crowd is referred to using the impersonal, all-inclusive 'man' or 'Jeder', which potentially permits the reader to see himself as an extension of the group of onlookers. One major difference, however, between the soldier figure in David's Belisarius viewing the beggar, and the crowd in Johanna Schopenhauer's scene beholding Ann Hatton, is that she does not allow us to see the expressions on their faces. We suspect that her onlookers give alms out of a charity motivated by guilt: the sense of dismay on the soldier's face is far more evocative than the act of giving by Schopenhauer's faceless, anonymous crowd.

The acknowledgement that this figure is indeed inspired by either Van Dyck's or David's *Belisarius* comes only at the end of this passage, as if to suggest that the attentive and educated reader (who knew Goethe's *Die Wahlverwandtschaften*) might have already made this connection:

> Die bildende Kunst hat sich diese auffallende, große Gestalt, diesen weiblichen Belisar, möchten wir sagen, oft zum Vorbild gewählt. In allen Kupferstich-magazinen, bei allen Ausstellungen der Maler fand man ihr sprechend ähnliches Bild, denn diese Züge drückten sich leicht der Phantasie ein.[56]

> [Pictorial art has often taken this striking, great figure, this female Belisarius, we might say, as its model. In every magazine of engravings, at every art exhibition the spitting image of her could be seen, since these features impressed themselves easily on the memory.]

The commentary on this picture switches rapidly out of its tragic, dramatic mode to make factual references to the many copies of 'diese auffallende, große Gestalt'. Whether this specifically refers to Ann Hatton or to a stereotypical image of the begging woman is rather ambiguous. Paradoxically, while the *lebendes Bild* aimed to make the scene more authentic and more real, the 'performance' is halted so sharply that it confronts the reader even more directly with the artifice of representation — be it in the form of the *lebendes Bild* or the paper illustration.

'Das Schöne Mädchen von Winandermere'

The construction of readerly sympathy in the second *lebendes Bild*, which follows on directly in the *Reise durch England und Schottland* from the description of the 'weiblicher Belisar', is of quite a different order. Yet in Johanna Schopenhauer's mind, these two images were closely linked and show certain parallels in their handling of subject matter. As she adds, again rather ambiguously, the second picture, that of a beautiful young country girl, usually hung next to that of the Belisarius figure in the art galleries which she visited.[57] What Johanna Schopenhauer means by 'hing gewöhnlich' is unclear, since the hanging order of paintings from gallery to gallery was not likely to be the same. This rather confused connection does however reinforce the notion that she actively seeks to order her viewing of Britain in terms of a collection of paintings which she calls to mind to evoke particular scenes.

If Ann Hatton represented calm grandeur, Molly, the fair girl of Windermere (or 'Winandermere' as it was also known at that time), embodied noble simplicity. She was 'einfach gekleidet, in jugendlichen Schmerz versunken' [simply dressed, sunk in youthful misery], simple in her gestures and poses: the references to the poses of Emma Hamilton, whom the Schopenhauers had met while living in Hamburg in the 1790s,[58] and of Henriette Hendel-Schütz are overt. Molly, like Ann Hatton, is presented as a tragic figure. She too falls prey to a man already married, she also subsequently contemplates suicide, but she at least retains beauty of form and movement, as demonstrated by the *Attitüden* which the travellers witness. The setting is clearly conceived as if it were a theatre stage. As the travellers draw near to the house where this figure will hold a series of graceful poses as if she were Emma Hamilton performing her *attitudes*, they see a small lawn, surrounded by a white, decorative railing, which spreads before them like a carpet.[59] As if from the wings, Molly slowly appears and her plastomimic performance begins:

> Ein junges Mädchen erhob sich langsam aus einer Laube, nahe am Hause, näherte sich der Einfassung und reichte schweigend unsern Begleiterinnen die Hand. Auch sie schwiegen, es war, als ob ihnen das Herz zu voll wäre zum Sprechen.[60]

> [A young girl slowly rose out of an arbour, close to the house, approached the railing, and silently reached out her hand to the ladies accompanying us. They too were silent; it was as if they were too overcome to speak.]

The moment when she reaches out to Johanna Schopenhauer's female companions and, we presume, touches them, is crucial. It not only creates a physical 'connection' between her and her spectators in which she is performing within the same spatial frame of reference. It also appears to 'touch' them emotionally, such that they are likewise reduced to silence. Indeed this scene demonstrates precisely how silence could, paradoxically, become a highly expressive medium by which to convey the excess of emotion through the medium of mime. That she reaches out towards them in a gesture implying contact emphasizes her proximity both spatially and emotionally.

Just as Ann Hatton was the commanding, dominant figure in the 'performance' of the Belisarius picture, Molly likewise appears to 'absorb' the spectators visually. They cannot break the silence, nor do they seem in control of the scene unfolding before them:

> Uns war es unmöglich, diese Stille zu unterbrechen; staunend konnten wir nur die schöne Gestalt des Mädchens betrachten, die uns bekannt erschien, aber vergebens strebten wir uns zu erinnern, wo wir diese Züge früher gesehen haben konnten.[61]

> [It was not possible for us to break the silence; we looked with amazement on the beautiful figure of the girl, who appeared familiar to us, but we tried in vain to remember where we could have previously seen these features.]

Had they been able to recall her face as being that of a well-known painting, this would have reduced the affective impact of the act of looking. This two-dimensional representation of herself could never have absorbed the spectators in the way that she appears to do in real life. Nor indeed would a picture convey to those observers at one remove, namely the readers, the artistic power of her performance.

The static pose which she adopts is described in terms of its statuesque properties:

> Blendend weiß, hätte man dies himmlische Gesicht, ohne die dunkeln blauen Augen, für eine Marmorbüste halten können.[62]

> [Brilliant white, this heavenly face could have been taken for a marble bust, were it not for the dark blue eyes.]

It seems to reverse the Pygmalion myth of incarnation, so popular at that time, by almost turning her back into a statue. Molly's clothing too has all the simplicity of Emma Hamilton's performances, 'halb arm' in colours which are plain — grey, white, and black. This not only served to focus attention on bodily movements rather than costume: it also reflected the mistakenly held eighteenth-century belief that colour, when applied to sculpture, detracted from the form and left the impression of ugliness. The colouring of sculpture remained a taboo topic until well into the nineteenth century when the issue of polychromy became the subject of critical debate. (Herder even went as far as to call a painted finish on sculptures 'Sandkorn, Tünche, fremder Anwuchs' [grains of sand, distemper, foreign growths].)[63]

This scene plays out that paradox epitomized in the notion of the *lebendes Bild*: namely that it is at once a picture brought to life and at the same time life petrified and immobilized. As the 'living statue' begins to weep, it recaptures its vitality:

> eine Träne funkelte in der Abendsonne an den langen seidnen Wimpern; man sah, diese Augen waren des Weinens gewohnt, sie schienen an Glanz dadurch zu gewinnen.[64]

> [A tear sparkled on the long silken lashes in the evening sun; one could see that these eyes were used to crying, and they appeared as a result to gain in radiance.]

The tears which Molly sheds could well have been inspired by Sarah Siddons's tragic performances. Siddons played a part as if possessed by it, allowing the storm of emotions associated with it to wash over her in a way that could never have been termed 'studied'.[65] Facial expression was everything. Just as theatre critics of the day gave detailed accounts of expression, Johanna Schopenhauer also particularly focuses in on her eyes and her mouth as conveying her tragic situation: 'den lieblichen Mund umschwebte ein halb schmerzliches, halb freundliches Lächeln' [a half pained, half friendly smile played on the lovely lips].[66] Because she focuses in on these details of facial expression, which she had not done in the case of Ann Hatton, and allows the 'narrative' of male disloyalty and abandonment to be told by the landlady who has accompanied the travellers, it is easier for the reader to imagine something of the figure's mental suffering, rather than sympathize solely with Molly through the tragic performance she gives.

As the description of Molly draws to a close and she withdraws to the bower whence she had appeared, the visitors ask the landlady who she is, since she seems familiar. That familiarity, they are told, comes not through having seen her in real life, but in recognizing her from a painting in London. Since they are enraptured to have seen her in real life, the picture to which they have been referred is summarily declared to be an inferior mode of representation: '[s]o hatten wir sie denn gesehen, und schöner bei weitem, als alle Gemälde, die Künstler oder unsre Phantasie von ihr bildeten' [thus we had seen her, and more beautiful by far than any picture which an artist or our imagination painted of her].[67] Again, this was confirmation of the fact that pictorial art could not capture as effectively what the three-dimensional experience had succeeded in doing.

Nevertheless, it seems important for the spectators, including the author, to catalogue and reduce what they see to a pictorial canon, indicating a desire to control and to order which shifts away from the emotional proximity of sympathetic engagement demonstrated earlier in the description. This desire is only momentarily overridden by the sublimity of the experience of beholding ('wir [. . .] konnten nur sehen' [we could only look]) which wholly engrosses them in the act of viewing.[68] Their failure to catalogue Molly within the 'gallery' they have in their memories acts as a reproach upon themselves: '[w]ir zürnten uns selbst, daß wir sie nicht gleich erkannt hatten' [we were angry with ourselves for not having recognized her at once].[69] In a way, the panoptic gaze of public expectation turns upon the self and the beholders find themselves lacking, failing to measure up against the self-conscious standards they have set themselves as educated connoisseurs of art.[70] Thus, in the final analysis, we see that the inclusion of these *tableaux vivants* and *attitudes* was not only about the evocation of pity in the reading public or, indeed, about the construction of the author as a woman with a social conscience. It was also, to a degree, about the display of female accomplishment as art critic and connoisseur at the start of the nineteenth century.

In the *Reise durch England und Schottland*, Johanna Schopenhauer was concerned to describe the British landscape in terms which railed against the potentially more trivial nature of picturesque tourism. Her work challenged in particular the tenets of disinterested contemplation and the autonomy of the aesthetic domain from moral, political, or utilitarian concerns and activities which had hitherto characterized German aesthetic discourse. If Goethe and Fernow sought to create works of art which propounded classical ideals of beauty and harmony, Johanna Schopenhauer was concerned precisely to show that man and nature were not at one. In the interests of industry, the relationship between labouring figures and their natural environment had become exploitative, energy-sapping, dehumanizing. Nature, and its representation in the landscape aesthetics to which she subscribes, therefore came to be suffused with moral and social criticism. Johanna Schopenhauer endeavoured to draw the reader into the scene by the construction of an affective, 'interested', bond between the observer and the observed. A feeling of sympathy with them was constructed according to the notion that we should be able to project ourselves into the same space that they occupied. We would thus sense at greater proximity the harshness of the environment in which they live and work, losing, if only momentarily, the notion that there was a dividing line between observer and observed. While Johanna Schopenhauer's response to the needs of the figures in the landscape was not itself unambiguous, she nevertheless insisted on the acknowledgement in landscape aesthetics of the harsher realities of the industrial world.

In including the *lebendes Bild* and the *Attitüde* in the *Reise durch England und Schottland*, it seems that Johanna Schopenhauer offered a reconstruction of the foreign experience which made it more vivid, more 'alive', and hence more authentic to the reader. The *tableau* and the *attitude*, which both actively exploited the emotional force of tragic situations, drew on readers' imaginative powers to construct such scenes in their minds and to allow themselves to become affectively involved in them. By using these two representational strategies, a different kind of visual and psychological engagement with the subjects in the narrative was therefore initiated. Not only did this suggest that in occupying the same physical space as the viewing subject, the expression of the tragic figure's suffering was an experience more acutely felt than if represented in a painting. The series of positions these figures held and the movements they made could also express a range of emotions which a single, flat, image could not. In so doing they could convey more clearly the mental, rather than merely physical, distress of these suffering figures. I think it no coincidence that the two female figures to whom our gaze is drawn are both made tragic subjects through male infidelity: perhaps Johanna Schopenhauer had a point to make about the suffering of women as they deferred to unfaithful husbands. Her version of tragedy is, then, constructed out of the misery and grotesqueness of real-life experience in which the boundaries between 'life' and 'art' are blurred. In showing the fluidity with which theatre, sculpture, and painting had the potential to adapt and adopt, she therefore allowed works of art to play a fundamental role in the presentation of social interaction. By interweaving *lebende Bilder* and *Attitüden* into her travel account, Johanna Schopenhauer thus sought to speak to the reader both in the 'universal' language of art and in the nineteenth-century language of social concern and sympathy.

Notes to Chapter 5

1. Johanna Schopenhauer, *Gabriele*, 3 vols (Leipzig: Brockhaus, 1821), I, Vorwort (unpaginated).
2. As Johanna Schopenhauer herself boasted to her son Arthur in a letter of 28 November 1806, 'Der Zirkel, der sich Sonntags und Donnerstags um mich versammelt, hat wohl in Deutschland und nirgends seines Gleichen; könnte ich dich doch nur einmahl herzaubern!' (*Die Schopenhauers: Der Familienbriefwechsel von Adele, Arthur, Heinrich Floris und Johanna Schopenhauer*, ed. by Ludger Lütkehaus (Zurich: Haffmans, 1991), p. 123).
3. See John Dixon Hunt, *The Figure in the Landscape: Poetry, Painting, and Gardening during the Eighteenth Century* (Baltimore: Johns Hopkins University Press, 1976), esp. ch. 5, 'The Landscape of Sensibility', pp. 196–245.
4. See in particular Anke Gilleir, *Johanna Schopenhauer und die Weimarer Klassik: Betrachtungen über die Selbstpositionierung weiblichen Schreibens* (Hildesheim: Olms-Weidmann, 2000).
5. See John Barrell, *The Dark Side of the Landscape: The Rural Poor in English Painting, 1730–1840* (Cambridge: Cambridge University Press, 1980), also Francis D. Klingender, *Art and the Industrial Revolution* (London: Paladin, 1968).
6. Gilpin, *Observations, Relative Chiefly to Picturesque Beauty*, II, 225.
7. Trevor D. Ford, 'Speleogenesis: The Evolution of the Castleton Caves', *Geology Today*, 12 (1996), 101–09.
8. Immanuel Kant, *Kritik der Urteilskraft* (1790), in *Werke*, ed. by Wilhelm Weischedel, 6 vols (Frankfurt a.M.: Insel, 1964), V, 233–620 (p. 349).
9. Johanna Schopenhauer, *Reise durch England und Schottland*, in *Sämmtliche Schriften*, 24 vols (Leipzig: Brockhaus, 1830–31), XV (1830), 190–91.
10. Ibid., p. 191.
11. Ibid.
12. Ibid., p. 192.
13. For an excellent essay on the aesthetics of the mine, see ch. 2, 'The Mine: Image of the Soul', in Theodore Ziolkowski's *German Romanticism and its Institutions* (Princeton: Princeton University Press, 1990), pp. 18–63.
14. Johanna Schopenhauer, *Sämmtliche Schriften*, XV, pp. 192–93.
15. Ibid., p. 193.
16. Friedrich Wilhelm Joseph von Schelling, *Philosophie der Kunst*, in *Sämmtliche Werke*, 14 vols (Stuttgart: Cotta, 1856–61), V: I (1859), 355–736 (p. 546).
17. *DKV*, I: 18, 501–07 (p. 504).
18. Ibid., p. 506.
19. Ibid., pp. 789–91 (p. 789).

20. Ibid.

21. *DKV*, I: 19, *Ästhetische Schriften, 1806–1815* (1998), pp. 632–36.

22. Ibid., p. 635.

23. Carl Ludwig Fernow, 3 vols, *Römische Studien* (Zurich: Gessner, 1806–08), II (1806), 11–130 (p. 12).

24. Ibid., p. 97 (Fernow's emphasis).

25. Ibid., pp. 31–32.

26. Richard Joseph Sulivan, *Tour Through Different Parts of England, Scotland, and Wales*, in *The British Tourists; or Traveller's Pocket Companion through England, Wales, Scotland, and Ireland. Comprehending the most celebrated Tours in the British Islands*, ed. by William Mavor, 6 vols (London: Newbery, 1798), III, 1–152 (p. 102).

27. Moritz, *Werke*, II, 101.

28. Richard Warner, *A Tour through the Northern Counties of England, and the Borders of Scotland*, 2 vols (London: Robinson, 1802), I, 167.

29. William Westall, *Great Britain Illustrated: A Series of Original Views* (London: Tilt, 1830), p. 46.

30. *Morning Chronicle*, 9 January 1779.

31. See Rüdiger Joppien, 'Die Szenenbilder Philippe Jacques de Loutherbourgs: Eine Untersuchung zu ihrer Stellung zwischen Malerei und Theater' (unpublished doctoral dissertation, University of Cologne, 1972), esp. pp. 209–23.

32. Ibid., p. 121.

33. For a lively description of the meeting between the Schopenhauers and the Hamiltons on 21 October 1800 in Hamburg, see Carola Stern, *Alles, was ich in der Welt verlange: Das Leben der Johanna Schopenhauer* (Cologne: Kiepenhauer and Witsch, 2003), pp. 85–86.

34. Birgitt Jooss, *Lebende Bilder: Körperliche Nachahmung von Kunstwerken in der Goethezeit* (Berlin: Reimer, 1999), p. 110.

35. *DKV*, I: 17, p. 237.

36. *DKV*, I: 19, pp. 707–15 (pp. 714–15).

37. Earlier studies include Kirsten Gram Holmström's *Monodrama. Attitudes. Tableaux Vivants. Studies on Some Trends of Theatrical Fashion 1770–1815* (Stockholm: Almqvist and Wiksell, 1967); August Langen, 'Attitüde und Tableau in der Goethezeit', *Jahrbuch der Schillergesellschaft*, 12 (1968), 194–258; Dagmar von Hoff and Helga Meise, 'Tableaux vivants: Die Kunst- und Kultform der Attitüden und lebenden Bilder', in *Weiblichkeit und Tod in der Literatur*, ed. by Renate Berger and Inge Stephan (Cologne: Böhlau, 1987), pp. 69–86; Michel Delon, 'L'Esthétique du tableau et la crise de la représentation classique à la fin du XVIIIe siècle', in *La Lettre et la Figure: La littérature et les arts visuels à l'époque moderne*, ed. by Wolfgang Drost and Géraldi Leroy (Heidelberg: Winter, 1989), pp. 11–29. I am grateful to Margaret Rose for suggesting this link between the performing figures in Schopenhauer's work and the *tableau vivant*, and for helping to access more recent secondary literature on this subject.

38. See the most recent studies of Johanna Schopenhauer's work: Gilleir, *Johanna Schopenhauer*; Ulrike Bergmann, *Johanna Schopenhauer: 'Lebe und sei so glücklich als du kannst'* (Leipzig: Reclam, 2002); also Cindy Brewer, 'Resignation and Rebellion: The Dual Narrative of Johanna Schopenhauer's *Gabriele*', *The German Quarterly*, 75.2 (2002), 181–95.

39. *London und Paris*, 2 (1811), 260–81.

40. See Jeanne R. Monty, 'The Myth of Belisarius in Eighteenth Century France', *Romance Notes*, 4 (1962), 127–31.

41. Ibid., p. 130.

42. Johanna Schopenhauer, *Sämmtliche Schriften*, XVI, 100–01.

43. See Philip H. Highfill, Kalman A. Burnim, and Edward A. Langhaus, *A Biographical Dictionary of Actors, Actresses, Musicians, Dancers, Managers and other Stage Personnel in London, 1660–1800*, 16 vols (Carbondale: Southern Illinois University Press, 1973–93), VII (1982), 171–75 (p. 172).

44. Moira Dearnley, '"Condem'd to wither on a foreign strand": The 1833–34 Manuscript Poems of Ann of Swansea', *New Welsh Review*, 11.1 (1998), 56–59 (p. 59).

45. Ivor J. Bromham, '"Ann of Swansea" (Ann Julia Hatton: 1764–1838)', in *Glamorgan Historian*, 7 (1971), ed. by Stewart Williams, pp. 173–86 (p. 178).

46. Ibid., p. 174.

47. John Thomas Barber, *A Tour throughout South Wales and Monmouthshire Comprehending a General Survey of the Picturesque Scenery, Remains of Antiquity, Historical Events, Peculiar Manners, and Commercial Situations, of that Interesting Portion of the British Empire*, (London: Cadell and Davies, 1803), p. 143.

48. See Arthur Schopenhauer, *Die Reisetagebücher* (Zurich: Haffmans, 1988) p. 79. Johanna Schopenhauer's account is not, in any case, linear and chronologically ordered. Her son's diary entries offer a more precise account of the dates of their various activities in London.

49. Johanna Schopenhauer, *Sämmtliche Schriften*, XVI, 101.

50. Ibid.

51. See Virginia E. Swain, 'Lumières et Vision: Reflections on Sight and Seeing in Seventeenth- and Eighteenth-Century France', *L'Esprit Créateur*, 28.4 (1988), 5–16 (p. 9).

52. H. G. Barnes, 'Bildhafte Darstellung in den "Wahlverwandtschaften"', *Deutsche Vierteljahrsschrift für Literaturwissenschaft*, 30 (1956), 41–70 (p. 47).

53. Fried, pp. 145–60.

54. Ibid., p. 148.

55. Ibid., p. 149.

56. Johanna Schopenhauer, *Sämmtliche Schriften*, XVI, 101–02.

57. Ibid., p. 102.

58. See Johanna Schopenhauer, *Reise nach England*, ed. by Konrad Paul (Berlin: Rütten and Loening, 1982), p. 312.

59. Ibid., p. 105.

60. Ibid.

61. Ibid.

62. Ibid.

63. Johann Gottfried Herder, *Werke*, 5 vols (Berlin: Aufbau, 1969) III, 96.

64. Ibid., pp. 105–06.

65. Michael R. Booth, 'Sarah Siddons', in *Three Tragic Actresses: Siddons, Rachel, Ristori*, ed. by Michael R. Booth, John Stokes, and Susan Bassnett (Cambridge: Cambridge University Press, 1996), p. 50.

66. Johanna Schopenhauer, *Sämmtliche Schriften*, XVI, 106.

67. Ibid. p. 107.

68. Ibid.

69. Ibid.

70. See Ann Bermingham, 'The Aesthetics of Ignorance: The Accomplished Woman in the Culture of Connoisseurship', *The Oxford Art Journal*, 16 (1993), 3–20 (p. 8).

CHAPTER 6

August Hermann Niemeyer:
'Die bodenlose Tiefe der menschlichen Seele'

In 1827, the University of Halle celebrated fifty years since its former Rector and Chancellor, August Hermann Niemeyer, had been awarded his doctorate.[1] This was an opportunity to honour his varied and impressive achievements. At just twenty-one he had published the first part of his five-volume *Charakteristik der Bibel* [*Characteristics of the Bible*] (1775–94) that won him immediate academic recognition. Four years later he was made Associate Professor of Theology at the University of Halle. By thirty he was professor and co-director of the Halle orphanage. In the early 1790s he rose to the position of vice-chancellor at the University of Halle and helped to steer it through the turbulent years following the Wöllner Edict of 1788, with its harsh clampdown on the theological teachings of progressives, such as Carl Friedrich Bahrdt. Like his great-grandfather August Hermann Francke (1633–1727), Niemeyer was also one of the most active representatives of Pietist educational theory in the Germany of his day. He was appointed director of the *Franckesche Stiftungen* in 1799, becoming their 'second founder'. Three years earlier, he had published the *Grundsätze der Erziehung und des Unterrichts für Eltern, Hauslehrer und Erzieher* [*Principles of Education and Teaching for Parents, Private Tutors and Educators*] (1796), his masterpiece on education which saw eight editions during his lifetime and translations into six different languages. Deported to France in 1807 following the Prussian defeats at Jena and Auerstädt, Niemeyer returned to Germany towards the end of the year to be offered a post at the newly founded University of Berlin, which he declined (it was subsequently taken up by Wilhelm von Humboldt), preferring to stay in Halle. Following the Prussian victory at Leipzig in 1813, Niemeyer was appointed rector and chancellor of the university, posts which he held until 1816 and 1819 respectively. He then retired to travel and to write about his travels, adding more titles to his already extensive oeuvre.

Niemeyer was not just a theologian and educational theorist. He wrote poetry, dramas, travel accounts, and oratorios. As a young student at Halle in the early 1770s, his future father-in-law, Friedrich von Köpken, had introduced him to other members of the Magdeburg Mittwochgesellschaft [Wednesday Society] including Wieland, Nicolai, and Karl Wilhelm Ramler. But it was especially the odes of Klopstock, whom Niemeyer met briefly in Hamburg in 1776, that inspired the young academic to pen his own verse. Niemeyer had also been an avid reader in his youth not just of Bodmer, Haller, Kleist, and Gellert, but also of English writers (possibly in translation), such as Milton, Young, Glover, Richardson, and Hervey.[2] In July 1802 when Goethe visited the Franckesche Stiftungen, Niemeyer was translating Terence's *Andria* for him, which Goethe then adapted to form the basis for his masked drama, *Die Fremde aus Andros* [*The Stranger from Andros*].[3] Niemeyer also made Schiller's acquaintance, maintaining correspondence with him and later receiving copies of *Wallenstein, Maria Stuart* [*Mary Stuart*], and *Die Jungfrau von Orleans* [*The Maid of Orleans*] in manuscript form to read before a small audience, prior to their public performance. The highly successful salon held by Niemeyer's wife, Agnes Wilhelmine, was attended by a variety of notables, including Johann Friedrich Reichardt, Johann Christian Reil, and Friedrich Daniel Ernst Schleiermacher. Thus the Niemeyers held a commanding position in the cultural and literary life of Halle. It came as no surprise, then, that during the festivities of 1827, congratulations should flow in not just from academic quarters but also from Goethe himself.

Seven years earlier, with much less pomp, Niemeyer had paused to reflect on the previous five decades of his life. In the foreword to the *Beobachtungen auf Reisen in und außer Deutschland* [*Observations on Travels within and outside Germany*], a collection of accounts of travel through northern Germany, England, and the Netherlands, he noted that this collection of narratives was a record of 'denkwürdige Ereignisse und Zeitgenossen' [memorable events and contemporary figures] gathered over the past fifty years.[4] It placed particular emphasis on the acquaintance he had made with a series of both less and more prominent individuals, and included 'Mittheilungen dieser Art — biographische, epistolographische, historische und reflectirende, besonders über einige denkwürdige Zeitperioden [. . .], so fern ich hoffen darf, daß sie noch itzt Theilnahme wecken können' [reports of the following kinds — biographical, epistolographical, historical, and reflective, particularly on several memorable periods, to the extent that I may hope that they can still even now arouse sympathy].[5] His interest, he elaborated, was not so much in describing historical events as in attempting to relate the trials and tribulations of past figures to the present, re-reading and reinterpreting them through the lens of current thought. The role of the individual in the making of history was a subject to which Niemeyer repeatedly returned. His own barely contained euphoria at having lived through a period of momentous historical change was evidence enough of his conception of history:

> Welche Zeit ist nicht überhaupt, schon in *welthistorischer Hinsicht*, vor einem jeden vorübergangen, der fünf, ja auch nur *vier* Decennien zurückdenken kann! [. . .] Liegt nicht in den Gränzen dieser vierzig Jahre — einem Zeitraum, der in anderen Perioden der Geschichte oft so leer erscheint — eine ganze Weltgeschichte voll lauter ungeahndeter Ereignisse?[6]

> [What an era, viewed from a *world-historical perspective*, has not passed before each individual who can think back five, indeed even only *four* decades! [. . .] Within the boundaries of these forty years — a span which often seems so empty in other periods of history — does not a complete world history lie, full of events previously undreamt of?]

As Niemeyer's excitement demonstrated, 'history' was not for him the dry collation of events long gone, nor indeed a past from which nothing could be learned for the future. Rather, he viewed the past as a vibrant collection of individual lives and histories. Samuel Johnson's remark, that 'He that would travel for the entertainment of others, should remember that the great object of remark is human life', was nowhere truer than in Niemeyer's travel account of England.[7] Indeed as Niemeyer's son-in-law Professor Johann August Jacobs noted in his 1831 biography of Niemeyer: 'Für ihn bot schon eine menschliche Seele für die Beschauung eine bodenlose Tiefe: sie in ihrem Adel, in ihrer Mischung, in ihrem Irrgarten der Gefühle zu erkennen, in sie ganz zu versetzen, war ihm hohe, erbauliche Lust' [For him, even a human soul offered, on inspection, boundless depths: to uncover these in its nobility, in its mixture, its labyrinth of emotions, to project oneself completely into it, was for him a great, uplifting delight].[8] Niemeyer's professional interest lay in seeing how educational establishments, orphanages and theological institutions operated outside Germany; his private concern was with the suffering of child labourers and the reintegration into society of those in prison and other penitentiary institutions.

There were therefore both strong historical and 'human interest' aspects to Niemeyer's account of his travel to England. Having read Christian August Gottlieb Goede, Carl Gottlob Küttner, Moritz, Wendeborn, Archenholtz, Gilpin, and Johanna Schopenhauer (to whose superior knowledge on food preparation in England he quickly deferred),[9] he knew just how hard it would be to carve his own niche.[10] Its individuality, Niemeyer asserted, did not lie in dry description of buildings, portrait collections, museums, or gardens. Indeed, he was all too aware that this approach did not revivify the foreign experience in the mind's eye of the reader: 'Es läßt oft kaum die Sehnsucht zurück, selbst an Ort und Stelle gewesen zu seyn' [It rarely leaves one with a yearning to have been on the spot oneself.][11] Rather, his concern was to make events which were geographically or chronologically distant from his readers come alive in their imaginations. The immediacy of his travelogue in the *Beobachtungen* was reinforced by the diary-entry style of presentation which characterized at least the first few pages: later information was organized more generally under subject headings. Niemeyer's presentation of information this way in his travel account probably had much to do with the form that some of it had been published in previously. Between 25 September 1819 and 5 August 1820, over thirty short installments, each mostly under ten pages in length, had appeared in the *Hallisches Patriotisches Wochenblatt* [*Halle Patriotic Weekly*]. These articles, ranging thematically in a somewhat haphazard fashion from English mailboats, to Parliament, Sunday pastimes, Windsor, schooling and religion in England, Lady Jane Grey's final hours, and porter breweries, nevertheless gave the reader insights into a variety of different aspects of life, mainly in the British capital. The order in which these articles appeared was not maintained in the monograph, and footnoted cross-references to other travel accounts on England which Niemeyer added as he reorganized his material suggest that he was concerned to embed the travelogue more firmly in the established corpus of travel writing on England.

The two volumes in the *Beobachtungen* which were devoted to his travels through England were not lightweight affairs. The first, just under 400 pages in length, contained an additional appendix of some sixty pages which included 'Aufsätze, Nachträge und Erläuterungen' [Essays, Supplements, and Elucidations]. The second, complete with coloured engravings of the gowns and hoods of the academic staff and students of the universities of Cambridge and Oxford, numbered some 460 pages. The opening to Niemeyer's travels in England saw him bowling up to London from Harwich on 15 June 1819; the close of the second volume described him preparing to depart for Hamburg on 5 August that same year. Given that he stayed in the country for not much more than one and a half months, Niemeyer's account was a particularly detailed and wide-ranging collation of descriptions, conclusions, and reflections. Its content was not strikingly unusual: the account recorded the standard sights of Westminster Abbey, St Paul's, and the Tower, as well as Newgate Prison and the King's Bench, Magdalen Hospital, and other charitable institutions. Thematically it concerned itself with education, religion, and the justice system. Socially, it vaunted meetings with celebrities of the day such as Herschel or Banks and marvelled at the talents of Siddons. Geographically though, it was limited, like so many travelogues on England of the period, to being chiefly an account of the capital with only brief forays out to Woodstock and Blenheim, Oxford and Cambridge.

Research on Niemeyer has focused primarily on his pedagogical and religious writings, while little attention has been paid to the style or rhetoric of his travel writing. Yet his account of travel to England was more than the dry enumeration of fact and a light revision or minor expansion of the brief handwritten notes made on his travels. It was a text consciously constructed to engage his readers affectively by allowing them to gain some understanding, through the inclusion of cameo portraits of the sufferings of both contemporary and historically situated individuals. This chapter begins by exploring how Niemeyer wove descriptions of unfortunates such as prostitutes and child-labourers, notably chimney sweeps, into his account and to which ends. In a second section, it examines how historical figures, particularly those whose fate was bound up with the Tower, were drawn into his travel narrative. It asks what they contributed to his travelogue in rhetorical terms and how they shaped the resulting picture of life in Britain. Finally, it discusses Niemeyer's own reservations regarding the use of sympathy and sensibility, as well as his responses to their deployment in the works of other travel writers on England.

'Ein Jammeranblick': London's Chimney Sweeps and Prostitutes

Scarcely ten pages after Niemeyer had enthusiastically recorded his arrival in Britain's capital, he was marvelling at the 'panorama' of the large crowds passing to and fro. The magnificence of this spectacle momentarily overshadowed, though, a less attractive reality — children on the streets begging for money or work. The black faces of the chimney sweeps stood in particularly stark contrast to the other passers-by:

> Es ist ein Jammeranblick, wenn man die sieben- bis achtjährigen Knäbchen (vielleicht selbst Mädchen), an denen nichts *weiß* ist als etwa das Auge, die Borstbesen in der Hand, einen Sack auf der Schulter, eine schwarze Binde um den Kopf, ihr kläglich tönendes Sweep! (Kehren!) ausrufen, oder in kleinen

> Gassen aus den Kellern elender Häuser, wo sie die Nacht zubringen, wie aus
> einem unterirdischen Nest, die kleinen Mohrenköpfe herausstecken und nach
> Luft schnappen sieht.[12]

> [It is a wretched sight to see the seven- to eight-year-old boys (perhaps even
> girls) who have no *white* on them except in their eyes, brush in hand, a sack
> over their shoulder, a black scarf around their head, calling out their pitiful-
> sounding 'Sweep!', or to see in small alleys or the cellars of awful houses where
> they spend the night, their small blackamoor heads poking out, as if from an
> underground nest, gasping for air.]

Niemeyer's description of the chimney sweeps likens them at the same time both
to exotic, foreign beings and to animals, emerging from their underground holes.
Such dehumanizing images appear to distance both observer and reader from these
exploited individuals: any pity that is encouraged derives precisely from the fact that
they are no longer treated as human beings. Indeed, Niemeyer goes on to insert
them into a broader, more general, enumeration of unpleasant figures such as rag
merchants, cat's meat sellers, and street sweepers who remove dirt and excrement
from the footpaths. While philanthropists had continually tried to improve
conditions for these people, he observes rather flatly, it has brought the poor little
comfort. Niemeyer emphasizes time and again his concern 'mich mit möglichst
vielen und den verschiedenartigsten Menschen aus allen Ständen zu berühren' [to
come into contact with as many people of the most different kinds from all classes]
and does not fail to visit the poorer areas of the City, Southwark and St Giles, in
a quest to view British society from as many different angles as possible.[13] Yet the
sheer number and diversity of impoverished figures he observes are such that his
powers of representation are pushed to their limits: 'Aber die Figuren sind doch zu
viel, um ein so großes Gemählde ganz genau ausführen und vollenden zu können'
[But the figures are too many that such a large-scale painting could be undertaken
and completed with great precision].[14] Indeed, he argues, it would require the
combined talents of the painters Angelika Kaufmann and Teniers (whether the
Elder or the Younger was unclear), and the caricaturists Hogarth and Thomas
Rowlandson, to convey accurately all that he has seen.

In the second volume of the *Beobachtungen*, Niemeyer is reminded of the chimney
sweeps again when he draws up a section on squares in London. Lord Montagu,
whose house was located in Portman Square, would give a free meal to the chimney
sweeps once a year — a practice not likely to be continued now that he had
died.[15] This time, Niemeyer devotes almost ten pages to the fate of these children,
analysing the dangerous nature of their work in a detail which made their suffering
far harder to ignore:

> Natürlich ist der zarte Körper der Kinder bey diesen gewaltsamen Operationen
> den empfindlichsten Beschädigungen ausgesetzt, und sehr häufig sind sie mit
> Quetschungen, Geschwüren, offenen Wunden und Brandschäden, besonders
> an Beinen, Knieen und Ellenbogen bedeckt [. . .].[16]

> [The delicate bodies of these children are, of course, exposed to the most
> severe injuries during these forced activities, and very often they are covered
> in bruises, ulcers, open wounds, and burns, particularly on the legs, knees, and
> elbows]

By enumerating the various injuries which these children suffered, he not only brought home to the reader how dangerous their work was. He also sought to evoke readerly sympathy through this detailed analysis of the injuries they suffered. While Niemeyer was of course concerned with the plight of the poor, his preoccupation with the chimney sweeps suggests that they were a powerful symbol for him less of poverty than of the misuse of children in the (adult) world of work.

Women, like children, were also subjects open to potential exploitation by society, a fact to which Niemeyer constantly returned. London's Magdalen Hospital, a kind of asylum set up in 1758 to remove penitent prostitutes from the streets, teach them moral discipline, and then find them a situation, was an institution which was naturally of great interest to Niemeyer. He was quick to affirm his non-judgemental stance towards the Magdalen Hospital's inmates:

> [Es] bleibt [. . .] auch der schreyendste Widerspruch, daß in den Urtheilen dieser Welt, die ganze Last der Schande auf den schwächen, in den meisten Fällen Anfangs nicht verführenden sondern verführten Theil zurückfällt [. . .].[17]

> [[It] remains [. . .] the most glaring contradiction that in the judgements of this world the whole burden of shame should fall on the weak party, who in most cases was not initially the seducer but the seduced]

While the men 'geck und triumphirend' [foppish and triumphant] can go their own way, the women are 'in ihrem ganzen Wesen zerstört, ohne Hülfe, ohne Rettung, selbst ohne den Throst des Mitleids' [destroyed to the very core of their being, without help, salvation, even without the consolation of sympathy].[18] Hogarth's *Harlot's Progress*, Niemeyer remarked, well described the situation in which many guileless young women found themselves on arrival from the provinces in London.[19] Thus while Niemeyer must have ultimately deplored these women's profession as immoral, the prevailing image we have from him is that of the prostitute as victim. The debauched life in the capital, the wicked designs of men and indeed society in general were to blame for the fate of such women. In the spirit of the Enlightenment, Niemeyer therefore saw this problem not as a private issue of sin and atonement but as a social problem that required public action. The first step on the road to public engagement with the problem was simply human concern: 'So viel vermag *reines Interesse auch für die gesunkene Menschheit*, so viel *durch Menschenliebe thätig werdende* Frömmigkeit' [*Pure interest shown towards sunken humanity, piousness activated by a love of mankind*, are capable of so much].[20] Thus Niemeyer's concern for these prostitutes embodied the optimism that their rehabilitation into society was not an impossibility: instead he supported wholeheartedly the creation of institutional solutions to this problem.

Instead of merely describing the situations in which such women found themselves, their own backgrounds or life histories, Niemeyer used the medium of the letter to inject a certain sense of authenticity into his account: 'Nicht ohne Rührung kann man die dankbaren Briefe lesen, welche die Entlassenen, die in ihre Familien zurückgekehrt oder in Dienste getreten sind, an die Vorsteher des Hauses schreiben' [One cannot read without being moved the grateful letters to the governor of the institution written by those who have been discharged, who have returned to their families or gone into service].[21] These letters served not only to authenticate Niemeyer's account by affirmingly categorically that he had indeed visited Magdalen Hospital, but also to reinforce his status as a sentient individual. By giving the initials of the correspondent and the date of the letter, it seemed beyond doubt that he was recording what he had seen with his own eyes:

> So schrieb eine S. M. an die Aufseherin unter dem 6. Februar 1818:
> Ich wage es itzt, Sie durch diese Zeilen zu bitten, allen den ehrwürdigen Damen zu bezeugen, wie hoch ich mich ihnen für alle die Güte verpflichtet fühle, die ich unter ihnen wo unverdient genoß, um der Gesellschaft der Tugendhaften wieder zurückgegeben zu werden.[22]

> [Thus wrote one S. M. to the warder on 6 February 1818:
> I am now venturing to ask you in these lines to demonstrate to the honorable ladies how obliged I feel to them for all the unmerited kindness which I enjoyed in your care, so that I might be returned to the society of the virtuous.]

The letter therefore opened with a formal show of gratitude by the prisoner, now reintegrated into society, who was looking back on her stay in this institution and could appreciate the worth of the values and codes it instilled in her. But then the style of the letter changed:

> Aber auch itzt fehlt es mir an Worten für meine Empfindung. Meine Augen sind voll Thränen und ich kann nur sagen: Lobe den Herrn meine Seele! [. . .] Möge Gott seine höchsten Segnungen über alle verbreiten, welche dieses wohlthätige Haus verwalten. Das ist mein tägliches Gebet. Ich fürchte nur, ich mißbrauche Ihre Geduld; aber mein Herz — ach! es ist zu voll, daß ich nicht aufhören möchte zu schreiben.[23]

> [But now once again I am lacking the words to describe my emotions. My eyes are full of tears and I can only say: Let my soul praise the Lord! [. . .] May God distribute his greatest blessings across all those who run this charitable house. This is my daily prayer. I only fear that I am trying your patience; but my heart — oh! It is too full, so that I do not want to cease writing.]

Here, then, the letter takes recourse to the topos of inexpressibility, key to the discourse of sentimentality. As the tears flowed and heartfelt thanks poured out, the letter sought to appeal to the reader's emotions directly through an open show of emotion. Its subservient tone did not, admittedly, set it on the same level as the high drama and tragedy in the historical scenes that Niemeyer portrayed later on in his *Beobachtungen*. But it was nevertheless a valuable demonstration that Niemeyer's chief concern was with the individual's response to extreme tribulation.

'Der Sieg der Kraft über das Leiden'

Niemeyer's account focused not only on the suffering of lesser individuals but also on the more famous. Unlike Moritz, he failed to find Parliament a particularly interesting source of material and moved swiftly on to the Tower. In contrast to other visitors, he was not there to be impressed by the crown jewels, weapons, or the wild animals housed in its menagerie. Rather it was the historical significance of the place that affected him most : 'So oft hatte ich mich in diese alte *Zeit* versetzt; itzt stand ich auf dem *Schauplatz* wo [diese Begebenheiten] vorgegangen waren' [Time and again I transported myself into this bygone *age*; now I was standing on the *stage* where [these events] had taken place].[24] Thus the 'theatre' of history was not merely conceived as a reliving of historical events but as an engaging spectacle in which the observers themselves became actors, drawn into the historical discourse. At Traitors' Gate, Niemeyer suggested that it was enough to stand on that very spot to be able to call to mind rich and vivid scenes from British (literary) history:

> Ein mit der Geschichte vertrauter Wegweiser könnte, sobald er einen Kreis von Zuhörern fände, [. . .] viele Tage zubringen, um ihnen an Ort und Stelle alle die Scenen zu vergegenwärtigen, bey denen man schon bey dem Lesen derselben in *Burnet, Hume* oder *Shakespeare*, von dem mannigfachsten Wechsel der Gefühle, bald der sanften Rührung, bald des empörten Hasses der Tyranney verweilt.[25]

> [A guide who is familiar with history could, as soon as he has found a circle of listeners, [. . .] spend many days recalling on the very spots all the scenes over which one lingers while reading them in *Burnet, Hume* or *Shakespeare*, the most diverse exchanges of feeling, one moment tender emotion, the next the indignant hatred of tyranny.]

Thus historical sites functioned as emotional *Erinnerungsorte* for him through the power of associationalism. Inspired perhaps by Hume, who himself was not averse to showing virtue in distress and evoking scenes of sentimental sympathy in his historical writing, Niemeyer sketched in the extremes that emotion could range across to reinforce the harrowing nature of the scenes which he aimed to make so vivid in his mind's eye, while closer descriptions were to follow.[26]

It was really within the Tower, the site which prompted his narration of the final days of Anne Boleyn, Jane Grey, and Mary, Queen of Scots, that Niemeyer began to offer his most detailed sympathetic portraits of historical individuals. It was the private grief and the personal suffering of these individuals, which had failed to gain a foothold in the annals of history, that appeared to move him most. Primarily concerned with factual detail, historical writing did not seem programmed to accommodate the less easily definable turbulence of emotions that powered human action: 'Von vielen der Schlachtopfer wilder und fanatischer Leidenschaften, hat die Geschichte nur im allgemeinen die Umrisse ihres Schicksals aufbewahrt' [History has only preserved the general outlines of the fates of many of the victims of wild and incredible passions].[27] To Niemeyer, then, it appeared that historical writing did not care for personal detail. Like any genre it was necessarily selective in the information that it presented and omitted. But in its canonization of certain figures, it repeatedly concentrated on particular aspects of their character or actions, gradually 'losing' to the passing of time other facets and features of their lives.

Niemeyer singled out two particular cases which he suggested would touch even the most cold-hearted: acts of tyranny against the young and against women. Perhaps for this reason he chose three queens on whom to focus in his travel account, well knowing that the Tower had also been the final home to a series of high-ranking male historical figures, not least the so-called 'Princes in the Tower', the young Edward V, and Richard, Duke of York.[28] But his interest in the three queens was not only fired by their historical or dramatic qualities. As he had noted in the introduction to the *Beobachtungen*, he was concerned to relate past to present. This historical section in his travel account

> bietet zugleich eine so natürliche Gelegenheit dar, längst vergangene Zeit mit der Gegenwart zu vergleichen, wo in demselben Lande, welches der Schauplatz der fürchterlichsten Willkühr der Herrscher war, wieder eine Königin, ihrem Gemahl und dem Parlament gegenüber, zu einem Kampfe über *Schuld* und *Unschuld* in den Schranken steht.[29]

> [offers at the same time such a natural opportunity to compare an era long gone with the present, where in the same country that saw scenes of the most dreadful despotism amongst its rulers, once more a queen is being challenged to a fight over *guilt* and *innocence* by her husband and parliament.]

This was more than an oblique reference to George IV's treatment of his wife, Caroline of Brunswick. Married in 1795 to this rather unattractive, noisy German woman, George was trying by 1806 to rid himself of her by claiming that she had given birth to an illegitimate child. Parliament was not in favour of his request for divorce. In 1814 he banned her from court and eventually she left England for the Continent, taking with her the support of the people of Britain. When George III died in 1820, the problem became acute, because it now meant that Caroline would be crowned queen. In July 1820, Caroline was cleared of the adultery charges, although a year later her husband barred her entry to the coronation in Westminster Abbey. This mistreatment of a female member of royalty at the hands of a tyrannical head of state found valuable parallels in British history, which Niemeyer found interesting to explore further.

Of the three women on whom he focused, it was Lady Jane Grey whom he considered the most worthy of our sympathy: the quality of her innocence and of her moral behaviour we should see as attractive; the exploitation of her virtue should offend us. Mary, Queen of Scots, had so often slipped from virtue — here he was perhaps thinking of her alleged involvement in her first husband's murder — that we should not want to engage with her emotionally. Indeed, he makes only the briefest of references to her. At first sight, this seems odd, since she was one of the most studied women in history. But perhaps Niemeyer felt, after the publication of numerous works on her — not least Christian Heinrich Spiess's 1784 sentimental play *Marie Stuart* and Schiller's *Maria Stuart* (1800), as well as further public debate in the eighteenth century about the authenticity of her letters[30] — that there was little more to be said within the context of his travel account. Schiller's concern had been less with historical truth, describing the process of writing *Maria Stuart* in a letter to Goethe in 1799 as slow since it required effort to give the imagination free rein over history.[31] Niemeyer, in an article about her in *Geschichte und Politik* (1802), based on John Whitaker's *Mary Queen of Scots Vindicated* (1788), had been more interested in focusing on the psychological development of the two queens, Mary and Elizabeth, as a means to understanding their actions better.

If shelves were filling with tracts arguing for and against the authenticity of Mary's self-incriminating letters and papers, Niemeyer sensed that the spotlight might better be turned on Anne Boleyn and Jane Grey, whose letters had not been subject to this same tug-of-war between political historians. As he stood in the Tower, he noted:

> Seit ich in der Nähe ihrer letzten Kerker und ihrer längst eingesunkenen Gräber stand, ist ihr Bild nur noch lebendiger vor meine Seele getreten, und hat mich veranlaßt, in den zuverlässigsten Quellen den kleinsten Umständen der Geschichte ihrer letzten Tage noch einmal nachzuforschen.[32]

> [Since I was near her last place of emprisonment and her graves which have long ago caved in, the picture of her has only become more vivid in my mind and has caused me to research the most minute details of the story of her last days in the most reliable sources.]

He envisaged his discussion of the lives of these two queens not only as an exercise in better understanding the psychological motivations underlying power politics. He also viewed it as a reflection upon the period under Henry VIII's rule: 'ein Bild der Verderbniß seiner Zeit, des kriechenden Gehorsams der Parlamente, der Gesunkenheit eines freyen Volks' [a picture of the depravity of his time, the crawling obedience of the parliaments, the submission of a free people].[33] None of Henry VIII's wives elicited more sympathy, Niemeyer suggested, than Anne Boleyn. Woven into his description of her last months is his translation of her letter of 6 May 1536 to Henry VIII in which she laments her fall from royal grace and considers her own imprisonment outrageous.[34] In his *Charakteristik der Bibel*, Niemeyer had demonstrated his concern to gain an understanding of individual experience through an historical and philological form of Bible criticism. There he had stressed the importance of capturing a subject's voice as a way of delineating their character. What is unique to each of us, he argued, is our mode of thinking, acting, speaking, and writing.[35] To offer a reassessment of Biblical figures according to their characteristics and mannerisms would therefore give us greater insight into why they acted as they did. Oral testimonies would greatly enhance the authenticity of the piece:

> Erzählungen, oder eigne Reden der Personen, welche wir zeichnen wollen, sind die eigentlichen Hülfsmittel. Die letzten würden noch dazu durch ihre Umschreibung oder Veränderung sehr oft verlieren, da sie zuweilen *bis auf den Ausdruck* charakteristisch sind. Denn eben durch unsre Reden pflegen wir unsern Charakter am genauesten abzumahlen.[36]

> [Narratives about, or speeches by the people themselves, whom we wish to portray, are our real aids. Moreover, the latter would lose much through paraphrase or alteration, because they are in places characteristic *right down to the very expression* of the speaker in question. Since it is precisely through our speech that we tend to paint our character most exactly.]

Writing in the same tradition as Moritz, Niemeyer had realized that to give an authentic account of an individual was not necessarily to describe them in great detail, but rather to grasp something of their character. In focusing on the medium of speech as encapsulating an individual's manner, Niemeyer showed a keen awareness of the rhetorical devices which could be used to create a sense that this was indeed a true representation of the individual in question.

In the *Beobachtungen* his use of epistolarity served a similar purpose. It allowed

Anne Boleyn to 'speak' on the page in an apparently intimate communication between her and her husband. This was a highly emotive vehicle for narrative which appeared to give direct access to interior feeling. Niemeyer was above all concerned to show the psychological pressure she suffered in the period between her imprisonment and her actual execution. He opens by stressing her human frailty, mentally and physically, in the face of uncertainty:

> Anfangs, als sie der Schlag so ganz unvorbereitet getroffen hatte, und sie noch in der grausamsten Ungewißheit über ihr Schicksal schwebte, litt Körper und Seele in gleichem Grade. Sie fiel oft in Krämpfe und Zückungen, und eine Ueberspannung, die sich bald durch lautes Weinen, bald durch unnatürliches Lachen äußerte [. . .][37]

> [Initially, when the blow hit her so unexpectedly and she was still suffering the most dreadful uncertainties about her fate, body and soul suffered to the same degree. She often had cramps and convulsions, and hysteria, which expressed itself sometimes through loud crying, sometimes unnatural laughter]

Niemeyer does not attempt to describe her mental suffering directly. Rather, the physiological effects which he portrays are representative of the psychological torture which she is undergoing. Her body 'speaks' for her mind. At the passing of sentence, though, Niemeyer puts direct speech into her mouth: 'O mein Vater, o mein Schöpfer, und du, der du bist der Weg, die Wahrheit und das Leben. Du weißt, daß ich dieses Schicksal nicht verdient habe!' [O my father, O my creator, and you, you who are the way, the truth, and the life. You know that I have not earned this fate!].[38] On returning to Anne's prison cell, Niemeyer does not fail to note how she is still capable of offering this feisty retort to the King:

> Aus einem unbedeutenden Fräulein erhoben Sie mich zur Gräfin; dann zur Königin; und nun da Sie mich in dieser Welt auf keine höhere Stufe stellen können, zur Märtyrerkrone im Himmel.[39]

> [From an insignificant woman, you raised me to countess; then to queen; and then, since you could not give me a higher rank in this world, to a martyr's crown in heaven.]

As he describes her walk to the scaffold, Niemeyer again refers back to the actual words that she is supposed to have spoken to capture the drama of the moment. Parts are given in quotation marks and in the subjunctive, 'das Gericht habe sie verdammt, dem müsse sie sich unterwerfen' [the court of law had apparently damned her, she would have to submit to it].[40] But her call 'Christo befehl' ich meinen Geist' [I commend my soul to Christ] as she lays her head on the block is given in direct speech before the axe falls. Set against the inherent drama of this situation is the removal of her corpse in a plain box, and the swift interment of her body before midday. Niemeyer's description closes with the dryly informative remark that Henry VIII then married Jane Seymour the next day.[41] That he should consider Anne Boleyn's story appropriate subject matter for Ernst von Houwald, writer of the sentimental tragedies *Das Bild*, *Die Heimkehr* and *Der Leuchtturm* [*The Picture, The Homecoming, The Lighthouse*] (1821), suggests that her biography was well suited to dramatic staging.[42] But Niemeyer's repeated comment that it 'erinnert itzt die Geschichte einer Königin unsrer Zeit' [reminds us of the history of a queen in our time] also indicated that what underpinned its tragedy were human passions, desires, and ambitions that continued to trouble the monarchy in a similar fashion almost three hundred years on.

Of the three queens in question, Jane Grey most evoked sympathy, prized above all for her purity, innocence, and high morals. As Niemeyer also noted, in other historical accounts Jane Grey appeared 'fast als ein Ideal weiblicher Schönheit, fleckenloser Tugend und einer ganz seltnen Geistesbildung' [almost an ideal of female beauty, unblemished virtue, and a most rare intellect].[43] The problem with this flawless presentation of Jane Grey's character was one with which both Nicholas Rowe and Wieland had grappled, and, arguably, one on which both had come unstuck. Rowe's *Lady Jane Gray*, first performed in 1715, disappointed both its critics and its audiences.[44] Jane Grey was presented as a martyr figure whose spotless virtue set her above human frailty, thereby rendering it well-nigh impossible for an audience to show real sympathy for a character apparently so far above ordinary weakness or emotion. Too innocent and virtuous to be truly credible, she showed no spectrum of emotions, only interminable grief. Niemeyer's comments in the *Beobachtungen* that Wieland's 'Lady Johanna' was too uniform suggested that he considered this dramatist to have fallen into the same trap.[45] Lessing certainly thought so. In his critique of Wieland's drama *Lady Johanna Gray*, first performed in Winterthur in July 1758, he savagely criticised the drama. In the sixty-third *Literaturbrief*, written in October 1759, he viciously attacked Wieland's notion of tragedy for being solely concerned with 'das Größe, Schöne und Heroische der Tugend auf die rührendste Art vorzustellen' [portraying great, beautiful, and heroic aspects of virtue in the most moving fashion].[46] This was all well and good, he noted, if each character involved was a moral being, but what of those who were evil? Lessing argued that it was precisely this combination of good and evil that made characters appear to be complex, lifelike, authentic individuals. Furthermore, he objected to the way in which Wieland had manipulated historical events, and had paced this work so that the real drama of Jane Grey's situation was not played out to full effect. Wieland had placed the heroine, Lady Jane Grey, in the centre of the action, constructing his play in such a way that its dramatic effect should derive from the sympathy that the audience had with her. The difficulty with this lay in the fact that there were no real internal tensions presented to the audience which would invite their interest in her soul-searching.

Niemeyer was less interested in according these queens a particularly British identity. True, he felt that they were part and parcel of the historical heritage of the British nation, and it was their lives and histories that were evoked by sites in London. But his final comment, before moving on in the main body of his travel account to examine statistics concerning the number of people living in Britain and its colonies, demonstrated that he still saw them as individuals in their own right, divorced even from the factual framework of history:

> Das Leben und das Ende dieser königlichen Frauen ging noch einmal vor mir vorüber. Welche von ihnen, aus dem *moralischen* Standpunct aufgefaßt, die gerechtesten Ansprüche an unsre Theilnahme habe, konnte nicht zweifelhaft seyn. Aber jede von ihnen ist auch von *dramatischen* Dichtern zur Heldin

gewählt; wie von *J. Banks* die *Anna Boleyn*; *Johanna Gray* von *Rowe* und *Wieland*; von unserm großen Zeitgenossen die *Maria Stuart*. Dacht' ich sie mir aus diesem Gesichtspuncte, so änderte sich die Ansicht; es könne, schien es mir, nur zwischen *Anna* und *Maria* die Entscheidung des *Dramaturgen* schwanken.[47]

[The lives and deaths of these royal women went through my mind once more. There was no doubt about which of them, from a *moral* standpoint, laid the most justified claim to our sympathy. But each of them has also been chosen as a heroine by *dramatic* poets; *Anne Boleyn* by *J. Banks*; *Jane Gray* [sic] by *Rowe* and *Wieland*; *Mary Stuart* by our great contemporary. If I considered them from this point of view, my opinion would change; the *dramatist's* decision could only waver, so it seems to me, between *Anne* and *Mary*.]

In sum, he was more concerned with the quality of their moral actions and decisions and their ability to evoke in us a sense of sympathy, than in their status as key figures in the political history of Britain.

The appendix to this first volume of the *Beobachtungen* allowed Niemeyer to continue his musings on the tragic nature of the fates of several of Henry VIII's wives. The very inclusion of this appendix is unusual, particularly since it is one that does not include factual information such as tables and charts relating to a country's trade and industry, or routes and maps that one might have expected in a travel account. Entitled 'Maria Stuart, Anna Boleyn, Johanna Grey, aus dem Standpunkt der dramatischen Poesie' [Mary Stuart, Anne Boleyn, Jane Grey, from the Standpoint of Dramatic Poetry], this appendix assessed which of these three historical figures might best serve the purposes of tragic drama.[48] The decision to include this appendix is one which Niemeyer may have borrowed from Hume's *History of England*, which he certainly knew. Hume's work also contained appendices which, as Mark Salber Phillips has observed, were similar in terms of content to the main text, but took on quite a different narrative form and therefore offered a different angle on the same material.[49] In the appendix, Niemeyer noted that by combing a nation's history, a rich crop of potentially tragic situations could be harvested.[50] Steadfastness in the face of suffering was particularly what rendered the actions of a great figure grappling with fate particularly tragic:

Wenn die tragische Handlung durch den *Sieg der Kraft über das Leiden* ästhetisch wird, so ist auch dieß bey allen dreyen der Fall, da es sogar schwer zu bestimmen ist, welche dieser hohen Frauen, sofern man der Geschichte glauben darf, vor und in dem entscheidenden Moment am meisten Muth und Standhaftigkeit gezeigt habe.[51]

[When tragic action is rendered aesthetic through the *victory of strength over suffering*, then for all three this is the case, since it is even difficult to determine which of these high-ranking women — to the extent that we may believe history — showed the most courage and steadfastness before and during the decisive moment.]

But in adding the proviso 'sofern man der Geschichte glauben darf', Niemeyer gave a cautious reminder that the 'facts' of history — so hotly debated with regard to the authenticity of letters attributed to Mary, Queen of Scots — were not necessarily clear-cut. Nevertheless it revealed Niemeyer's concern to remain faithful to the 'truth', such as could be determined, rather than departing from fact in an attempt to exaggerate the tragedy of the individual's situation.

The essence of tragedy should lie quite simply in the constellation of events and circumstances and in the network of given relationships, he argued. As such no further embellishment of the plot was required on the part of the dramatist: if deepest sympathy, fear, compassion, hatred, and love were the levers of tragic drama, Niemeyer commented, then simply reading the history of the event would already suffice to move us, and art would scarcely need to do more.[52] Our imagination was potentially powerful enough to conjure up for us in our mind's eye the events narrated in a prose description. We did not necessarily need to see them performed on stage to comprehend the essential tragedy of the situation. Moreover, the tragedy of a given situation did not arise solely from the moral conflict to which the protagonist was subjected:

> Aber das Interesse, das wir an einem menschlichen Charakter und einem menschlichen Schicksal nehmen, geht nicht *allein* von dem *sittlichen* Werth der handelnden Personen aus. Das Leiden tragischer Helden und Heldinnen kann auch ein selbstgeschaffnes und verschuldetes seyn, und es kann sich dabey dennoch eine hohe menschliche Kraft zeigen, die uns Theilnahme und selbst Bewunderung abzwingt.[53]

> [But the interest which arises from a human character and human fate does not *solely* derive from the *moral* value of the acting figure. The suffering of tragic heroes and heroines can also be self-incurred and self-inflicted, and yet it can also demonstrate great human strength, which exacts sympathy and even admiration from us.]

A tragic situation could also be brought about by the motivations and actions of the protagonists themselves. Tragedy could be engendered by the respect that the audience accorded the suffering individual. But it could also be elicited in the reader or observer of tragic actions not simply by viewing the behaviour of a heroic individual but also by recognizing our own weaknesses.[54] In projecting ourselves into their position and finding that we would fall short — that we would equally be subject to the same temptations — this was also a way of engaging our sympathies. The psychologist, the *Seelenmahler*, as Niemeyer termed him, played a significant role in newer forms of tragedy. For the modern dramatist it was important to look from a perspective other than that of the 'bloße Sittenlehrer' [mere moralist]: even if moral codes still determined how we valued character, the psychological suffering that the protagonist underwent was increasingly what interested a nineteenth-century audience.[55]

Sympathetic Identification and *Empfindeley*

'Sympathie', as Niemeyer had broadly defined it in the *Grundsätze der Erziehung*, 'nennt man die bekannte Einrichtung der Natur, wonach das Gewahrwerden teils körperlicher, teils geistiger Zustände in anderen ähnliche Zustände in uns hervorbringt' [sympathy is what one calls the familiar provision made by nature in which the awareness of partly bodily, partly mental, states in others generates similar conditions in ourselves].[56] The predisposition for sympathy, he added, promised an individual's development into a benevolent character and pointed to a goodness of heart.[57] Too great a leaning towards sympathy tended towards *Empfindeley*; too little signified hardness of character.[58] In the earliest phase of his literary production, he was unashamedly influenced by the works of Klopstock. Niemeyer's poetry (particularly his *Ode an Klopstock* [*Ode to Klopstock*]) and religious dramas (*Abraham, Lazarus, Thirza und ihre Söhne* [*Thirza and her Sons*], and *Mehala*) openly acknowledged a debt to his great master. But as Christian Soboth has demonstrated, Niemeyer's adoration of Klopstock began to wane in the period between 1784 and 1785: such shows of passionate emotion now ill befitted the freshly appointed Professor of Theology, and co-director of the Halle orphanage.[59] By 1803 he admitted in the *Briefe an christliche Religionslehrer* [*Letters to Christian Religious Teachers*] that his earlier fascination with Klopstock retrospectively awakened in him only 'unangenehme Empfindungen' [unpleasant emotions].[60]

Perhaps it was for this reason that Niemeyer was rather touchy about the success of Moritz's account with the British public. He certainly voiced consternation at the popularity of Moritz's picturesque description of the scene around Richmond. This had come to embody for both English and foreign readers the idyllic English landscape, the harmony of nature and art which it emphasized transporting the viewer into a different realm.[61] Niemeyer commented:

> Wirklich merkwürdig ists, daß man die ganze Stelle aus *Moritz* Reisen, ins Englische übersetzt und sogar in die [. . .] *Picture of London* aufgenommen hat. Dadurch ist *Moritz* Namen Unzähligen, die dieß jedes Jahr neu erscheinende Buch benutzen, bekannt geworden, indeß man von vielen unsrer Classiker nichts weiß.[62]

> [It is really odd that the whole passage from *Moritz's* travels has been translated into English and even incorporated into the [. . .] *Picture of London*. As a result, *Moritz's* name has become familiar to countless people who use this book which appears in a new edition each year, while nothing is known of many of our classic authors.]

Given that Niemeyer had himself enthused of Richmond that nature, or rather its creator, had built a magnificent temple there 'in welchem jede fühlende Brust zu einer heitern Andacht begeistert werden muß' [in which every sentient breast must be inspired to joyous devotion], it seems rather inconsistent that he should be so critical of the inclusion of this whole passage from Moritz's account in the *Picture of London*. Perhaps, though, he was really more irritated by the canonical status which Moritz had acquired as a commentator on England: a status which appeared to put all subsequent writings in the shade.

Johanna Schopenhauer, while treated generally with great respect by Niemeyer in the *Beobachtungen*, also briefly came in for criticism. In her description of the statue of Händel in Poets' Corner in Westminster Abbey, she had been at pains to describe the posture of the great composer at work penning the *Messiah*. Niemeyer quoted that she 'läßt ihn "sitzend schreiben und aufhorchen, um die Melodie der Sphären auf dem Papier festzuhalten"' [has him 'sitting writing and listening attentively, in order to catch the melody of the spheres on paper'].[63] However,

Niemeyer cut through this rather romanticizing description of Händel by noting flatly that there was no evidence whatsoever for him adopting either a sitting position or writing. As a result, Schopenhauer's suggestions that he was presented as listening to the music of the spheres seemed at best fanciful and sentimentalized, at worst calling her authority as a spectator into doubt.[64] These criticisms give us a close indication of the priorities which Niemeyer set in travel writing: that it should first and foremost be an accurate recording of what the traveller had witnessed, and that sentimental description, while important, occupied a supplementary rather than a superior role.

In his account of travel to England, Niemeyer therefore demonstrated that biography had become a prime vehicle for the evocation of the vibrancy of another place and age. It was a valuable means by which to awaken and stimulate the reader's sensibility through its portrayal of individual human experience. The biographical approach which he adopted focused both on semi-anonymous figures (the chimney sweeps, the 'S.M'. of the letter to the directors of Magdalen Hospital) and on key individuals in British history (Anne Boleyn, Jane Grey). The confrontation between the spectator and the sufferer in the scenes of the sweeps or the penitentiary raised a series of questions about the moral relationship between viewer and viewed. Here, one suspects that in Niemeyer's account the travel writer and reader do not wholly participate in that process of 'affective projection' where the sufferer is replaced by the spectator's (and reader's) own image. Rather, it was social difference — and the authority and power which people like Niemeyer commanded to alleviate the suffering of the poor — that was played out here as a motivator for change.

Niemeyer was explicitly preoccupied with the experiences of compassion, pity, and identification not just in the realm of 'life' but also in 'art'. Indeed, at times it seems as if there is no real definition of the differences between the respective referents of history, biography, or travel writing in his work. This reinforces the fact that other non-fictional genres, especially historical writing, had also witnessed a shift away from the systematic recording of fact towards an interest in what moved and motivated the people who were implicitly also the subjects of its study. Thus the human mind took centre stage as audiences became less concerned with deeds and actions, and more focused on an individual's inward life and perception. Central to Niemeyer's travelogue is the issue of how sympathy can be mobilized and how both other figures in the text and we as readers respond when faced with the spectacle of tragedy, suffering, and accident. While Niemeyer was keen to revivify dramatic episodes from Britain's past, his demonstration of the universal and specific relevance of past events for British politics and the monarchy in the 1820s did not go unstressed. Thus sympathy fuelled a fascination with the dramatic and the tragic that clearly shaped Niemeyer's 'reading' both of contemporary issues and of the broader cultural and architectural heritage of England.

Notes to Chapter 6

1. The background to Niemeyer's life and work draws in part on information given in the exhibition 'Licht und Schatten: August Hermann Niemeyer. Ein Leben an der Epochenwende um 1800', held between 23 May and 7 November 2004 at the Franckesche Stiftungen zu Halle, and the exhibition catalogue edited by Brigitte Klosterberg (Halle: Verlag der Franckeschen Stiftungen, 2004). I would also like to thank the organizers and participants of the conference '"Seyd nicht träge in dem was ihr thun sollt." Zu Leben und Werk August Hermann Niemeyers (1754–1828)', Franckesche Stiftungen zu Halle, 17–19 June 2004. My attendance at this conference helped me substantially in writing this chapter.

2. August Hermann Niemeyer, *Beobachtungen auf Reisen in und außer Deutschland. Nebst Erinnerungen an denkwürdige Lebenserfahrungen und Zeitgenossen in den letzten fünfzig Jahren*, 4 vols (1820–26), I (1820), 5.

3. This was later performed, albeit with limited critical acclaim, in the Lauchstädter Theater in the summer of 1803. See Schiller's letter of 4 July 1803 to his wife: 'Die Fremde aus Andros, welche gleich in den ersten Wochen hier gegeben worden, hat nichts getan, und es ist am Schluß sogar von einigen gepfiffen worden' [*The Stranger from Andros*, which was performed here in the very first few weeks, has not done well, and towards the end even received whistles from some.] (*NA*, XXXII: *Briefe 1803–1805* (1984), 48).

4. Niemeyer, *Beobachtungen*, I (1820), v.

5. Ibid., p. xi.

6. Ibid., pp. vi (Niemeyer's emphasis).

7. Samuel Johnson, *The Idler. In Two Volumes* (Dublin: Wilson, 1762), no. 98 (Saturday, 23 February 1760), pp. 286–89 (p. 288).

8. *August Hermann Niemeyer: Zur Erinnerung an Dessen Leben und Wirken*, ed. by A. Jacobs, completed by J. G. Gruber (Halle: Buchhandlung des Waisenhauses, 1831), pp. 59–420 (p. 87).

9. Niemeyer, *Beobachtungen*, I, 129.

10. August Hermann Niemeyer, *Grundsätze der Erziehung und des Unterrichts für Eltern, Hauslehrer und Schulmänner*, 7th edn, 3 vols (Halle: Waisenhaus Buchhandlung, 1818), III, 389; Niemeyer, *Beobachtungen*, I, 98.

11. Niemeyer, *Beobachtungen*, I, xiii–xiv.

12. Ibid., p. 111 (Niemeyer's emphasis).

13. Ibid., p. 121.

14. Ibid., pp. 121–22.

15. Niemeyer, *Beobachtungen*, II, 10.

16. Ibid., p. 15.

17. Niemeyer, *Beobachtungen*, I, p. 276.

18. Ibid.

19. Ibid., p. 278.

20. Ibid., p. 267 (Niemeyer's emphasis).

21. Ibid., p. 288.

22. Ibid.

23. Ibid., p. 289.

24. Ibid., p. 206 (Niemeyer's emphasis).

25. Ibid., pp. 207–08 (Niemeyer's emphasis).

26. See Mark Salber Phillips, *Society and Sentiment. Genres of Historical Writing in Britain, 1740–1820* (Princeton: Princeton University Press, 2000), pp. 65–71.

27. Niemeyer, *Beobachtungen*, I, 211.

28. Curiously, the drama and inherent tragedy of the murders of these two princes does not appear to have been exploited by eighteenth-century historians: Hume's *History of England* only makes passing reference to their deaths, although specific studies such as Horace Walpole's *Historic Doubts on the Life and Reign of Richard III* (1768) dealt with this matter in greater detail.

29. Niemeyer, *Beobachtungen*, I, 212 (Niemeyer's emphasis).

30. Public opinion had gradually come to accept that Mary's letters were authentic, although in 1754

Mr Goodall, keeper of the Advocate's Library in Edinburgh, felt that he could prove that they were forgeries.

31. Schiller, *NA*, XXX: *Briefe 1798–1800* (1961), p. 73.

32. Niemeyer, *Beobachtungen*, I, 212.

33. Ibid., p. 214.

34. Ibid., p. 217.

35. August Hermann Niemeyer, *Charakteristik der Bibel*, 3rd edn, 5 vols (Halle: Gebauer, 1778–82), I (1778), 8.

36. Ibid., p. 9 (Niemeyer's emphasis).

37. Niemeyer, *Beobachtungen*, I, 220.

38. Ibid.

39. Ibid.

40. Ibid., pp. 221–22.

41. Ibid., p. 222.

42. Ibid., p. 368.

43. Ibid., p. 227.

44. For a detailed analysis of the reception and structure of *Lady Jane Gray*, see Landon C. Burns, *Pity and Tears: The Tragedies of Nicholas Rowe*, Salzburg Studies in English Literature, 8 (Salzburg: Salzburg University, 1974), esp. pp. 207–33.

45. Ibid., p. 362.

46. Gotthold Ephraim Lessing, *Werke und Briefe*, ed. by Wilfried Barner and others, 12 vols (Frankfurt a.M.: Deutscher Klassiker Verlag, 1985–2003), IV: *Werke: 1758–1759* (1997), p. 645.

47. Ibid., p. 235 (Niemeyer's emphasis).

48. Ibid., p. 357.

49. Salber Phillips sees Hume's appendices as allowing the historian to 'give full attention from time to time to aspects of society that in the main stream of political narrative could find only a limited scope' (p. 52).

50. Niemeyer, *Beobachtungen*, I, 357.

51. Ibid. (Niemeyer's emphasis).

52. Ibid. (Niemeyer's emphasis).

53. Ibid., p. 359 (Niemeyer's emphasis).

54. Ibid.

55. Ibid.

56. Niemeyer, *Grundsätze der Erziehung*, footnote, p. 162.

57. Ibid., p. 154.

58. Ibid., pp. 155–56.

59. Christian Soboth, 'Klopstockbegeisterung und erste literarische Versuche', in *Licht und Schatten: August Hermann Niemeyer. Ein Leben an der Epochenwende um 1800*, ed. by Brigitte Klosterberg (Halle: Verlag der Franckeschen Stiftungen, 2004), pp. 58-59.

60. August Hermann Niemeyer, *Briefe an christliche Religionslehrer*, 2 vols (Halle: Waisenhaus-Buchhandlung, 1803), II, 326. See also Goethe's initial enthusiasm for Klopstock, which subsequently waned: 'Ich verehrte ihn, mit der Pietät, die mir eigen war; ich betrachtete ihn wie meinen Oheim [. . .]. Sein Vortreffliches ließ ich auf mich wirken und ging übrigens meinen eigenen Weg' [I honoured him with my own brand of piety; I considered him like my own uncle [...]. I allowed his excellent qualities to influence me and then incidentally, went my own way] (*DKV*, II: 12, *Eckermann. Gespräche mit Goethe* (1999), p. 123).

61. Hollmer and Meier, 'Die Erde ist nicht überall einerlei!', p. 267.

62. Niemeyer, *Beobachtungen*, I, 145 (Niemeyer's emphasis).

63. Ibid., footnote, p. 177.

64. Ibid.

CONCLUSIONS

This study has pursued two related questions in its exploration of continuity and change in late eighteenth- and early nineteenth-century German travel writing on England. It has sought firstly to identify some of the most important narrative devices in non-fictional travel writing which were deployed to engage the reader's sympathy and, secondly, it has asked how they relate to other aesthetic currents in Germany at this time. In underscoring the importance of travel writing to the salient intellectual enterprises of the period, it has therefore also explored how those who wrote and read travel accounts responded to the sentimental interests of the age. Travel writing by no means abandoned its traditional concerns with social, historical, geographical, and economic interests. Nevertheless, between about 1783 and 1830, it was also subject to a substantial amount of formal experimentation that changed the shape of travel accounts, altering both their character and the ways in which they could be read.

Analysing the representational structures in travel writing has first and foremost allowed us to point up the strengths and weaknesses in the genre. One of the problems with which all travellers were confronted was the implicit demand by their readership that they produce a comprehensive, detailed account of their journey through England. For those who travelled by coach, there was often little to be said about the stretches of countryside between towns and in some of the more remote locations, even less to be said about the towns themselves. Given the number of travel accounts published which had a dubious provenance and whose authors almost certainly never clapped eyes on the Channel, let alone set foot in London, it was essential for those bona fide travellers to demonstrate incontrovertibly the authenticity of their writings. Thoroughness of description and broadness of scope were what many travel writers aimed for in order to achieve precisely this. Nevertheless, all travellers were under the same pressure to produce an account that was individual, made pleasurable reading, and was novel. The sheer range of accounts on England by the start of the nineteenth century made this a desperately awkward enterprise — and as Niemeyer testily observed, the reading public in the early 1820s were still regularly being served up extracts from Moritz's account of 1783. These immense constraints on the travelogue coerced travel writers into configuring their experience of England in different stylistically enterprising and entertaining ways, which made the travel account a highly creative literary form.

The malleability of the travelogue as a genre gave writers a surprising freedom in two main areas: creative expression and criticism of a social and political nature. Even in the foregoing analyses of just six accounts of travel to England, we have demonstrated that their authors drew on political oratory and declamation, theatrical performance, *tableaux vivants*, landscape painting, anecdotal narration, historical biography, and tragic drama, in order to revivify the foreign scene in the mind's eye of the reader. Travel writing therefore occupied a position at the intersection of an impressive range of aesthetic discourses of the time. This meant that it was also itself underpinned by and a response to the work of respected thinkers and aestheticians of the period and that travelogues in their most successful form were sophisticated, complex, and highly artistic products — a far cry from the status of 'coffee-table literature' which travel writing has acquired today. The stylistic diversity of the travel accounts which we have explored here not only allowed them to demonstrate the author's affective engagement with the foreign in a range of different ways. It also permitted them to voice criticism both less and more subtly of the political situation back home, of the standing of German women in comparison to their English counterparts, or of the encroachment of industry on the natural landscape, using a range of persuasive strategies.

How successful such strategies were is, to a degree, a matter of opinion. But to modern sensibilities at least, the apparently excessive shows of emotion and the recurring anecdotes about the torments of family life do not make Gad's account a particularly rewarding read. Horstig's travelogue could likewise be considered less demanding, although his eye for the picturesque and for the play of light on water creates description that is intriguing and unusual. The accounts which pose the greatest interpretative challenges are those which are also the most provocative, critical, querying, either of what they saw in England, or of what they realized that Germany lacked. Moritz, for example, was faced with the representational challenge of conveying to the German reader how the expression of democracy worked, how alive and lively that concept could be made on the front benches in Parliament, and how it was that even humble figures could make their political opinions heard: in short, that the British public both literally and figuratively had a voice in political affairs. Schopenhauer's account is challenging to the extent that it draws on a range of issues concerning the observer and the observed in pictorial art (the frame, the status of the observer inside the picture, the (in)appropriateness of the poor as subject matter). She also projects the classical subject of Belisarius onto the begging poor of nineteenth-century London, thereby expecting and indeed requiring of her readers that they recognize and evaluate the innate symbolic convergences and divergences thus created. Niemeyer is more concerned to give new life to biographical material on royal personages such as Anne Boleyn and Lady Jane Grey and in so doing to remind us of the personal struggle and suffering which they overcame before their deaths.

Representing England is, then, not just about describing places, buildings, or collections. It involves defining the actors who people such scenes — both groups and individuals — and the significance they carry. In Niemeyer's travelogue the queens convey transhistorical norms and values, while in Moritz's account the figures he chooses are very much of the moment. Moreover, he selects one figure from the crowd to stand symbolically for the *Volk* at large and we conclude from the lines which this one man utters that he speaks for the people as a whole. Schopenhauer's figures in the Derbyshire mines are drawn in a less individual and more impressionistic manner: we are not invited to project ourselves into their position with the same energy that Moritz had done for his characters, most obviously because they were suffering individuals while the carter was not. The figures of Ann Hatton and Molly of Windermere, rather like 'S.M'. in Niemeyer's account, likewise stand symbolically for all poor or unfortunate women. However, Schopenhauer's description, particularly of Ann Hatton's performance, constructs a certain proximity between viewer and viewed, reader and subject, that the letter cannot generate because the correspondent's (narrative) presence is only implied and she is never seen.

Through a range of different rhetorical means — the deployment of direct speech in reported narrative, the shared private language of epistolarity, the description of theatrical performance — certain figures included in travel accounts were therefore made the focus of the narrative and the proposed object of the reader's sympathy. Schopenhauer's travelogue sought to construct a form of character identification that invited empathy even when it was likely that the characters portrayed and the readership she had in mind differed in various quite obvious ways — social standing, income, level of education, to name a few. For Gad, situational empathy was what underpinned the issues of plot and circumstance which she sketched in within the framework of her anecdotes, while 'spontaneous empathy' best describes her own response to the scenes described, into which she tries to draw her (arguably unwilling) readership. Niemeyer clearly saw an empathy for past (and in their dramatized forms, fictional) situations as enhancing the relevance of current predicaments. Although the travel writers in this discussion therefore approached the deployment of sympathetic portrayal in different ways, they were all concerned to show that empathy could be devoted to socially desirable ends, be it the alleviation of the suffering of the poor, the disapproval of women and children performing industrial labour, of women begging, or of the mistreatment of women by their husbands.

But to what extent did these travellers reflect on the relationship between the traveller and the foreign spectacle? How far did they themselves comment on the cognitive and stylistic interplay of observing and observed? Gad was crucially aware of her role as observer and reporter of the scenes described. Indeed, her augmented presence in those scenes in the first volume where she lamented the unfortunate affairs of the heart of her fellow travellers only reinforced her narrative dominance in the text. Moreover, her own discursive interventions in the form of footnotes constantly drew the reader's attention away from the suffering subject to the worldly-wise, all-advising narrator. As a result, these constant switches between observer and observed make it difficult for the reader to develop feelings of sympathy with the subject: perhaps this was why Gad's work achieved little critical acclaim and why the second volume was strikingly different in approach. Niemeyer, one senses, rarely allowed himself to be swept along by a wave of sympathetic engagement. That is not to say that he did not demonstrate humanitarian concern for the plight of the poor and that he did not portray them sensitively, but he retained a certain reserve, perhaps developed in the course of his professional life at the Franckesche Stiftungen. Sympathetic absorption into the scenes he described would have meant that he dispensed with a critical-analytical stance: and Niemeyer was, more than any of the other travellers, concerned not only to portray scenes of suffering individuals, but to suggest a long-term (institutional) solution to their problems. Augmenting the significance of the sweeps and the prostitutes brought these figures into closer focus and picked them out from among the other groups of unfortunates whom Niemeyer listed. Nevertheless, he does not wholly succeed in convincing his readers that these are people like ourselves and we feel that we are always distanced observers. This is also true of the dramatic scenes in the Tower, which, although vivid and psychologically coherent, seem to be assessed more for their contribution to what constitutes 'good' tragic theatre than for their sympathetic appeal to a reading or viewing audience.

The points at which otherness is modulated into relatedness, and with it a greater sense of human sympathy, are motivated by very different forces in each of the travelogues. For Moritz it is the chance to play a political role in enlightened Britain — an opportunity he would not find in Berlin. For both La Roche and Schopenhauer (and, to a degree, Gad) it is the sight of downtrodden, suffering women. In all three accounts by these female travel writers it is also interesting to note, however, that their sympathetic engagement with the foreign, their open demonstration of a relatedness to the subject, becomes problematic. The shift of register in Schopenhauer's account as the poor draw near to beg, La Roche's self-consciousness about the stance which she can adopt as a sentient woman travelling and about her own deployment of the language of sentiment, and Gad's fierce insistence in her second volume on the intellectual merits of women, all point to a certain rhetorical nervousness. While they were no less skilled at negotiating the modulation of public and private interests than their male counterparts, one senses their precarious position as women travelling, and their desire to locate themselves within the discourse of sentimentality (which had brought women greater freedom to enter the literary sphere), while also negotiating around the scientific demands of travel writing still operating at that time.

All the travellers discussed here were, though, concerned to offer a realistic, seemingly truthful, representation of the foreign which at the same time bore witness to their role as figures in movement and as figures who were humanly moved by what they saw. The narrative techniques used to this end drew on a range of aesthetic strategies which were essential elements in this process of 're-presenting' the foreign: not only of *portraying* but also of *revivifying* the experience of journeying through England for a German readership. Empathy (and its cognates 'sympathy' and 'fellow feeling') largely continues to be considered in relation to the novelist's craft of fiction, and indeed the techniques on which the travel writers under discussion drew were often embedded in what we might consider 'literary' narrative strategies. Yet this study has demonstrated that empathy was also fundamental in forging those emotional connections across the social and cultural differences that lie at the very heart of non-fictional travel writing.

.

BIBLIOGRAPHY

Primary Sources

Periodicals

Allgemeine Deutsche Bibliothek
Allgemeine Literatur-Zeitung
Athenäum
Berliner Abendblätter
Berlinische Monatsschrift
Critical Review
Deutsche Kronik
Deutsche Monatsschrift
Deutsches Museum
Frankfurter Gelehrte Anzeigen
Genius der Zeit
Geschichte und Politik
Hallisches Patriotisches Wochenblatt
Die Horen
Irene
Journal des Luxus und der Moden
Der Kosmopolit
London und Paris
Morgenblatt für gebildete Stände
Morning Chronicle
Neue Allgemeine Deutsche Bibliothek
Neue Bibliothek der schönen Wissenschaften und der freyen Künste
Neue Hallische Gelehrte Zeitungen
Neues Hamburgisches Magazin
Teutscher Merkur
Vossische Zeitung
Zeitung für die elegante Welt

Contemporary Books and Pamphlets

ADDISON, JOSEPH, *Remarks on Several Parts of Italy, &c In the Years 1701, 1702, 1703* (London: Tonson, 1705)
ALISON, ARCHIBALD, *Essays on the Nature and Principles of Taste* (London: Robinson, 1790)
—— *Ueber den Geschmack, dessen Natur und Grundsätze*, verdeutscht und mit Anmerkungen und Abhandlungen begleitet von K. H. Heydenreich, 2 vols (Leipzig: Weygand, 1792)
AMARANTHES [GOTTLIEB SIGMUND CORVINUS], *Nutzbares, galantes und curiöses Frauenzimmer-Lexicon* (Leipzig: Gleditsch, 1715)
ANON., *A Complete and Accurate Account of the Very Important Debate in the House of Commons, on Tuesday, July 9, 1782. In Which The Cause of Mr Fox's Resignation, and the Great Question*

of AMERICAN INDEPENDENCE *came under Consideration*, 3rd edn (London: Stockdale and Axtell, 1782)

ANON., *The Speech of the Right Honourable Charles James Fox, At a General Meeting of the Electors of Westminster, Assembled in Westminster-Hall, July 17, 1782, In which are Accurately Given the Reasons for Withdrawing himself from the Cabinet, Taken in Short-hand by W. Blanchard of Dean-Street, Fetter Lane* (Dublin: Mills, 1782)

ANON., *The Speech of the Right Honourable Charles James Fox, in the House of Commons, on Tuesday the 9th Instant* [July 1782], *in Defence of his Resignation, A New Edition Corrected* (London: Debret and Stockdale, 1782)

ANON., *History of the Westminster Election, Containing Every Material Occurrence, from its Commecement [sic] on the First of April (1784), to the Final Close of the Poll . . . To which is Prefixed, a Summary Account of the Proceedings of the Late Parliament, so Far as they Appear Connected with the East India Business, and the Dismission of the Portland Administration . . . By Lovers of Truth and Justice* (London: Debret, 1784)

ANON., *The Speeches of the Right Honourable Charles James Fox, in the House of Commons*, 6 vols (London: Longman, Hurst, Reed, Rees, Orne and Brown, 1815)

ARCHENHOLTZ, JOHANN WILHELM VON, *England und Italien*, Nachdr. der dreiteiligen Erstausg. Leipzig 1785, mit Varianten der fünfteiligen Ausg. Leipzig 1787, ed. and notes, Michael Maurer, 3 vols (Leipzig: Dykische Buchhandlung, 1785/1787; repr. Heidelberg: Winter, 1993)

AUSTIN, GILBERT, *Chironomia; or, a Treatise on Rhetorical Delivery* (London: Cadell and Davies, 1806)

BARBER, JOHN THOMAS, *A Tour throughout South Wales and Monmouthshire Comprehending a General Survey of the Picturesque Scenery, Remains of Antiquity, Historical Events, Peculiar Manners, and Commercial Situations, of that Interesting Portion of the British Empire* (London: Cadell and Davies, 1803)

BASEDOW, JOHANN BERNHARD, *J. B. Basedow's Ausgewählte Schriften* (Langensalza: Beyer, 1880)

BERCHTOLD, LEOPOLD [COUNT], *An Essay to Direct and Extend the Inquiries of Patriotic Travellers; with Further Observations on the Means of Preserving the Life, Health, and Property of the Experienced in their Journies by Land and Sea*, 2 vols (London: Robinsons, 1789)

BLANCKENBURG, FRIEDRICH VON, *Versuch über den Roman* (Leipzig: David Siegers Wittwe, 1774)

BOCCAGE, MADAME DU [ANNE MARIE LEPAGE FIQUET DU BOCCAGE], *Letters concerning England, Holland and Italy. By the Celebrated Madam du Boccage, Member of the Academies of Padua, Bologna, Rome and Lyons. Written during her Travels in those Countries*, 2 vols (London: Dilly, 1770)

—— *Lettres De Madame du Boccage: Contenant Ses Voyages En France, En Angleterre, En Hollande Et En Italie, Faits Pendant Les Années 1750. 1757. & 1758* (Dresden: Walther, 1771)

—— *Reisen der Madame du Bocage durch England, Holland, Frankreich und Italien in Briefen, aus dem Französischen übersetzt* (Dresden: Hibscher, 1776)

BREITINGER, JOHANN JACOB, *Critische Dichtkunst worinnen die Poetische Mahlerey in Absicht auf die Erfindung im Grunde untersuchet und mit Beyspielen aus den berühmtesten Alten und Neuern erläutert wird*, 2 vols (Zurich: Orell, 1740)

BÜSCH, JOHANN GEORG, *Bemerkungen auf einer Reise durch einen Teil der Vereinigten Niederlande und Englands* (Hamburg: Bohn, 1786)

—— 'Ueber Anekdoten, insonderheit über die Anekdoten unserer Zeit', *Historisch-politisches Magazin, nebst litterarischen Nachrichten* (1787), 272–86

BÜSCHEL, JOHANN GABRIEL BERNHARD, *Neue Reisen eines Deutschen nach und in England im Jahre 1783. Ein Pendant zu des Herrn Professor Moriz Reisen* (Berlin: Maurer, 1784)

BURKE, EDMUND, *A Philosophical Enquiry into the Origin of our Ideas of the Sublime and Beautiful*, ed. by Adam Philips (Oxford: Oxford University Press, 1990)

Charaktere der vornehmsten Dichter aller Nationen; nebst kritischen und historischen Abhandlungen über Gegenstände der schönen Künste und Wissenschaften von einer Gesellschaft von Gelehrten. (Nachträge zu Sulzers allgemeiner Theorie der schönen Künste), ed. by Johann Gottfried Dyk and Georg Schaz, 8 vols (Leipzig: Dyk, 1792–1808)

CAMPE, JOACHIM HEINRICH, *Väterlicher Rath für meine Tochter. Ein Gegenstück zum Theophron. Der erwachsenen weiblichen Jugend gewidmet* (Braunschweig: Verlag der Schulbuchhandlung, 1789)

DOBSON, AUSTIN, ed., *Diary and Letters of Madame D'Arblay (1778–1840)*, 6 vols (London: Macmillan, 1904–05)

ENGEL, JOHANN JAKOB, 'Ueber Handlung, Gespräch und Erzehlung', *NBsWfK*, 16 (1774), 177-256

ERSCH, JOHANN SAMUEL and JOHANN GOTTFRIED GRUBER, *Allgemeine Encyclopädie der Wissenschaften und Künste in alphabetischer Folge* (Leipzig: Brockhaus, 1818–89)

FERNOW, CARL LUDWIG, *Römische Studien*, 3 vols (Zurich: Gessner, 1806–08)

FORSTER, GEORG, *A Voyage Round the World, in his Brit. Majesty's Sloop Resolution, commanded by Capt. Cook, during the years 1772, 1773, 1774, and 1775*, 2 vols (London: White, Robson, Elmsly, Robinson, 1777)

FUNCK, HEINRICH, ed., *Goethe und Lavater: Briefe und Tagebücher* (Weimar: Goethe-Gesellschaft, 1901)

GAD (Domeier), Esther, 'Einige Aeußerungen über Hrn. Kampe'ns Behauptungen, die weibliche Gelehrsamkeit betreffend', *DK*, 3 (1798), 577–90

——*Briefe während meines Aufenthalts in England und Portugal an einen Freund von E. Bernard geb. Gad*, 2 vols (Hamburg: Campe, 1802–3)

——*Gesammelte Blätter* (Leipzig: Reclam, 1806)

GATTERER, JOHANN CHRISTOPH, 'Von der Evidenz in der Geschichtkunde', in *Die Allgemeine Welthistorie die in England durch eine Gesellschaft von Gelehrten ausgefertiget worden. In einem vollständigen und pragmatischen Auszuge*, ed. by Friedrich Eberhard Boysen, 37 vols (Halle: Gebauer, 1767–90), 1 (1767), 1–38

GENLIS, MADAME DE, *The Traveller's Companion for Conversation being a Collection of Such Expressions as Occur Most Frequently in Travelling and in the Different Situations of Life, in six languages, English, German, French, Italian, Spanish and Russian*, fifth edition, augmented and improved (Florence: Marenigh, 1821)

GESSNER, SALOMON, *Brief über die Landschaftmahlerey an Herrn Fuesslin, den Verfasser der Geschichte der besten Künstler in der Schweitz* (Zurich: Orell, Geßner, Füeßli and Compagnie, 1770)

GILPIN, WILLIAM, *An Essay upon Prints: Containing Remarks upon the Principles of Picturesque Beauty* (London: Robson, 1768)

——*Observations on the River Wye, and Several Parts of South Wales, Relative Chiefly to Picturesque Beauty; Made in the Summer of 1770* (London: Blamire, 1782)

——*Observations, Relative Chiefly to Picturesque Beauty, Made in the Year 1772, On Several Parts of England; Particularly the Mountains, and Lakes of Cumberland, and Westmoreland*, 2 vols (London: Blamire, 1786)

——*Three Essays: On Picturesque Beauty; on Picturesque Travel, and on Sketching Landscape* (London: Blamire, 1792)

——*Observations on the Western Parts of England: Relative Chiefly to Picturesque Beauty; to which are Added, a Few Remarks on the Picturesque Beauties of the Isle of Wight* (London: Cadell and Davies, 1798)

GOETHE, JOHANN WOLFGANG VON, *Sämtliche Werke*, 40 vols, ed. by Dieter Borchmeyer and others (Frankfurt a.M.: Deutscher Klassiker Verlag, 1985–)

GRIMM, JOHANN FRIEDRICH KARL, *Bemerkungen eines Reisenden durch Deutschland, Frankreich, England und Holland in Briefen an seine Freunde*, 3 vols (Altenburg: Richter, 1775)

GROTE, CARL WILHELM [CARL TREUTHOLD], *Zeitlosen: Eine Blüthenlese aus den Gaben der Freunde und eignen Dichtungen*, Erstes Gewinde (Wesel: Becker, 1817)

HASSENCAMP, ROBERT, 'Briefe von Joh. Heinr. Jung-Stilling an Sophie v. La Roche', *Euphorion*, 2 (1895), 579–87

HERDER, JOHANN GOTTFRIED, *Werke*, 5 vols (Berlin: Aufbau, 1969)

HIPPEL, THEODORE VON, *Sämmtliche Werke*, 14 vols (Berlin: Reimer, 1827–39)

HOME, HENRY [LORD KAMES], *Grundsätze der Critik*, aus dem Englischen übersetzt von Johann Nicolaus Meinhard, 3 vols (Leipzig: [n. pub.], 1763–66)

——*Elements of Criticism. With the Author's Last Corrections and Additions*, 6th edn, 2 vols (Edinburgh: Bell, Creech, Cadell and Robinson, 1785)

HORN, FRANZ, ed., *C. M. Wieland's Briefe an Sophie von La Roche, nebst einem Schreiben von Gellert und Lavater* (Berlin: Christiani, 1820)

HORSTIG, CARL GOTTLIEB, 'Ueber die Natur und das Wesen schöner Empfindungen. Veranlaßt durch Alisons Versuch über den Geschmack', *NBsWfK*, 46 (1792), 3-20

——'Ueber das Pittoreske in der Malerey', *Nachträge zu Sulzers allgemeiner Theorie der schönen Künste* (Leipzig: Dyk, 1792–1808), II: 1 (1793), 31–40

——'Fortsetzung über die Natur und das Wesen schöner Empfindungen', *NBsWfK*, 49 (1793), 195-228

——'Ueber den Werth der Symbole', *Der Genius der Zeit*, 3:9 (September 1794), 1-11

——*Briefe über die mahlerische Perspektive* (Leipzig: Dyck, 1797)

——*Tageblätter unsrer Reise in und um den Harz. Mit 16 in Kupfer gestochenen Zeichnungen großer Naturscenen* (Dresden: Gerlach, 1803)

——*Reise nach Frankreich, England und Holland zu Anfange des Jahres 1803* (Berlin: Maurer, 1806)

——'Einfluß der Umgebung', *MgS*, 261 (31 October 1808), 1041-42

——'Reflexe von Horstig', in *Zeitlosen: Eine Blüthenlese aus den Gaben der Freunde und eignen Dichtungen*, ed. by Carl Wilhelm Grote (Wesel: Becker, 1817), pp. 177-95

HUMBOLDT, ALEXANDER VON, *Ansichten der Natur*, ed. by Hanno Beck and others Forschungsunternehmen der Humboldt-Gesellschaft, 40 (Darmstadt: Wissenschaftliche Buch-gesellschaft, 1987)

HUMBOLDT, WILHELM VON, *Werke*, ed. by Andreas Flitner and Klaus Giel, 3rd edn, 5 vols (Stuttgart: Cotta, 1980–81)

HUME, DAVID, *A Treatise of Human Nature*, 3 vols (London: Noon, 1739–40)

ISELIN, ISAAK, *Über die Geschichte der Menschheit*, 2 vols (Karlsruhe: Schmieder, 1784)

JACOBS, AUGUST, ed., *August Hermann Niemeyer: Zur Erinnerung an Dessen Leben und Wirken*, completed by Johann Gottfried Gruber (Halle: Buchhandlung des Waisenhauses, 1831)

JENISCH, DANIEL, *Theorie der Lebens-Beschreibung. Nebst einer Lebens-Beschreibung Karls des Großen: einer Preisschrift* (Berlin: Fröhlich, 1802)

JOHNSON, SAMUEL, *The Idler. In Two Volumes* (Dublin: Wilson, 1762)

KANT, IMMANUEL, *Werke*, ed. by Wilhelm Weischedel, 6 vols (Frankfurt a.M.: Insel, 1964)

KAYSER, ALBRECHT CHRISTOPH, 'Ueber den Werth der Anekdoten', *TM* (1784), 82–86

KLISCHNIG, KARL FRIEDRICH, *Erinnerungen aus den zehn letzten Lebensjahren meines Freundes Anton Reiser* (Berlin: Vieweg, 1794)

LA ROCHE, SOPHIE VON, *Die Geschichte des Fräuleins von Sternheim*, ed. by Barbara Becker-Cantarino, 2 vols (Stuttgart: Reclam, 1983)

——*Pomona für Teutschlands Töchter*, 4 vols (Speyer: Enderische Schriften, 1783–84; repr. Munich: Saur, 1987)

—— *Mein Schreibetisch*, 2 vols (Leipzig: Gräff, 1799; repr. Karben: Wald, 1996)

—— *Tagebuch einer Reise durch Holland und England von der Verfasserin von Rosaliens Briefen* (Offenbach a.M.: Weiß and Brede, 1788; repr. Karben: Wald, 1997)

LESSING, GOTTHOLD EPHRAIM, *Werke und Briefe*, ed. by Wilfried Barner and others, 12 vols (Frankfurt a.M.: Deutscher Klassiker Verlag, 1985–2003)

LESSING, GOTTHOLD EPHRAIM, MOSES MENDELSSOHN and FRIEDRICH NICOLAI, *Briefwechsel über das Trauerspiel*, ed. by Jochen Schulte-Sasse (Munich: Winkler, 1972)

LÜTKEHAUS LUDGER, ed., *Die Schopenhauers: Der Familienbriefwechsel von Adele, Arthur, Heinrich Floris und Johanna Schopenhauer* (Zurich: Haffmans, 1991)

MAASS, JOHANN GEBHARD EHRENREICH, *Versuch über die Gefühle, besonders über die Affecten*, 2 vols (Halle: Reinecke, 1811)

MAURER, MICHAEL, ed., *Ich bin mehr Herz als Kopf. Sophie von La Roche. Ein Lebensbild in Briefen* (Munich: Beck, 1983)

MEISSNER, EDUARD, *Bemerkungen aus dem Taschenbuche eines Arztes während einer Reise von Odessa durch einen Theil von Deutschland, Holland, England und Schottland* (Halle: Renger, 1819)

MERIAN, MARIA SYBILLA, *Der Raupen wunderbare Verwandelung und sonderbare Blumen-nahrung*, 2 vols (Nürnberg: Funken, 1679)

MORITZ, KARL PHILIPP, 'Vorschlag zu einem Magazin einer Erfahrungs-Seelenkunde', *DM*, 1782:I, 485–503

—— *Travels, Chiefly on Foot, Through Several Parts of England, in 1782. Described to a Friend, by Charles P. Moritz, a Literary Gentleman of Berlin. Translated from the German by a Lady* (London: Robinson, 1795)

—— *Schriften zur Ästhetik und Poetik*, ed. by Hans Joachim Schrimpf (Tübingen: Niemeyer, 1962)

—— *Werke*, ed. by Horst Günther, 3 vols (Frankfurt a.M.: Insel, 1993)

NEIGEBAUR, JOHANN DANIEL FERDINAND, *Handbuch für Reisende in England* (Leipzig: Brockhaus, 1829)

NIEMEYER, AUGUST HERMANN, *Charakteristik der Bibel*, 3rd edn, 5 vols (Halle: Gebauer, 1778–82)

——, ed., *Leben Johann Wesleys, Stifters der Methodisten, nebst einer Geschichte des Methodismus von J. Hampson*, 2 vols (Halle: Buchhandlung des Waisenhauses, 1793)

NIEMEYER, AUGUST HERMANN, *Grundsätze der Erziehung und des Unterrichts für Eltern, Hauslehrer und Erzieher*, unveränderter Nachdruck der ersten Auflage, Halle 1796, ed. by Hans-Hermann Groothoff and Ulrich Herrmann (Paderborn: Schöningh, 1970)

—— *Briefe an christliche Religionslehrer*, 2 vols (Halle: Waisenhaus-Buchhandlung, 1803)

—— *Leben, Charakter und Verdienste D. Joh. Aug. Nösselts, nebst einer Sammlung einiger zum Theil ungedruckten Aufsätze, Briefe und Fragmente* (Halle: Buchhandlung des Hallischen Waisenhauses, 1809)

—— *Grundsätze der Erziehung und des Unterrichts für Eltern, Hauslehrer und Schulmänner*, 7th edn, 3 vols (Halle: Waisenhaus Buchhandlung, 1818)

—— *Beobachtungen auf Reisen in und außer Deutschland. Nebst Erinnerungen an denkwürdige Lebenserfahrungen und Zeitgenossen in den letzten fünfzig Jahren*, 4 vols (Halle: Buchhandlung des Hallischen Waisenhauses, 1820–26)

—— *Doktor Martin Luther in seinem Leben und Wirken. Im Jahr der dritten Säcularfeyer der Kirchenverbesserung*, mit einem Vorwort von Aug. H. Niemeyer (Halle: Buchhandlung des Hallischen Waisenhauses, 1817)

PEROUX JOSEPH NICOLAUS and HEINRICH RITTER, *Pantomimische Stellungen von Henriette Hendel* (Frankfurt a.M.: Peroux, 1809)

PIOZZI, ESTHER [HESTER] LYNCH, *Letters to and from the late Samuel Johnson, LL.D. To which are added some poems never before printed*, 2 vols (London: Strahan and Cadell, 1788)

——*Bemerkungen auf der Reise durch Frankreich, Italien und Deutschland*, trans. by M. Forkel, preface Georg Forster, 2 vols (Frankfurt a.M.: Barrentrapp and Wenner, 1790)

POPE, ALEXANDER, *Selected Poems* (London: Bloomsbury Poetry Classics, 1994)

POSSELT, FRANZ, *Apodemik oder die Kunst zu reisen. Ein systematischer Versuch zum Gebrauch junger Reisenden aus den gebildeten Ständen überhaupt und angehender Gelehrten und Künstler insbesondere*, 2 vols (Leipzig: Breitkopf, 1795)

PRICE, UVEDALE, *An Essay on the Picturesque, as Compared with the Sublime and the Beautiful; and on the Use of Studying Pictures, for the Purpose of Improving Real Landscape* (London: Robson, 1794)

REHBERG, FRIEDRICH, *Drawings Faithfully Copied from Nature at Naples, and with Permission Dedicated to the Right Honourable Sir William Hamilton* (London: Fores, 1797)

REISER, ANTON, *Theatronamia; oder, Die Wercke der Finsterniß, in denen öffentlichen Schau-Spielen von den alten Kirchen-Vätern verdammet, welches aus ihren Schrifften zu getreuer Warnung kürzlich entworffen* (Ratzeburg: Nissen, 1681)

ROSENWALL, P. [GOTTFRIED FRIEDRICH PETER RAUSCHNICK], *Mahlerische Ansichten und Bemerkungen auf einer Reise durch Holland, die Rheinlande, Baden, die Schweiz und Württemberg*, 2 vols (Mainz: Kupferberg, 1824)

ROUSSEAU, JEAN-JACQUES, *Du Contrat Social et autres œuvres politiques*, introduced by Jean Ehrard (Paris: Garnier, 1975)

SCHAUER, HANS, ed., *Herders Briefwechsel mit Caroline Flachsland. Nach den Handschriften des Goethe- und Schiller-Archivs herausgegeben*, 2 vols (Weimar: Goethe-Gesellschaft, 1926–28)

SCHELLING, FRIEDRICH WILHELM JOSEPH VON, *Sämmtliche Werke*, 14 vols (Stuttgart: Cotta, 1856–61)

SCHILLER, FRIEDRICH, *Werke. Nationalausgabe*, ed. by Julius Petersen and others, 43 vols (Weimar: Hermann Böhlaus Nachfolger, 1943–)

SCHLEGEL, AUGUST WILHELM VON, *Sämmtliche Werke*, ed. by Eduard Böcking, 12 vols (Leipzig: Weidmann, 1846)

——*Vorlesungen über Ästhetik I (1798–1803)*, ed. by Ernst Behler (Paderborn: Schöningh, 1989)

SCHLICHTEGROLL, FRIEDRICH, ed., *Nekrolog auf das Jahr 1790–1800. Enthaltend Nachrichten von dem Leben merkwürdiger in diesem Jahre verstorbener Personen*, 23 vols (Gotha: Perthes, 1791–1806)

SCHLÖZER, AUGUST LUDWIG, *Entwurf zu einem Reise-Collegio, mit einer Anzeige seines Zeitungs-Collegii* (Göttingen: Vandenhoeck, 1777)

SCHOPENHAUER, ARTHUR, *Die Reisetagebücher* (Zurich: Haffmans, 1988)

SCHOPENHAUER, JOHANNA, *Gabriele*, 3 vols (Leipzig: Brockhaus, 1821)

——*Sämmtliche Schriften*, 24 vols (Frankfurt a.M.: Brockhaus, 1830–31)

——*Reise nach England*, ed. by Konrad Paul (Berlin: Rütten and Loening, 1982)

SCHRIMPF, HANS JOACHIM, *Schriften zur Ästhetik und Poetik* (Tübingen: Niemeyer, 1962)

SCHÜTZ, FRIEDRICH WILHELM VON, *Briefe über London. Ein Gegenstück zu des Herrn von Archenholz England und Italien* (Hamburg: Bachmann and Sundermann, 1792)

SMITH, ADAM, *The Theory of Moral Sentiments* (London: Miller, 1759)

STERNE, LAURENCE, *A Sentimental Journey through France and Italy* (Oxford: Oxford University Press, 1998)

SULIVAN, RICHARD JOSEPH, *Tour through Different Parts of England, Scotland, and Wales*, in *The British Tourists; or Traveller's Pocket Companion through England, Wales, Scotland, and Ireland. Comprehending the most celebrated Tours in the British Islands*, ed. by William Mavor, 6 vols (London: Newbery, 1798), III, 1–152

SULZER, JOHANN GEORG, *Kurzer Begriff aller Wissenschaften und anderen Theilen der Gelehrsamkeit worin jeder nach seinem Inhalt, Nuzen u. Vollkommenheit kuerzlich beschr. wird*, 2nd edn (Leipzig: Langenheim, 1759)

——*Allgemeine Theorie der schönen Künste in einzeln, nach alphabetischer Ordnung der Kunstwörter auf einander folgenden, Artikeln abgehandelt*, 2 vols (Leipzig: Weidmann, 1771)

——*Allgemeine Theorie der schönen Künste in einzeln, nach alphabetischer Ordnung der Kunstwörter auf einander folgenden, Artikeln abgehandelt*, 2nd edn, 4 vols (Leipzig: Weidmann, 1792–94)

TIECK, LUDWIG, *Schriften*, ed. by Achim Hölter, 12 vols (Frankfurt a.M.: Deutscher Klassiker Verlag, 1991)

VARNHAGEN, RAHEL, *Rahel. Ein Buch des Andenkens für ihre Freunde*, 3 vols (Berlin: Duncker and Humblot, 1834)

VOLKMANN, JOHANN JACOB, *Neueste Reisen durch England, vorzüglich in Absicht auf die Kunstsammlungen, Naturgeschichte, Oekonomie, Manufakturen und Landsitze der Großen. Aus den besten Nachrichten und neuern Schriften zusammengetragen*, 4 vols (Leipzig: Fritsch, 1781–82)

WAGNER, KARL, ed., *Briefe an Johann Heinrich Merck von Göthe, Herder, Wieland und andern bedeutenden Zeitgenossen, mit Merck's biographische Skizze* (Darmstadt: Diehl, 1835)

WARNER, RICHARD, *A Tour through the Northern Counties of England, and the Borders of Scotland*, 2 vols (London: Robinson, 1802)

WATZDORF, HEINRICH VON, *Briefe zur Charakteristik von England gehörig; geschrieben auf einer Reise im Jahre 1784* (Leipzig: Dyk, 1786)

WENDEBORN, GEBHARD FRIEDRICH AUGUST, *Beyträge zur Kenntniß Grosbritanniens vom Jahr 1797* (Lemgo: Meyer, 1780)

—— *Der Zustand des Staats, der Religion, der Gelehrsamkeit und der Kunst in Großbritannien gegen das Ende des achtzehnten Jahrhunderts*, 4 vols (Berlin: Spener, 1785–88)

WESTALL, WILLIAM, *Great Britain Illustrated: A Series of Original Views* (London: Tilt, 1830)

WHITAKER, JOHN, *Mary Queen of Scots Vindicated*, 3 vols (London: Murray, 1787)

WOLFF, KURT, ed., *Johann Heinrich Mercks Schriften und Briefwechsel*, 2 vols (Leipzig: Insel, 1909)

WORTLEY MONTAGU, MARY, *Lady Wortley Montagu: Essays and Poems and 'Simplicity, A Comedy'*, ed. by Robert Halsband and Isobel Grundy (Oxford: Clarendon Press, 1977)

ZEDLER, JOHANN HEINRICH, *Grosses vollständiges Universal-Lexicon aller Wissenschafften und Künste welche biszhero durch menschlichen Verstand Witz erfunden und verbessert worden*, 64 vols (Leipzig: Zedler, 1732–54)

Secondary Sources

Books and Articles

ABBEY, J. R., *Travel in Aquatint and Lithography, 1770–1860* (London: Dawsons, 1972)

ADAMS, PERCY G., *Travelers and Travel Liars, 1660–1800* (Berkeley: University of California Press, 1962)

—— *Travel Literature and the Evolution of the Novel* (Kentucky: University Press of Kentucky, 1983)

AHRBECK, HANS, 'Über August Hermann Niemeyer', *Gedenkschrift für Ferdinand Josef Schneider (1879–1954)*, ed. by Karl Bischoff (Weimar: Hermann Böhlaus Nachfolger, 1956), pp. 124–49

ALBRECHT, ANDREA, 'Bildung und Ehe "genialer Weiber". Jean Pauls Diesjährige Nachlesung an die Dichtinnen als Erwiderung auf Esther Gad und Rahel Levin Varnhagen', *Deutsche Vierteljahrsschrift für Literaturwissenschaft und Geistesgeschichte*, 80 (2006), 378–407

ANDREWS, MALCOLM, *The Search for the Picturesque: Landscape Aesthetics and Tourism in Britain, 1760–1800* (Aldershot: Scolar Press, 1989)

ASSING, LUDMILLA, *Sophie von La Roche, die Freundin Wielands* (Berlin: Janke, 1859)

BACHLEITNER, NORBERT, 'Die Rezeption von Henry Homes *Elements of Criticism* in Deutschland, 1763–1793', *arcadia*, 20 (1985), 115–33

BANN, STEPHEN, *The Clothing of Clio: A Study of the Representation of History in Nineteenth-Century Britain and France* (Cambridge: Cambridge University Press, 1984)

BARKER-BENFIELD, G. J., *The Culture of Sensibility: Sex and Society in Eighteenth-Century Britain* (Chicago: University of Chicago Press, 1992)

BARNES, H. G., 'Bildhafte Darstellung in den "Wahlverwandtschaften"', *Deutsche Vierteljahrsschrift für Literaturwissenschaft*, 30 (1956), 41–70

BARRELL, JOHN, *The Dark Side of the Landscape: The Rural Poor in English Painting, 1730–1840* (Cambridge: Cambridge University Press, 1980)

BATTEN, CHARLES, *Pleasurable Instruction: Form and Convention in Eighteenth-Century Travel Literature* (Berkeley: University of California Press, 1978)

BECKER-CANTARINO, BARBARA, *Der lange Weg zur Mündigkeit: Frau und Literatur (1500–1800)* (Metzler: Stuttgart, 1987)

——'Sophie von La Roche (1730–1807): Kommentiertes Werkverzeichnis', *Das achtzehnte Jahrhundert*, 17 (1993), 28–49

BENEDICT, BARBARA M., 'The "Curious Attitude" in Eighteenth-Century Britain: Observing and Owning', *Eighteenth-Century Life*, 14 (1990), 59–98

——*Curiosity: A Cultural History of Early Modern Enquiry* (Chicago: University of Chicago Press, 2001)

BERGHAHN, KLAUS L., 'German Literary Theory from Gottsched to Goethe', in *The Cambridge History of Literary Criticism*, general editors H. B. Nisbet and Claude Rawson, 9 vols (Cambridge: Cambridge University Press, 1989–2001), IV (1997), 522–45

BERGMANN, ULRIKE, *Johanna Schopenhauer: 'Lebe und sei so glücklich als du kannst'* (Leipzig: Reclam, 2002)

BERMINGHAM, ANN, *Landsape and Ideology: The English Rustic Tradition, 1740–1860* (London: Thames and Hudson, 1987)

——'The Aesthetics of Ignorance: The Accomplished Woman in the Culture of Connoisseurship', *The Oxford Art Journal*, 16 (1993), 3–20

——'Landscape-O-Rama: The Exhibition Landscape at Somerset House and the Rise of Popular Landscape Entertainments', in *Art on the Line: The Royal Academy Exhibitions at Somerset House, 1780–1836*, ed. by David Solkin (London: Paul Mellon Centre for Studies in British Art, 2001)

BLANKE, HORST W., *Politische Herrschaft und soziale Ungleichheit im Spiegel der Anderen: Untersuchungen zu den deutschsprachigen Reisebeschreibungen vornehmlich im Zeitalter der Auklärung* (Waltrop: Spenner, 1997)

BLEDSOE, ROBERT S., 'Empathetic Reading and Identity Formation', *Lessing Yearbook*, 33 (2001), 201–31

BLUMENBERG, HANS, *Die Legitimität der Neuzeit*, 3rd edn (Frankfurt a.M.: Suhrkamp, 1997)

BOECK, KARL, *Die Bildung des Gefühls nach A. H. Niemeyers 'Grundsätze der Erziehung und des Unterrichts'* (Paderborn: Schöningh, 1908)

BOHLS, ELIZABETH, *Women Travel Writers and the Language of Aesthetics, 1716–1818*, Cambridge Studies in Romanticism, 13 (Cambridge: Cambridge University Press, 1995)

BOOTH, MICHAEL R., JOHN STOKES and SUSAN BASSNETT, EDS, *Three Tragic Actresses: Siddons, Rachel, Ristori* (Cambridge: Cambridge University Press, 1996)

BOULBY, MARK, 'Karl Philipp Moritz and the 'Psychological' Study of Language', *German Life and Letters*, 29 (October 1975), 15–26

——*Karl Philipp Moritz: At the Fringe of Genius* (Toronto: University of Toronto Press, 1979)

BOVENSCHEN, SILVIA, *Die imaginierte Weiblichkeit: Exemplarische Untersuchungen zu kultur-geschichtlichen und literarischen Präsentationsformen des Weiblichen* (Frankfurt a.M.: Suhrkamp, 1979)

BOYLE, NICHOLAS, *Goethe: The Poet and the Age* (Oxford: Clarendon, 1991–)

BRANDES, HELGA, 'Die Entstehung eines weiblichen Lesepublikums im 18. Jahrhundert. Von den Frauenzimmerbibliotheken zu den literarischen Damengesellschaften', *in Lesen und Schreiben im 17. und 18. Jahrhundert: Studien zu ihrer Bewertung in Deutschland, England und Frankreich*, ed. by Paul Goetsch (Tübingen: Narr, 1994)

BRANDSTETTER, GABRIELE, 'Figura: Körper und Szene. Zur Theorie der Darstellung im 18. Jahrhundert', in *Theater im Kulturwandel des 18. Jahrhunderts: Inszenierung und Wahrnehmung von Körper — Musik — Sprache*, ed. by Erika Fischer-Lichte and Jörg Schönert, Deutsche Gesellschaft für die Erforschung des achtzehnten Jahrhunderts, 5 (Göttingen: Wallstein, 1999), pp. 23–51

BRENNER, PETER J., *Der Reisebericht in der deutschen Literatur*, Internationales Archiv für Sozialgeschichte der deutschen Literatur, Sonderheft 2 (Tübingen: Niemeyer, 1990)

——, ed., *Der Reisebericht: Die Entwicklung einer Gattung in der deutschen Literatur* (Frankfurt a.M.: Suhrkamp, 1989)

——*Reisen in die Neue Welt: Die Erfahrung Nordamerikas in deutschen Reise- und Auswandererberichten des 19. Jahrhunderts*, Studien und Texte zur Sozialgeschichte der Literatur, 35 (Tübingen: Niemeyer, 1991)

BREUER, DIETER, 'Die Sprache der Affekte: Ihre Beschreibung im Lehrbuch des 18. Jahrhunderts, insbesondere bei Johann Christian Adelung', in *Zur historischen Semantik des deutschen Gefühlswortschatzes: Aspekte, Probleme, Beispiele seiner lexicographischen Erfassung*, ed. by Ludwig Jäger (Aachen: Rader, 1988), pp. 192–214

BREWER, CINDY, 'Resignation and Rebellion: The Dual Narrative of Johanna Schopenhauer's *Gabriele*', *The German Quarterly*, 75.2 (2002), 181–95

BRINKER-GABLER, GISELA, ed., *Deutsche Literatur von Frauen* (Munich: Beck, 1988)

BROMHAM, IVOR J., '"Ann of Swansea" (Ann Julia Hatton: 1764–1838)', in *Glamorgan Historian*, 7 (1971), ed. by Stewart Williams, pp. 173–86

BURKE, PETER, ed., *New Perspectives on Historical Writing*, 2nd edn (Cambridge: Polity Press, 2001)

BURNS, LANDON C., *Pity and Tears: The Tragedies of Nicholas Rowe*, Salzburg Studies in English Literature, 8 (Salzburg: Salzburg University, 1974)

BUSHART, BRUNO, ed., *Die Entdeckung der Wirklichkeit: Deutsche Malerei und Zeichnung, 1765–1815*, exhibition catalogue, Museum Georg Schäfer, Schweinfurt, 15 June–2 November 2003 (Leipzig: Seemann Henschel, 2003)

CATHOLY, ECKEHARD, 'Karl Philipp Moritz. Ein Beitrag zur "Theatromanie" der Goethezeit', *Euphorion*, 45 (1950), 100–23

CHARD, CHLOE, *Pleasure and Guilt on the Grand Tour: Travel Writing and Imaginative Geography, 1600–1830* (Manchester: Manchester University Press, 1999)

CHARTIER, ROGER, *L'ordre des livres. Lecteurs, auteurs, bibliothèques en Europe entre XIVe et XVIII siècle* (Aix-en-Provence: Alinéa, 1992)

——*On the Edge of the Cliff: History, Language, and Practices* (London: Johns Hopkins University Press, 1997)

COPLEY, STEVEN and PETER GARSIDE, eds, *The Politics of the Picturesque: Literature, Landscape and Aesthetics since 1770* (Cambridge: Cambridge University Press, 1994)

CORFIELD, PENELOPE J., EDMUND M. GREEN and CHARLES HARVEY, 'Westminster Man: Charles James Fox and his Electorate, 1780–1806', *Parliamentary History*, 20 (2001), 157–85

DASTON, LORRAINE and PARK, KATHARINE, *Wonders and the Order of Nature 1150–1750* (New York: Zone Books, 1998)

DAVIES, MAURICE, *Turner as Professor: The Artist and Linear Perspective* (London: Tate Gallery, 1992)

DAVIS, NATALIE ZEMON, *Women on the Margins: Three Seventeenth-Century Lives* (Cambridge, MA: Harvard University Press, 1995)

DEARNLEY, MOIRA, '"Condem'd to wither on a foreign strand": the 1833–34 Manuscript Poems of Ann of Swansea', *New Welsh Review*, 11.1 (1998), 56–59

DELL'ORTO, Vincent J., 'Karl Philipp Moritz in England: A Psychological Study of the Traveller', *Modern Language Notes*, 91 (1976), 453–66

DELON, MICHEL, 'L'Esthétique du tableau et la crise de la représentation classique à la fin du XVIIIe siècle', in *La Lettre et la Figure: La littérature et les arts visuels à l'époque moderne*, ed. by Wolfgang Drost and Géraldi Leroy (Heidelberg: Winter, 1989), pp. 11–29

DERRY, JOHN W., *Charles James Fox* (London: Batsford, 1972)

DÜRBECK, GABRIELE, *Einbildungskraft und Aufklärung: Perspektiven der Philosophie, Anthropologie und Ästhetik um 1750*, Studien zur deutschen Literatur, 148 (Tübingen: Niemeyer, 1998)

EBERLE, MATTHIAS, *Individuum und Landschaft: Zur Entstehung und Entwicklung der Landschaftsmalerei* (Gießen: Anabas, 1986)

EGER, ELIZABETH, CHARLOTTE GRANT, CLÍONA Ó GALLCHOIR and PENNY WARBURTON, EDS, *Women, Writing and the Public Sphere, 1700–1830* (Cambridge: Cambridge University Press, 2001)

EGGERS, MICHAEL, *Texte, die alles sagen. Erzählende Literatur des 18. und 19. Jahrhunderts und Theorien der Stimme*, Reihe Kulturpoetiken, 1 (Würzburg: Königshausen and Neumann, 2003)

ELLIS, MARKMAN, *The Politics of Sensibility: Race, Gender and Commerce in the Sentimental Novel*, Cambridge Studies in Romanticism, 18 (Cambridge: Cambridge University Press, 1996)

ELSASSER, ROBERT, *Über die politischen Bildungsreisen der Deutschen nach England vom Anfang des 18. Jahrhunderts bis 1815*, Heidelberger Abhandlungen zur mittleren und neueren Geschichte, 51 (Heidelberg: Winter, 1917)

ENGELL, JAMES, *The Creative Imagination: Enlightenment to Romanticism* (Cambridge, MA: Harvard University Press, 1981)

EYBISCH, HUGO, *Anton Reiser: Untersuchungen zur Lebensgeschichte von K. Ph. Moritz und zur Kritik seiner Autobiographie* (Leipzig: Voigtländer, 1909)

FISCHER, TILMANN, *Reiseziel England: Ein Beitrag zur Poetik der Reisebeschreibung und zur Topik der Moderne (1830–1870)*, Philologische Studien und Quellen, 184 (Berlin: Schmidt, 2004)

FORD, TREVOR D., 'Speleogenesis: The Evolution of the Castleton Caves', *Geology Today*, 12 (1996), 101–09

FOUCAULT, MICHEL, *The Order of Things: An Archaeology of the Human Sciences*, trans. not given (London: Tavistock, 1970)

FREVERT, UTE, 'Bürgerliche Meisterdenker und das Geschlechterverhältnis: Konzepte, Erfahrungen, Visionen an der Wende vom 18. zum 19. Jahrhundert', in *Bürgerinnen und Bürger: Geschlechterverhältnisse im 19. Jahrhundert*, ed. by Ute Frevert, Kritische Studien zur Geschichtswissenschaft, 77 (Göttingen: Vandenhoeck and Ruprecht, 1988), pp. 17–48

——, ed., *Bürgerinnen und Bürger: Geschlechterverhältnisse im 19. Jahrhundert*, Kritische Studien zur Geschichtswissenschaft, 77 (Göttingen: Vandenhoeck and Ruprecht, 1988)

FRIED, MICHAEL, *Absorption and Theatricality: Painting and Beholder in the Age of Diderot* (Los Angeles: University of California Press, 1980)

FRIEDRICHSMEYER, SARA and BARBARA BECKER-CANTARINO, *The Enlightenment and its Legacy: Studies in German Literature in Honor of Helga Slessarev* (Bonn: Bouvier, 1991)

FUCHS, ANNE, '". . . in Madrid müßten zwei Ochsen an einer Traube ziehen": Fremdverstehen in Karl Philipp Moritz' "Reisen eines Deutschen in Italien"', *Weimarer Beiträge*, 44 (1998), 42–53

FUCHS, ANNE and THEO HARDEN, eds, *Reisen im Diskurs: Modelle der literarischen Fremderfahrung von den Pilgerberichten bis zur Postmoderne* (Heidelberg: Winter, 1995)

FULDA, DANIEL, *Wissenschaft aus Kunst: Die Entstehung der modernen deutschen Geschichtsschreibung, 1760–1860* (Berlin: de Gruyter, 1996)

GILLEIR, ANKE, *Johanna Schopenhauer und die Weimarer Klassik: Betrachtungen über die Selbstpositionierung weiblichen Schreibens* (Hildesheim: Olms-Weidmann, 2000)

—— 'Die Vielstimmigkeit der Aufklärung: Georg Forsters *Ansichten vom Niederrhein*', *Das achtzehnte Jahrhundert*, 27 (2003), 171–88

GRAEWE, RICHARD, 'Horstigs Tagebuch einer Fußreise nach Hildesheim 1797', *Alt-Hildesheim. Jahrbuch für Stift und Stadt Hildesheim*, 42 (1971), 27–35

—— *Carl Gottlieb Horstig 1763–1835: Das Lebensbild eines vielseitigen Genies aus Goethes Freundeskreis* (Hildesheim: August Lax, 1974)

GRIEP, WOLFGANG, ed., *Sehen und Beschreiben: Europäische Reisen im 18. und frühen 19. Jahrhundert* (Heide: Eutiner Landesbibliothek, Westholsteinische Verlagsanstalt Boyens und Co., 1991)

GRIEP, WOLFGANG and HANS-WOLF JÄGER, eds, *Reise und soziale Realität am Ende des 18. Jahrhunderts* (Heidelberg: Universitätsverlag, 1983)

GRIEP, WOLFGANG and ANNEGRET PELZ, *Frauen reisen: Ein bibliographisches Verzeichnis deutschsprachiger Frauenreisen 1700 bis 1810*, Eutiner Kompendien, 1 (Bremen: Temmen, 1995)

GRUNDY, ISOBEL, 'Books and the Woman: An Eighteenth-Century Owner and her Libraries', *English Studies in Canada*, 20 (1994), 1–22

HAHN, BARBARA, '"Geliebtester Schrifsteller". Esther Gads Korrespondenz mit Jean Paul', *Jahrbuch der Jean Paul Gesellschaft*, 25 (1990), 7–42

—— *Unter falschem Namen. Von der schwierigen Autorschaft der Frauen* (Frankfurt: Suhrkamp, 1991)

HEIDMANN VISCHER, UTE, *Die eigene Art zu sehen: Zur Reisebeschreibung des späten achtzehnten Jahrhunderts am Beispiel von Karl Philipp Moritz und anderen Englandreisenden*, Zürcher Germanistische Studien, 30 (Berlin: Lang, 1993)

HENTSCHEL, UWE, 'Goethe und die Reiseliteratur am Ende des achtzehnten Jahrhunderts', *Jahrbuch des Freien Deutschen Hochstifts* (1993), 93–127

HIGHFILL, PHILIP H., KALMAN A. BURNIM and EDWARD A. LANGHAUS, *A Biographical Dictionary of Actors, Actresses, Musicians, Dancers, Managers and other Stage Personnel in London, 1660–1800*, 16 vols (Carbondale: Southern Illinois University Press, 1973–93)

HILZINGER, SONJA, *Anekdotisches Erzählen im Zeitalter der Aufklärung: Zum Struktur- und Funktionswandel der Gattung Anekdote in Historiographie, Publizistik und Literatur des 18. Jahrhunderts* (Stuttgart: M und P Verlag für Wissenschaft und Forschung, 1997)

HIPPLE, WALTER JOHN JR., *The Beautiful, the Sublime, & the Picturesque in Eighteenth-Century British Aesthetic Theory* (Carbondale: Southern Illinois University Press, 1957)

HOFF, DAGMAR VON and HELGA MEISE, 'Tableaux vivants — Die Kunst- und Kultform der Attitüden und lebenden Bilder', in *Weiblichkeit und Tod in der Literatur*, ed. by Renate Berger and Inge Stephan (Cologne: Böhlau, 1987), pp. 69–86

HOLLMER, HEIDE and ALBERT MEIER, '"Die Erde ist nicht überall einerlei!" Landschaftsbeschreibungen in Karl Philipp Moritz' Reiseberichten aus England und Italien', in *Erschriebene Natur: Internationale Perspektiven auf Texte des 18. Jahrhunderts*, ed. by Michael Scheffel and Dietmar Götsch, Jahrbuch für Internationale Germanistik Reihe A: 66 (Berlin: Lang, 2001), pp. 263–88

HOLMSTRÖM, KIRSTEN GRAM, *Monodrama. Attitudes. Tableaux Vivants. Studies on Some Trends of Theatrical Fashion 1770–1815* (Stockholm: Almqvist and Wiksell, 1967)

HOWARD, PETER, *Landscapes: The Artists' Vision* (London: Routledge, 1991)

HUNT, JOHN DIXON, *The Figure in the Landscape: Poetry, Painting, and Gardening during the Eighteenth Century* (Baltimore: Johns Hopkins University Press, 1976)

HUSSEY, CHRISTOPHER, *The Picturesque: Studies in a Point of View* (London: G. P. Putnam's Sons, 1927)

JARVIS, ROBIN, *Romantic Writing and Pedestrian Travel* (Basingstoke: Macmillan, 1997)

JONES, ROBERT W., *Gender and the Formation of Taste in Eighteenth-Century Britain: The Analysis of Beauty* (Cambridge: Cambridge University Press, 1998)

JOOSS, BIRGIT, *Lebende Bilder. Körperliche Nachahmung von Kunstwerken in der Goethezeit* (Berlin: Reimer, 1999)

JUNOD, KAREN, 'Drawing Pictures in Words: The Anecdote as Spatial Form in Biographies of Hogarth', in *The Space of English*, ed. by David Spurr and Cornelia Tschichold (Tübingen: Narr, 2005), pp. 119–34

KAISER, HELMUT, *Maria Sybilla Merian: Eine Biographie* (Düsseldorf: Artemis and Winkler, 1997)

KALLICH, MARTIN, *The Association of Ideas and Critical Theory in Eighteenth-Century England: A History of a Psychological Method in English Criticism* (The Hague: Mouton, 1970)

KEEN, SUZANNE, *Empathy and the Novel* (Oxford: Oxford University Press, 2007)

KELLY, JOHN ALEXANDER, *German Visitors to English Theaters in the Eighteenth Century* (Princeton: Princeton University Press, 1936)

KENNY, NEIL, *Curiosity in Early Modern Europe: Word Histories*, Wolfenbütteler Forschungen, 81 (Wiesbaden: Harrasowitz, 1998)

KLEIN, LAWRENCE E., 'Gender and the Public/Private Distinction in the Eighteenth Century: Some Questions about Evidence and Analytic Procedure', *Eighteenth-Century Studies*, 29 (1995), 97–109

KLINGENDER, FRANCIS D., *Art and the Industrial Revolution* (London: Paladin, 1968)

KLOSTERBERG, BRIGITTE, ed., *Licht und Schatten: August Hermann Niemeyer. Ein Leben an der Epochenwende um 1800* (Halle: Verlag der Franckeschen Stiftungen, 2004)

KÖHLER, ASTRID, *Salonkultur im klassischen Weimar: Geselligkeit als Lebensform und literarisches Konzept* (Stuttgart: M & P Verlag für Wissenschaft und Forschung, 1996)

KOŠENINA, ALEXANDER, *Karl Philipp Moritz. Literarische Experimente auf dem Weg zum psychologischen Roman* (Göttingen: Wallstein, 2006)

KRAUS WORLEY, LINDA, 'Sophie von La Roche's Reisejournale. Reflections of a Traveling Subject', in *The Enlightenment and its Legacy. Studies in German Literature in Honor of Helga Slessarev*, ed. by Sara Friedrichsmeyer and Barbara Becker-Cantarino (Bonn: Bouvier, 1990), pp. 91–103

KUBY, EVA, 'Über Stock und Stein – August Hermann Niemeyer unterwegs in Europa', in *»Seyd nicht träge in dem was ihr thun sollt.« August Hermann Niemeyer (1754-1828): Erneuerung durch Erfahrung, Hallesche Forschungen* 24, ed. by Christian Soboth (Tübingen: Niemeyer/ Halle: Verlag der Franckeschen Stiftungen, 2007), pp. 37-55

KUCZYNSKI, INGRID, 'Verunsicherung und Selbstbehauptung: Der Umgang mit den Fremden in der englischen Reiseliteratur des 18. Jahrhunderts', in *Reisen im Diskurs: Modelle der literarischen Fremderfahrung von den Pilgerberichten bis zur Postmoderne*, ed. by Anne Fuchs and Theo Harden (Heidelberg: Winter, 1995), pp. 55–70

LABBE, JACQUELINE, *Romantic Visualities: Landscape, Gender and Romanticism* (New York: St. Martin's, 1998)

LANDSHEERE, GILBERT DE, 'August Hermann Niemeyer', *Prospects: The Quarterly Review of Comparative Education*, 28.3 (September 1998), 509–24

LANGEN, AUGUST, 'Zur Lichtsymbolik der deutschen Romantik', in *Märchen, Mythos, Dichtung: Festschrift zum 90. Geburtstag Friedrich von der Leyens am 19. August 1963*, ed. by Hugo Kuhn and Kurt Schier (Munich: Beck, 1963), pp. 447–85

LANGEN, AUGUST, 'Attitüde und Tableau in der Goethezeit', *Jahrbuch der deutschen Schiller-gesellschaft*, 12 (1968), 194–258

LANGNER, MARGRIT, *Sophie von La Roche: Die empfindsame Realistin*, Beiträge zur Literatur-, Sprach- und Medienwissenschaft, 126 (Heidelberg: Winter, 1995)

LARGE, DUNCAN, '"Sterne-Bilder": Sterne in the German-Speaking World', in *The*

Reception of Laurence Sterne in Europe, ed. by Peter de Voogd and John Neubauer (London and New York: Continuum, 2004), pp. 68–84

LEASK, NIGEL, *Curiosity and the Aesthetics of Travel Writing, 1770–1840* (Oxford: Oxford University Press, 2002)

LOSTER-SCHNEIDER, GUDRUN, *Sophie La Roche: Paradoxien weiblichen Schreibens im 18. Jahrhundert* (Tübingen: Narr, 1995)

LOUWERSE, MAX and DON KUIKEN, 'The Effects of Personal Involvement in Narrative Discourse', *Discourse Processes* 38.2 (2004), 169–72

MĄCZAK ANTONI and HANS JÜRGEN TEUTEBERG, EDS, *Reiseberichte als Quellen europäischer Kulturgeschichte: Aufgaben und Möglichkeiten der historischen Reiseforschung*, Wolfenbütteler Forschungen, 21 (Wolfenbüttel: Herzog August Bibliothek, 1982)

MARSHALL, DAVID, *The Surprising Effects of Sympathy: Marivaux, Diderot, Rousseau, and Mary Shelley* (Chicago: University of Chicago Press, 1988)

MARTENS, WOLFGANG, *Literatur und Frömmigkeit in der Zeit der frühen Aufklärung*, Studien und Texte zur Sozialgeschichte der Literatur, 25 (Tübingen: Niemeyer, 1989)

——'Zur Einschätzung von Romanen und Theater in Moritz' "Anton Reiser"', in *Karl Philipp Moritz und das 18. Jahrhundert: Bestandsaufnahmen — Korrekturen — Neuansätze*, ed. by Martin Fontius and Anneliese Klingenberg (Tübingen: Niemeyer, 1995), pp. 101–09

MARTIN, ALISON E., 'German Travel Writing and the Rhetoric of Sensibility: Karl Philipp Moritz's *Reisen eines Deutschen in England im Jahr 1782*', in *Cross-cultural Travel. Papers from the Royal Irish Academy International Symposium on Literature and Travel, National University of Ireland, Galway, November 2002*, ed. by Jane Conroy (Berlin: Lang, 2003), pp. 81–88

——'Sympathy and Spectacle: *lebende Bilder, Attitüden* and Visual Representation in Johanna Schopenhauer's Travel Writing', *PEGS*, 73 (2004), pp. 19–38

——'Travel, Sensibility and Gender: The Rhetoric of Female Travel Writing in Sophie von La Roche's *Tagebuch einer Reise durch Holland und England*', *German Life and Letters*, 57 (2004), 127–42

——'The Traveller as *Landschaftsmaler*: Industrial Labour and Landscape Aesthetics in Johanna Schopenhauer's *Reise durch England und Schottland*', *Modern Language Review*, 99 (2004), 991–1005

MATHESON, P. E., *German Visitors to England 1770–1795 and their Impressions* (Oxford: Clarendon Press, 1930)

MAURER, MICHAEL, 'Das Gute und das Schöne: Sophie von La Roche (1730–1807) wiederentdecken?', *Euphorion*, 79 (1985), 111–38

——*Aufklärung und Anglophilie in Deutschland* (Göttingen: Vandenhoeck and Ruprecht, 1987)

——, ed., *O Britannien, von deiner Freiheit einen Hut voll: Deutsche Reiseberichte des 18. Jahrhunderts* (Munich: Beck, 1992)

——, ed., *Neue Impulse der Reiseforschung* (Berlin: Akademie, 1999)

McKEON, MICHAEL, 'Prose Fiction: Great Britain', in *The Cambridge History of Literary Criticism*, IV (1997), pp. 238–63

MENNE, KARL, 'Aus dem Leben des Hallischen Kanzlers Aug. Herm. Niemeyer', *Studien zur vergleichenden Literaturgeschichte*, 4 (1904), 348–66

MILCH, WERNER, *Sophie La Roche, die Großmutter des Brentanos* (Frankfurt a.M.: Societäts-Verlag, 1935)

MILSTEIN, BARNEY M., *Eight Eighteenth Century Reading Societies. A Sociological Contribution to the History of German Literature*, German Studies in America, 11 (Berlin: Lang, 1972)

MINDER, ROBERT, *Glaube, Skepsis und Rationalismus: Dargestellt aufgrund der autobiographischen Schriften von Karl Philipp Moritz* (Frankfurt a.M.: Suhrkamp, 1974)

MINTER, CATHERINE J., 'Literary Empfindsamkeit and Nervous Sensibility in Eighteenth-Century Germany', *MLR*, 96 (2001), 1016–28

MONK, SAMUEL H., *The Sublime: A Study of Critical Theories in XVIII-Century England* (Ann Arbor: University of Michigan Press, 1960)

MONTY, JEANNE R., 'The Myth of Belisarius in Eighteenth Century France', *Romance Notes*, 4 (1962), 127–31

MULLAN, JOHN, *Sentiment and Sociability. The Language of Feeling in the Eighteenth Century* (Oxford: Clarendon Press, 1988)

MÜLLER, KLAUS-DETLEF, 'Die Autobiographie der Goethezeit: Historischer Sinn und gattungsgeschichtliche Perspektiven', in *Die Autobiographie: Zur Form und Geschichte einer literarischen Gattung*, ed. by Günter Niggl (Darmstadt: Wissenschaftliche Buchgesellschaft, 1989), pp. 459–81

MÜLLER, LOTHAR, 'Die Erziehung der Gefühle im 18. Jahrhundert: Kanzel, Buch und Bühne in Karl Philipp Moritz' "Anton Reiser" (1785–1790)', *Der Deutschunterricht*, 48.2 (1996), 5–20

NAUMANN, URSULA, 'Das Fräulein und die Blicke: Eine Betrachtung über Sophie von La Roche', *Zeitschrift für deutsche Philologie*, 107 (1988), 488–516

NENON, MONIKA, *Autorschaft und Frauenbildung. Das Beispiel Sophie von La Roche* (Würzburg: Königshausen and Neumann, 1988)

NISBET, H. B. and CLAUDE RAWSON, EDS, *The Cambridge History of Literary Criticism*, iv: *The Eighteenth Century* (Cambridge: Cambridge University Press, 1997)

NORTON, ROBERT E., *Herder's Aesthetics and the European Enlightenment* (Ithaca: Cornell University Press, 1991)

PAPE, WALTER, ' "Die Sinne triegen nicht": Perception and Landscapes in Classical Goethe', in *Reflecting Senses: Perception and Appearance in Literature, Culture, and the Arts*, ed. by Walter Pape and Frederick Burwick (Berlin: de Gruyter, 1995), pp. 96–121

——and FREDERICK BURWICK, EDS, *Reflecting Senses: Perception and Appearance in Literature, Culture, and the Arts* (Berlin: de Gruyter, 1995)

PEER, WILLIE VAN and HENK PANDER MAAT, 'Perspectivation and Sympathy: Effects of Narrative Point of View', in *Empirical Approaches to Literature and Aesthetics*, ed. by Roger J. Kreuz and Mary Sue MacNealy (Norwood: Ablex, 1996), pp. 143–54

PELZ, ANNEGRET, ' "Ob und wie Frauenzimmer reisen sollen?" Das "reisende Frauenzimmer" als eine Entdeckung des 18. Jahrhunderts', in *Sehen und Beschreiben. Europäische Reisen im 18. und frühen 19. Jahrhundert*, ed. by Wolfgang Griep, Eutiner Forschungen, 1 (Heide: Westholsteinische Verlagsanstalt, 1991), pp. 125–35

——'Reisen Frauen anders? Von Entdeckerinnen und reisenden Frauenzimmern', in *Reisekultur: Von der Pilgerfahrt zum modernen Tourismus*, ed. by Hermann Bausinger, Klaus Beyrer, and Gottfried Korff (Munich: Beck, 1991), pp. 174–78

——*Reisen durch die eigene Fremde: Reiseliteratur von Frauen als autogeographische Schriften* (Cologne: Böhlau, 1993)

PETSCHAUER, PETER, 'Sophie von LaRoche, Novelist between Reason and Emotion', *The Germanic Review*, 57 (1982), 70–77

——'Christina Dorothea Leporin (Erxleben), Sophia (Gutermann) von La Roche, and Angelika Kaufmann: Background and Dilemmas of Independence', *Studies in Eighteenth-Century Culture*, 15 (1986), 127–43

PFISTER, MANFRED, 'Intertextuelles Reisen, oder: Der Reisebericht als Intertext', in *Tales and 'their telling difference'. Festschrift für Frank K. Stanzel*, ed. by Herbert Foltinek, Wolfgang Riehle, and Waldemar Zacharasiewicz (Heidelberg: Winter, 1993), pp. 109–32

PHILLIPS, MARK SALBER, *Society and Sentiment. Genres of Historical Writing in Britain, 1740–1820* (Princeton: Princeton University Press, 2000)

PICKERODT, GERHART, 'Das "poetische Gemählde": Zu Karl Philipp Moritz' "Werther"-Rezeption', *Weimarer Beiträge*, 36 (1990), 1364–68

POINTON, MARCIA, *Strategies for Showing: Women, Possession, and Representation in English Visual Culture, 1665–1800* (Oxford: Oxford University Press, 1997)

Pomian, Krzysztof, *Collectors and Curiosities: Paris and Venice, 1500–1800*, trans. by Elizabeth Wiles-Porter (Cambridge: Polity Press, 1990)

Prüsener, Marlies, 'Lesegesellschaften im 18. Jahrhundert. Ein Beitrag zur Lesergeschichte', *Archiv für Geschichte des Buchwesens*, 13 (1973), 370–594

Purver, Judith, '"Zufrieden mit stillerem Ruhme"?: Reflections on the Place of Women Writers in the Literary Spectrum of the Late Eighteenth and Early Nineteenth Centuries', *PEGS*, 64–65 (1993–95), 72–93

——'Revolution, Romanticism, Restoration (1789–1830)', in *A History of Women's Writing in Germany, Austria and Switzerland*, ed. by Jo Catling (Cambridge: Cambridge University Press, 2000), pp. 68–87

Real, Willy, *Untersuchungen zu Archibald Alisons Theorie des Geschmacks* (Frankfurt a.M.: Akademische Verlagsgesellschaft, 1973)

Redmond, James, ed., *The Theatrical Space*, Themes in Drama, 9 (Cambridge: Cambridge University Press, 1987)

Reid, Loren D., 'Did Charles Fox prepare his Speeches?', *Quarterly Journal of Speech*, 24 (1968), 17–26

——*Charles James Fox* (London: Longmans, 1969)

Reill, Peter Hanns, 'Narration and Structure in Late Eighteenth-Century Historical Thought', *History and Theory*, 25 (1986), 286–98

——'Science and the Science of History in the Late Enlightenment and Early Romanticism in Germany', in *Dimensionen der Historik: Geschichtstheorie, Wissenschaftsgeschichte und Geschichtskultur heute*, ed. by Horst Walter Blanke, Friedrich Jaeger, and Thomas Sandkühler (Cologne: Böhlau, 1998), pp. 253–62

Rigney, Ann, *The Rhetoric of Historical Representation: Three Narrative Histories of the French Revolution* (Cambridge: Cambridge University Press, 1990)

——'Narrativity and Historical Representation', *Poetics Today*, 12 (1991), 591–605

Riley, Helene M. Kastinger, *Die weibliche Muse: Sechs Essays über künstlerisch schaffende Frauen der Goethezeit*, Studies in German Literature, Linguistics and Culture, 8 (Columbia: Camden House, 1986)

Robertson, J. G., 'Sophie von La Roche's Visit to England in 1786', *MLR*, 28 (1932), 196–203

Robson-Scott, W. D., *German Travellers in England, 1400–1800* (Oxford: Blackwell, 1953)

Röthlisberger, Marcel, *Claude Lorrain: The Paintings*, 2 vols (New York: Hacker Art Books, 1979)

Rudert, Karin, 'Die Wiederentdeckung einer "deutschen Wollstonecraft": Esther Gad Bernard Domeier für Gleichberechtigung der Frauen und Juden', *Quaderni. Università degli studi die Lecce, Facoltà di magistero, Dipartimento di lingue e letterature straniere*, 10 (1988), 213–61

Sauder, Gerhard, *Empfindsamkeit*, 3 vols (Stuttgart: Metzler, 1974)

——'Reisen eines Deutschen in England im Jahr 1782: Karl Philipp Moritz', in *'Der curieuse Passagier': Deutsche Englandreisende des achtzehnten Jahrhunderts als Vermittler kultureller und technologischer Anregungen*, ed. by Marie-Luise Spieckermann, Beiträge zur Geschichte der Literatur und Kunst des 18. Jahrhunderts, 6 (Heidelberg: Winter, 1983), pp. 93–108

——'Empfindsame Reisen' in *Reisekultur: Von der Pilgerfahrt zum modernen Tourismus*, ed. by Hermann Bausinger, Klaus Beyrer, and Gottfried Korff (Munich: Beck, 1991), pp. 276–83

Saul, Nicholas, *History and Poetry in Novalis and in the Tradition of the German Enlightenment*, Bithell Series of Dissertations, 8 (London: Institute of Germanic Studies, 1984)

Schäfer, Walter E., 'Anekdotische Erzählformen und der Begriff Anekdote im Zeitalter der Aufklärung', *Zeitschrift für deutsche Philologie*, 104 (1985), 185–204

Scheffel, Michael and Dietmar Götsch, eds, *Erschriebene Natur: Internationale Perspektiven auf Texte des 18. Jahrhunderts* (Berlin: Lang, 2001)

SCHIETH, LYDIA, *Die Entwicklung des deutschen Frauenromans im ausgehenden 18 Jh., ein Betrag zur Gattungsgeschichte* (Frankfurt a.M.: Lang, 1987)

SCHINGS, HANS-JÜRGEN, *Der mitleidigste Mensch ist der beste Mensch: Poetik des Mitleids von Lessing bis Büchner* (Munich: Beck, 1980)

SCHLICHTMANN, SILKE, *Geschlechterdifferenz in der Literaturrezeption um 1800?*, Untersuchungen zur deutschen Literaturgeschichte, 107 (Tübingen: Niemeyer, 2001)

SCHMITT, HANNO, 'On the Importance of Halle in the Eighteenth Century for the History of Education', *Paedagogica Historica*, 32 (1996), 85–100

SCHNEIDER, HELMUT J., 'The Staging of the Gaze: Aesthetic Illusion and the Scene of Nature in the Eighteenth Century', in *Reflecting Senses: Perception and Appearance in Literature, Culture, and the Arts*, ed. by Walter Pape and Frederick Burwick (Berlin: de Gruyter, 1995), pp. 77–95

——'The Cold Eye: Herder's Critique of Enlightenment Visualism', in *Johann Gottfried Herder: Academic Disciplines and the Pursuit of Knowledge*, ed. by Wulf Kopke (Columbia: Camden House, 1996), pp. 53–60

SCHNEIDER, NORBERT, *Geschichte der Landschaftsmalerei: Vom Spätmittelalter bis zur Romantik* (Darmstadt: Wissenschaftliche Buchgesellschaft, 1999)

SCHÖN, ERICH, 'Weibliches Lesen: Romanleserinnen im späten 18. Jahrhundert', in *Untersuchungen zum Roman von Frauen um 1800*, ed. by Helga Gallas and Magdalene Heuser (Tübingen: Niemeyer, 1990)

SCHULTZ, ARTHUR R., 'Goethe and the Literature of Travel', *Journal of English and Germanic Philology*, 48 (1949), 445–68

SEIBERT, PETER, *Der literarische Salon: Literatur und Geselligkeit zwischen Aufklärung und Vormärz* (Stuttgart: Metzler, 1993)

SELLING, ANDREAS, *Deutsche Gelehrten-Reisen nach England, 1660–1714* (Frankfurt a.M.: Lang, 1990)

SHAW, LEROY R., 'Henry Home of Kames: Precursor of Herder', *Germanic Review*, 35 (1960), 16–27

SMITH, GREG, *The Emergence of the Professional Watercolourist: Contentions and Alliances in the Artistic Domain, 1760–1824* (Aldershot: Ashgate, 2002)

SOBOTH, CHRISTIAN, 'Klopstockbegeisterung und erste literarische Versuche', in *Licht und Schatten: August Hermann Niemeyer. Ein Leben an der Epochenwende um 1800*, ed. by Brigitte Klosterberg (Halle: Verlag der Franckeschen Stiftungen, 2004), pp. 58–59

SPIECKERMANN, MARIE-LUISE, ed., *Der curieuse Passagier: Deutsche Englandreisende des achtzehnten Jahrhunderts als Vermittler kultureller und technologischer Anregungen* (Heidelberg: Winter, 1983)

STAGL, JUSTIN, *A History of Curiosity: The Theory of Travel, 1550–1800* (Chur: Harwood, 1995)

STERN, CAROLA, *Alles, was ich in der Welt verlange: Das Leben der Johanna Schopenhauer* (Cologne: Kiepenhauer and Witsch, 2003)

STEWART, WILLIAM E., *Die Reisebeschreibung und ihre Theorie im Deutschland des 18. Jahrhunderts* (Bonn: Bouvier, 1978)

SUTHERLAND, JAMES, ed., *The Oxford Book of Literary Anecdotes* (Oxford: Oxford University Press, 1975)

SWAIN, VIRGINIA E., 'Lumières et Vision: Reflections on Sight and Seeing in Seventeenth- and Eighteenth-Century France', *L'Esprit Créateur*, 28.4 (1988), 5–16

TEUTEBERG, HANS JÜRGEN, 'Der Beitrag der Reiseliteratur zur Entstehung des deutschen Englandbildes zwischen Reformation und Aufklärung', in *Reiseberichte als Quellen europäischer Kulturgeschichte: Aufgaben und Möglichkeiten der historischen Reiseforschung*, ed. by Antoni Mączak and Hans Jürgen Teuteberg (Wolfenbüttel: Herzog August Bibliothek, 1982), pp. 73–113

THOMAS, KEITH, *Man and the Natural World: Changing Attitudes in England, 1500–1800* (London: Allen Lane, 1983)

TODD, JANET, *Sensibility: An Introduction* (London: Methuen, 1986)

TURNER, CHERYL, *Living by the Pen: Women Writers in the Eighteenth Century* (London: Routledge, 1992)

TURNER, KATHERINE, *British Travel Writers in Europe, 1750–1800: Authorship, Gender and National Identity* (Aldershot: Ashgate, 2001)

ULRICH, EDITHA, 'Reiseberichte als Medium der Fremderfahrung. Esther Bernards Wandlung in Briefen über England', in *Entdeckung und Selbstentdeckung. Die Begegnung europäischer Reisender mit dem England und Irland der Neuzeit*, ed. by Otfried Dankelmann (Frankfurt a.M.: Lang, 1999), pp. 11–49

VAN SANT, ANN JESSIE, *Eighteenth-Century Sensibility and the Novel: The Senses in Social Context* (Cambridge: Cambridge University Press, 1993)

VICKERY, AMANDA, 'Golden Age to Separate Spheres? A Review of the Categories and Chronology of English Women's History', *The Historical Journal*, 36 (1993), 383–414

WATT, HELGA SCHUTTE 'Woman's Progress: Sophie La Roche's Travelogues 1787–1788', *The Germanic Review*, 69.2 (1994), 50–60

WEIGEL, SIGRID, 'Der schielende Blick: Thesen zur Geschichte weiblicher Sprachpraxis', in *Die verborgene Frau: Sechs Beiträge zu einer feministischen Literaturwissenschaft*, ed. by Inge Stephan and Sigrid Weigel (Berlin: Argument, 1983)

WHALE, JOHN, *Imagination under Pressure, 1789–1832: Aesthetics, Politics and Utility*, Cambridge Studies in Romanticism, 39 (Cambridge: Cambridge University Press, 2000)

WHITE, ISABEL A., ',Die zu oft wiederholte Lektüre des Werthers': Responses to Sentimentality in Moritz's *Anton Reiser*', *Lessing Yearbook*, 26 (1994), 93–112

WORLEY, LINDA KRAUS, 'Sophie von La Roche's Reisejournale: Reflections of a Traveling Subject', in *The Enlightenment and its Legacy: Studies in German Literature in Honor of Helga Slessarev*, ed. by Sara Friedrichsmeyer and Barbara Becker-Cantarino (Bonn: Bouvier, 1991), pp. 91–103

WUTHENOW, RALPH-RAINER, *Die erfahrene Welt: Europäische Reiseliteratur im Zeitalter der Aufklärung* (Frankfurt a.M.: Insel, 1980)

ZIOLKOWSKI, THEODORE, *German Romanticism and its Institutions* (Princeton: Princeton University Press, 1990)

Unpublished Theses

CHEETHAM, MARK, 'Revision and Exploration: German Landscape Depiction and Theory in the Late 18th Century' (unpublished doctoral thesis, University College London, 1982) DXI99984

HAMBLYN, RICHARD, 'Landscape and the Contours of Knowledge: The Literature of Travel and the Sciences of the Earth in Eighteenth-Century Britain' (unpublished doctoral thesis, University of Cambridge, 1994) PhD19172

HILEY, ALISON, 'German-speaking Travellers in Scotland, 1800–1860, and their Place in the History of European Travel Literature', 2 vols (unpublished doctoral thesis, University of Edinburgh, 1985) D68055/86

JOPPIEN, RÜDIGER, 'Die Szenenbilder Philippe Jacques de Loutherbourgs: Eine Untersuchung zu ihrer Stellung zwischen Malerei und Theater' (unpublished doctoral thesis, University of Cologne, 1972) 1V1279

LINK, MANFRED, 'Der Reisebericht als literarische Kunstform von Goethe bis Heine' (unpublished doctoral thesis, University of Cologne, 1963) DKG63LINK.MANF

LOWRY, HELEN, '"Reisen, sollte ich reisen! England sehen!": A study in Eighteenth-Century Travel Accounts. Sophie von La Roche, Johanna Schopenhauer and others (Karl

Philipp Moritz, Johann Wilhelm von Archenholz)' (unpublished doctoral thesis, Queen's University at Kingston, Canada, 1999) AAT NQ35971

MYERS, AMY SLAUGHTER, 'Fictions of Theater: Theatrical Sensibility in Lessing, Rousseau, Schiller and Moritz' (unpublished doctoral dissertation, Johns Hopkins University, 1999) UMI 9950576

INDEX

BRITISH COMPARATIVE
LITERATURE ASSOCIATION

The British Comparative Literature Association, founded in 1975, aims at promoting the scholarly study of literature without confinement to national or linguistic boundaries, and in relation to other disciplines. Through its regular publication *Comparative Critical Studies*, conferences, workshops, the John Dryden Translation Prize competition and other activities, the Association:

- encourages research along comparative, intercultural and interdisciplinary lines, as well as in the fields of general literary studies and literary theory
- fosters the exchange and renewal of critical ideas and concepts
- keeps its members informed about national and international developments in the study of literature
- provides a forum for personal and institutional academic contacts, both within Britain and with Associations and individuals in other countries.

Membership of the BCLA is open to academic members of universities and other institutions of higher learning as well as to graduate students and to other persons with appropriate scholarly interests, both in Britain and abroad. The BCLA is affiliated to the International Comparative Literature Association (ICLA), and membership of the BCLA includes membership of the ICLA.

President Professor Gillian Beer (Cambridge)
Secretary Mrs Penny Brown (Manchester)
Treasurer Dr Robin MacKenzie (Edinburgh)

www.bcla.org

Enquiries
Mrs Penny Brown
School of Languages, Linguistics and Cultures
University of Manchester
Manchester M13 9PL
E-mail: penny.brown@manchester.ac.uk